THE CULTURES OF EUROPE:

THE IRISH CONTRIBUTION

James P. Mackey
(Editor)

Published 1994
The Institute of Irish Studies
The Queen's University of Belfast,
Belfast

This book has received support from the Cultural Traditions Programme of the Community Relations Council, which aims to encourage acceptance and understanding of cultural diversity.

British Library Cataloguing-in-Publication Data. A catalogue record for this book is available from the British Library.

ISBN 085389 494 9

Printed by W & G Baird Ltd., Antrim
Cover designed by Rodney Miller Associates

The Cultures of Europe: The Irish Contribution

Edited by J. P. Mackey

For the City of Derry's
International Meeting Point for the Appreciation of Cultures
1992

The Institute of Irish Studies
The Queen's University of Belfast

CONTENTS

1. ENCOUNTER OF CULTURES

James P. Mackey

Europe is a garden of cultures: it looks larger and they more varied as old fences fall. But cultures can smother as they flourish, as easily as they can combine to contribute to the rich variety of human experience. Since they either precede or succeed all military/economic expansion, they can be used to colonise and subdue as often as to sustain and to enrich. The new and enlarged Europe cannot be rid of internal and external colonialism until it learns how to let its cultures relate without mutual threat, and how to make them humanise the more materialist forces which each in its own degree contains. Thirty years ago, realising that the economic and political unity of Europe could foreshadow a human disaster unless true cultural rapprochement kept in step, Strasbourg hosted a conference on 'L'Europe des personnes et des peuples'. Today, Europe's cultures have not yet begun to catch up, much less to find a more humane formula for unity than the levelling and standardising formula of a union driven almost entirely by economic concerns.

I

As the Northland Films video on Derry's Impact 92 (International Meeting Point for the Appreciation of Cultures) put it: 'All over Europe and the Soviet Union right now the bewildering question is . . . how at a time of powerful momentum for political and economic unity, do we simultaneously accommodate the resurgent national and ethnic identities clamouring for recognition and autonomy? Derry may not have all the answers but it is certainly an appropriate place in which to pursue the questioning process, because here, of necessity, the process has already begun'. And it goes on to describe Impact 92 as 'an ambitious and far reaching combination of conferences, seminars, music, drama and pageantry – a confident flourish of artistic and cultural activity that would grace any of the great capitals of Europe'.

This volume contains a selection of the papers read at one of these conferences. But before introducing the selection, it is worth saying something about the uniqueness of this conference, held in the city of Derry, 12–17 of March, 1992.

Although culture in its broadest sense refers to the entire distinctive creativity of any people, from the management of their space to the performance of their symphonies, culture in the high sense is often restricted to artists and academics and to those who have enough formal, and usually academic training to talk to them. And, although academia does play a pivotal part in the critique and preservation of culture both broad and high, this restriction usually means that conferences involve academics talking to each other; that is to say, talking to themselves. It is therefore difficult to exaggerate the leap of imagination when Derry's Centre for Creative Communications invited to this particular conference, an international group of leading academics to talk to its own citizenry. The experiment proved healthy for the academics, freed from their jargon and loosed from their footnotes, and it proved good for the citizens also in their own efforts to come to grips with the problems of engineering an encounter of cultures which would result, not in the destruction of one by another, the common vandalism of all colonialism, but in the mutual enrichment which is compatible with enhanced variety and uniqueness. If this volume made no other contribution to the emerging Europe, it might at least recommend this imaginative exercise to other cities: bringing together academics from different cultures to speak, not to themselves, but to the citizens, to the obvious advantage of both.

It has become fashionable quite recently in conferences and exhibitions devoted to their memory throughout Europe, to describe the Celts as the first Europeans (e.g. 'I Celti: La Prima Europa' exhibition at the Palazzo Grassi, Venice 1991). But of course the Romans followed in their tracks, subjected them to one of the most effective killing machines ever devised, and as is ever the way with colonising powers, vandalised their cultures, leaving only the peripheries of Europe undespoiled, mainly the Goidels, the Goidelic or Gaelic speaking peoples of Ireland and (from the 9th century and for many centuries thereafter) of most of Scotland. It was not that these peripheral areas escaped Roman influence, of course; it came to them particularly with Christianity, but without the military and economic enforcement of power-hungry colonisers; and so there are lessons still to be learned about the manner in which *that* influence was received *and* transmitted in a new form back to continental Europe as Roman overlordship receded. That is one reason why a peripheral region can tell us something about healthy encounters of cultures which old imperial centers may never have learned.

And Derry, geographically, a peripheral city in a peripheral European region, can bring forward other reasons for being the obvious choice for a conference on the encounter of cultures. It has itself had recent experience of conflicting cultures finding a new and mutually enriching *modus vivendi*. In addition, its people and those of its hinterland played a substantial role in fashioning the culture and politics of the emerging United States of America, arguably the dominant culture which at the present time Europe, like many other parts of the world, has to encounter and survive. And indeed the Protestant community of Northern Ireland played a very particular role in carrying a culture to the emerging United States, and carrying some of its elements back in inevitably changed forms to Northern Ireland. So, then, to the selection of papers from the conference.

II

The first picture, painted by Máire Herbert, is of an important and influential grouping in the Early Irish Church, the *familia* of Colum Cille who later lent his name to the Irish name for Derry. This grouping, whose influence was widespread in Ireland and in the north of the neighbouring island for many centuries, adapted the system of overlordship practised by their royal cousins to ideals of monasticism imported from the wider church in general and Gaul in particular. Thus they encultured the Christian church in their own indigenous social structures, yet the new forms of ecclesial Christianity show no evidence of impinging upon their sense of fully belonging to the universal church. They forged strong links between asceticism and learning, between involvement with continental Christian authors and a powerful scholarly interest in the natural world which predated Christianity amongst the Irish learned classes. They worked out ideals of church-state relationships suited to their own indigenous structures, resulting in a good deal of church-initiated law the aim of which was general social well-being. This experiment in christianising a non-Romanised culture did not survive the combined effects of the Viking and the Anglo-Norman invasions. But if its general formula had been followed more widely by Christian missionaries who went out from Europe in the 17th and succeeding centuries, less damage would have been done to so many other cultures, and Christianity might not have quite so fully fashioned itself to that imperial image which increasingly hinders some of its major ecclesiastical forms to this day.

When it came to painting the picture of the reverse influence of the Irish, now following in the tracks of receding Roman power, it was felt that a continental rather than an Irish scholar should have the commission. Perhaps the choice of a Breton prejudiced a favourable portrait! In the event Gwenaël Le Duc offered a refreshingly different assessment of the Irish contribution to European culture during the first millenium. Joining neither the recent sceptics nor the earlier fulsome admirers of the Irish as harbingers of the Middle Ages, he paints an intriguing picture of improvers of all they receive, yes, but a practical people, entrepeneurs almost, grammarians of language, and careful accountants of successes and failures in matters spiritual; people whose contribution to education was more crucial than ostentatious, more incisive than voluminous.

Fiona Stafford leaps many centuries to take up the story, still of Irish cultural influence abroad. Her focus is on the fascinating and controversial figure of one Macpherson, a Scot who in the mid-18th century brought ancient Gaelic myths, gods and heroes, but particularly Fionn and his company (or Fingal, as the Scots had come to call him), to the admiring notice of an astonishingly wide readership that spanned most of Europe and the United States. But now the story, as she tells it, reveals something of the frightening ambivalence of cultural influence travelling through time and space; and how that depends as much on the receivers as on the senders. For if, at one end, Macpherson himself was desperately trying to save something of a dying culture, in his conviction that great men and culture were giving way to little men and lesser, at the other end of this particular spectrum, Matthew Arnold, with a mind limply bound to the social Darwinism of his age, was reading in the same pages the visage of the mystic, melancholy Celt, a useful object lesson perhaps to the over materialised Anglo-Saxon, but essentially a loser and overdue for eradication. And in the meantime, on another spectrum, this ancient material, preserved for so long in oral tradition and manuscript, translated now into English and the style of the 18th century and then into the main European languages, was feeding the forces of romantic, cultural nationalism in Europe and the United States. It was put to that, again ambivalent, use by the Protestants of Ireland in the late 18th century – the Catholics of Ireland followed the by now well-marked route to the myths and heroes of the past in the course of creating their version of cultural nationalism a century or so later. Ancient cultural survivals and revivals which might have served to unite, served instead to divide, and do so to this day.

The story of the manner and circumstance in which that cultural nationalism became in Ireland at the end of the 18th century, the militant, separatist nationalism of 1798 and the following century, was told to the conference by Marianne Elliott. Her paper is not reproduced here, but the material may be found in her published works on the United Irishmen and on Wolfe Tone. She described the classical republicanism of Greece and Rome as the dominant political ideology which through Italian Humanism, the French *philosophes*, and such assorted British characters as Locke and Cromwell, reached Ireland in the 18th century. At its heart was an idea, not of democracy in its modern forms, but of civic virtue: the idea that all government should place the common good over private privilege and material advantage, and that a popular element should always be active and vigilant to that end. Another clear example of cultural content coming to Ireland from the old centre of Europe, and receiving there its own modification. One of the most significant modifications was supplied by the Ulster-born philosopher, Francis Hutcheson; for he added to the idea of popular sovereignty as the criterion of virtue in government, the quite radical idea of the right of active resistance in the conspicuous absence of such virtue. His rhetoric could be said to have caused armed revolution no more than the rhetoric of the French *philosophes* caused Robespierre's reign of terror; although, naturally, armed revolutionaries could afterwards appeal to such rhetoric. But it is not, in any case, with the story of the development of militant, separatist nationalism that we continue in this volume. If we have to be selective – and for purposes of publication, we do – we take the continuing direction of our story from John Barkley.

John Barkley describes the enormous influence of Hutcheson on Ulster Presbyterians in particular, and in the process he presents another source of influence upon the promotion of civic virtue in public life and the preference for the pursuit of the common weal over private interest: the religious ideas of the Reformed, coming once more from central Europe, stressing the convenant between God and people, and accordingly suspicious of the posturing of all intermediary authorities. It is probably fair to say that John Barkley in his life and work is a living representative of that fruitful union of classical republicanism with the religious freedom of the Reformed tradition. He himself, in his paper, begins to describe how these ideals were carried by Irish Presbyterians to North America, and nurtured there by their fidelity and suffering. But it was felt that it should be left to a historian from the United States to continue the story of the manner in which these ideals, carried by the dispossessed, achieved a success in the making of the modern United States of America which, unfortunately, they still await in Northern Ireland.

Marilyn Westerkamp traces these men and their ideas to the Western Frontier; though she remarks that their ideas were forged in action rather than phrased in words. From the point of view of the largely Anglican establishment which dominated the government in the East, these Scots-Irish looked like the colonised; to the Indians they looked more like colonisers. They forged out of their religious convictions and out of their experience as laity in managing the clergy of their own church, a radical egalitarianism which they then introduced by strategem, determination and opportunism to the government of the emerging country. The native Americans benefitted least, if at all, from this religiously inspired political culture – a salutary reminder, once again, that travelling cultures can do damage as well as confer benefit on that which they encounter; all depends on how they are presented and received.

The translantic connection, though now in the reverse direction, receives further attention from Stewart Brown, who came himself from the United States to a chair at Edinburgh. He considers the influence of Irish Protestants, and especially Ulster Presbyterians, on religious revivals and cultural identities. To a large extent, the revivalist piety of the First and Second Awakenings in North America, which had helped to define the identity of the new American republic, had first taken shape among the Presbyterian communities in Ulster and the West of Scotland during the seventeenth century. In 1859, this revivalist piety returned to Ireland, now in an American guise, when the 'prayer meeting' revival of 1857–58 in the United States travelled across the waters to stir a dramatic revival that swept through much of Ulster. From Ulster, the revival spread to Scotland, England and Wales, and (to a lesser degree) the Continent, and for a time, Ulster formed the centre of a translantic revival movement. The revival of 1859, however, also served to transform traditional Presbyterian communities in Ulster, encouraging the development of an individualistic piety and voluntary forms of church organisation, with close ties to American religious culture. The transformation also meant that they now perceived themselves more a part of a religiously pluralist Britain than of Ireland, thereby losing much of the ethos and circumstance which had once made them such a promising catalyst for political improvement on the Irish scene. Such are the vagaries of cultural transmissions in the religio-political dimension.

III

Of course it is salutary for any conference on the cultures of Europe to remember, and Declan Kiberd did remind us (since the example of North America is not altogether typical), that Europe itself is an invention, not just of Europeans, but of other peoples who owe much of their suffering as well as some of their enrichment to the colonising practices of certain European powers. And Ireland is in a particularly good position to remind the rest of Europe of this dimension of the argument. As a post-colonial country sharing the EEC with some post-imperial countries, it can tell other Europeans about the barbarism as well as the beauty of the traditions that have made us what we are.

. Kiberd pointed out that Ireland after 1921 suffered its own version of post-colonial petrification, that cultural numbness which induces a people newly given their country back, to keep it as their erstwhile over-lords would wish it to remain, in the image and likeness of departed superiors. Hence, although Ireland had produced great subversive anti-colonial literature, and indeed continued to produce it, standard literary criticism and the standard performance and teaching of great works conspired to rob these of their power to subvert. And it was left to artists and writers in other parts of the world, themselves in need of a radical vision of post-colonial existence, to see our literature restored to its properly liberating and creative functions. Kiberd himself refers to Mustafa Matura's *Playboy of the West Indies*, and from that weaves a story that helps recover the power of our own literature. But since it was almost a premise of the Derry conference that when we wished to hear of Irish influence in some other countries we invited a native of these countries, rather than tell ourselves about it, we were fortunate to find in E. A. Markham a poet from Montserrat who had spent some years as writer-in-residence and lecturer in Northern Ireland, and who therefore represents in his personal history the story he tells of cultural influences going and coming to Europe along this particular trajectory. And it is of course especially fitting and welcome that he should put his case mainly in the form of a poem.

The latter chapters would be enough to remind us, if Kiberd once again had not explicitly done so, that the Irish mind is not only available in the Irish language. And yet it would be an obvious abuse of the truth of this remark if it became an excuse for failure to say any more about the deep and complex issue of languages. Christopher Whyte uses the image of an actual journey from Slovenia to Macedonia to illustrate the intricate inter-relationship of languages – each as rooted in its own place as its boundaries are impossible to draw – and the potential poverty of the pure monoglot, if one could be found. Beside that he sets the picture of the Scot who cannot even pronounce the placenames of his own Highlands, much less understand what they have to tell him. So that nowhere more than in the language section of the conference did one glean the impression that in the act of travel from place to place and time to time, forced replacement caused great spiritual impoverishment, where otherwise there would be much mutual enrichment.

Nuala Ni Dhomhnaill is by no means unaware of the damage that can be caused when attempts to revive a dying language are put at the service of cultural nationalism, but she offers an account parallel to the Scottish poet's, of the process by which she too came to write in Gaelic, and from that there emerges all that is positive in her account also of the crucial importance of languages. She strikes again the note of the land and its language, but develops it now into a major theme, in line with the ancient Gaelic genre of Dinnsheanchas, a genre in which, century after century, our ancestors told their *paysage interieure* onto the physical and thereby named landscape, so that a kind of covenantal relationship came to exist through the language between the landscape and our ancestors, with all that they were and did and knew; and now our own land and language open up to us the possibilities of a process of symbolic mimesis, in which lies the essence of artistic creation. It was fortuitous, she thinks, that Irish escaped much of the influence of the Enlightenment, for the language preserved in the story-telling mode an access to the spiritual dimension which then survives the conceptual/empirical reductionism of that age, and allows us to recover much that was thereby lost.

IV

Culture is a large and varied entity and its vagaries are best studied in sub-sets. Politics is one of these, language another. There were other sub-sets still to which the Derry conference paid close attention but which, for economy's sake, cannot be included in this volume. One section of the conference dealt with music, for instance, as an expression, a carrier and a (re)fashioning of people's culture, as it travels abroad and returns. It is a particular pity that the lectures from that section cannot be reproduced here, since music so seldom features in investigations of this nature, and since it is another proof of the imagination behind the Derry conference

that it was included there, through the lectures and performances of
Ann Buckley, Tomás O Canainn, Len Graham and Pádraigín Ní
Uallacháin.

Fine Art, too, was more widely represented at the conference than
Gwen Le Duc's short section in his chapter would suggest. Hilary
Richardson told and illustrated the story of old Irish art, an extraordinary
marriage of pre-historic 'Celtic' forms surviving on this peripheral island,
with motifs of early Christian centuries that bind this art to places as far
removed as Armenia – another powerful illustration of the way in which
cultures, when they travel with their bearers, can unite and enrich, without threatening in the least, the unique genius and value of each people,
each land, each cultural unit.

There was attention to intra-cultural as well as inter-cultural problems
and prospects – to the fact that within a cultural unit some groups or
classes can be oppressed, colonised by larger or more powerful ones. The
resulting impoverishment of all and the resulting enrichment when the
oppression is lifted, were described in some of these microcosms also;
when Meg Bateman, for instance, presented examples of women's self-
expression in Scottish Gaelic oral poetry, as the voice of the colonised
within the colony. Nina Witosjek lectured on the invisible (invisible in the
prevailing literature on the subject, that is) colonisation of the ones she
calls the 'Babus of Mittel Europa', the preservers and defenders still of a
set of philosophical, aesthetic, moral and even religious values which
they identify as a truly European inheritance, in spite of the terrible
destructive colonisation engineered by Russian communism. Perhaps it
is as well therefore that the present collection ends with a piece by that
very European man, Garret FitzGerald, who, confident of the ability of
the citizens of different European countries and cultures to combine
different types and levels of allegiance, confident, that is to say, of the
ability of the cultures of Europe to coexist for mutual enrichment,
concentrates instead upon some common values which Europe as a
whole may have to offer to a wider world.

But there was much more in the conference. It is indeed a pity that this
volume could not contain much more. Nonetheless, it is a cause for
unqualified gratitude that the Cultural Traditions Group of Northern
Ireland's Community Relations Council gave a generous subvention,
without which collections of this kind find it difficult to find a publisher.

2. THE LEGACY OF COLUM CILLE AND HIS MONASTIC COMMUNITY

Máire Herbert

The idealised image of the island of saints and scholars has been, for long, a dominant feature of the received view of the early Irish church. Yet there have been quite contrary perceptions of the nature and character-istics of the christian church in Ireland. One school of thought has stressed the manner in which Irish organisation and outlook were anti-thetical to those of the Graeco-Roman tradition, while the opposing view emphasises the manner in which the Irish church was cognisant of, and participated in, the contemporary culture of Western Christendom.[1] The notion of an inspirational 'Celtic' spirituality, which transformed the Latin Christianity which it had received, is countered by the view of an Irish ecclesiastical world which sought the assimilation of the Irish church into the mainstream of the western Church. With so much work yet to be done on the documentary sources relating to the early Irish church, neither position can claim an unassailable base of all available evidence. Moreover, the strands of the history of early Irish christendom are diverse and complicated, and less than amenable to simple generalisa-tion. I do not propose, therefore, to attempt a premature characterisation of the nature of early Irish christianity. Instead, I should like to focus on the narrative of one particularly important and influential grouping within the Irish church, the monastic *familia* of Colum Cille. I hope to show something of its intellectual and institutional life, and of the man-ner in which it interacted with the wider community, both secular and ecclesiastical. The Columban monastic federation had its roots here in the north-west of Ireland, the native place of its founder-saint, but its influence extended far beyond this place of origin. My focus in the pre-sent paper is on the period in which its ideals had their widest currency, the period before the Viking incursions at the close of the eighth century AD.

Colum Cille, our founder saint, is the subject of what seems to be the oldest surviving Irish literary work, a poetic eulogy known as the *Amra*, composed shortly after the saint's death in the year 597.[2] The *Amra* is composed in the Irish language, in the native tradition of praise-poetry, yet its vocabulary and subject-matter draw extensively on Christian-Latin materials. It is a praise-poem for an aristocrat, whose high-born Uí

Néill ancestry is celebrated. Yet it praises Colum Cille, not as the bearer of the noble and warlike qualities of his ancestors, but as the exemplar of Christian monasticism. The *Amra* therefore witnesses on many levels to the interaction of native and Christian traditions in the Irish Church around the year 600. Moreover, it provides our earliest insight into the governing ideals of Irish monasticism, by praising the saint's learning as well as his asceticism.[3] We are told, not only of his extensive study of the Scriptures, but also that he used the works of Basil and of Cassian. It is evident, therefore, that for Colum Cille and his community their practice of monasticism was based on the teachings of leading authorities, whose writings may have been transmitted to Ireland from Gaul.[4] The *Amra* writer, who may have been a Columban monk, reveals the saint's community as intellectually aware of its links with the wider world of Christendom. Yet the poem also reveals, in its language and structure, its links with vernacular Irish culture. Furthermore, it witnesses to an aspect of the saint's learning which may owe more to his Irish intellectual milieu than to Latin reading, that is, his interest in the natural world, in the movements of the sun and moon, and the course of the sea.

Another closely contemporary text, the *Alphabet of Piety*, was written by Colmán moccu Beógnae, who seems to have been an associate of Colum Cille, and visited the saint in Iona. This provides a further witness to the monastic ideas of the *Amra*, drawing on Cassian and on the Wisdom literature of the Bible in its delineation of Christian conduct.[5] Among its dicta, moreover, it proposes that what is best for the mind is breadth and humility. This we may read as a further affirmation of the range of intellectual interests which the *Amra* ascribed to Colum Cille.

To discover something of the saint's monasticism in public life, we must now turn to another major source, the *Vita Columbae*, a Latin Life of Colum Cille, composed about a century after his death by his Iona successor Adomnán.[6] The *Amra* only briefly refers to the saint's departure to Scotland, but the *Vita* dwells mainly on his monastic life in Iona. Like all saints' lives, Adomnán's work bears the imprint of its genre and of the sources and literary exemplars used by its compiler. Yet I believe that it brings us into close contact with Colum Cille, since one of its principal sources is a now-lost memoir of the saint, compiled mainly from first-hand testimonies from fellow-monks a few decades after his death.[7] Here we get the small-change of community life, reading, copying of psalms, the reception of visitors to Iona, the abbot overseeing the daily round of monastic work. Yet we also glimpse the royal dynast of the *Amra*, who 'left chariots for clerical life'. We see Colum Cille, the kinsman of kings, able to deal on equal terms with rulers on both sides of the Irish Sea. He visits the kings of Dál Riata and Pictland. He returns to Ireland to attend a royal conference. Herein lies a key, I believe, to the public and organisational face of Columban monasticism. As the lands of the founder's Uí Néill kin extended widely both in the north of Ireland and in the midlands, so too it would appear that family donations of lands had led to the foundation of Columban churches in both Uí Néill kingdoms. Political contacts with the rulers of the Irish kingdom of Dál Riata on the west coast of Scotland seem to have facilitated the foundation of Iona and dependent churches on other islands and on the Scottish mainland. In their organisation, each church was assigned its own ruler, yet each was subject to the ultimate headship of Colum Cille in Iona. The founder, in fact, combined headship both of temporalities and of the spiritual life of his monastic organization. The temporalities, the subordinate churches and their dues, in accordance with secular practice were regarded as inheritable by the kin. Thus Colum Cille's successors in Iona, with very few exceptions, were to be fellow Uí Néill kinsmen. Certainly this organ-isational mode does not fit readily into the mould of contemporary Western Christendom. But, in fact, the Columban community had to evolve its own system, since its monastic authorities such as Cassian pro-vided no suitable guidance. Colum Cille simply adopted family secular practice, the system of overlordship practised by his relations. This was a practical organisational decision. The evidence provides no indication that it in any way impinged on the Columban community's sense of com-munion in their monastic life with the great exemplars of the universal church.

Indeed, two seventh-century Irish poems in praise of Colum Cille reveal a substantial thematic continuity with the *Amra* in their praise of his monastic virtues of asceticism and learning.[8] Here, however, there is more reference to the saint's overseas journeying, and to the extent of his fame both in Ireland and in Britain. We are conscious of the fact that Colum Cille, because of his secular status, was inevitably a prominent churchman in Ireland, but we are also reminded that his exile in Scotland did not diminish his ties with his homeland. The evidence of the *Vita Columbae* in fact reveals Iona as a hub of contact between Ireland and Britain, and as a centre where news, both secular and ecclesiastical, from both sides of the Irish Sea was recorded. Our earliest Irish historical doc-uments, the annals, have as their primary source Iona's chronicle of its diverse incoming information up to the mid-eighth century.[9]

Taking a lead from the life of the founder, the Columban monastic *familia* continued after his death to combine internal commitment to monastic practice with external engagement with the political and social life of the kingdoms in which the community was active. The *Vita Columbae* revealed Colum Cille, not only acting as monastic father, but also, for instance, as the prime mover of an alliance between his royal kinsman, the Uí Néill king, and his secular overlord, the king of Dál Riata. The fact that his successors were members of the same kin-group must have ensured their similar involvement in the networks of Uí Néill and Dál Riata political contacts.

In fact, it was such a royal contact which further extended the influence of the Columban community to Northumbria around the year 635. The Bernician prince, Oswald, had been an exile in Dál Riata, and on his attainment of kingship he looked for Christian teachers from among the Irish from whom he had received baptism during his exile. Thus Aidan was sent from Iona to establish the new foundation of Lindisfarne, from which Iona-trained monks preached and taught throughout Northumbria, and indeed, further south.[10]

While Iona's influence was thus reaching its apogee in Britain, however, some hints of conflict were beginning to surface. These first appear in Ireland, in a letter dated about the year 632, from a churchman called Cummian addressing himself to Ségéne, abbot of Iona, and the hermit Beccán. Cummian's letter implies disagreement on the part of Iona with collective decisions taken by other Irish churches regarding the calculation of the date of Easter.[11] On what were Iona's objections based? We can only deduce that it was confident of the superiority of its own calculations, and of its well-established scholarship. There is also a hint of argument based on the practice of the elders, which we may interpret, not merely as loyalty to the practices of Colum Cille, but also as adherence to Cassian's dictum that monastic practice should be guided by established experience.

Furthermore, however, I think that there may have been contrasting perspectives on the position of an Irish monastic community in the wider world of Christendom. Cummian stresses the unity in observance of Hebrews, Greeks, Latins and Egyptians, as against 'an insignificant group of Britons and Irish who are almost at the end of the earth, and if I may say so, but pimples on the face of the earth'.[12] The Columban abbot in Iona, at the centre of a far-flung federation of monasteries extending over several political frontiers, on an island on which Gaulish sailors or Munster bishops might arrive at any time, seems to have felt no such sense of peripherality. Moreover, opinion in Iona certainly seems to have rejected the view that the Easter question was a doctrinal matter rather than one of custom and discipline in which there was no obligation of uniformity.

The debate did not cease, however, and the next scene of confrontation was Northumbria. While the north of England received its Christian teachers from among the Irish, a Roman-inspired mission had been active in the south of Britain, and it was inevitable that the disparities in observance between the two should become evident. Yet it would appear that the culminating debate between the two sides at the Synod of Whitby in 664 may have come about as much because of political factors as of ecclesiastical. Thus, the king's son took up a position alongside the churchman Wilfrid, the strong advocate of Roman custom, in opposition to his father, who had inherited close links with the Irish mission. Ultimately, however, when the argument was stated in terms of whether the authority of Colum Cille should be upheld against that of St. Peter, the king himself gave judgement in favour of Peter and the Roman side lest, he said, when he came to the gate of heaven, the one who held the keys might not turn his back on him.[13] The arguments of the Synod of

Whitby as given by Bede, have many echoes of those in Cummian's letter. Once more, the Columban community and their followers are characterized as those from 'the two remotest islands of the Ocean,' who 'foolishly attempt to fight against the whole world'. Yet they do not appear to have been swayed by this view, nor indeed by the proposition that their dissidence was doctrinal, and hence sinful. In the end, it was the king's judgement – and his outflanking of his son's manoeuvres – which caused Colman of Lindisfarne and some of his followers to withdraw to Iona. It did not mean the end of scholarly and ecclesiastical contacts between the Columban community and North Britain, but it did now contract the Columban sphere of influence in Britain to the kingdoms of the Scots and Picts. The most negative legacy of Whitby may have been what is least visible and documented – an attitude shift in Iona which tended to place undue emphasis on custom and observance as the index of its fidelity to its monastic inheritance.

Yet this did not mean that its intellectual and public life stagnated. Iona abbots travelled back and forth to Ireland, and on one such occasion, in the latter decades of the seventh century, the abbot Failbe may have recruited to the community its future outstanding leader, Adomnán. Next to Colum Cille himself, Adomnán's achievements dominate the record of the Columban *familia*. Like his famous predecessor, he was a close relative of Ireland's most powerful kings. Indeed, his first documented public act as abbot was to go to Northumbria as an ambassador on behalf of the Uí Néill to ransom prisoners taken in a raid in the year 685.[14] Thus, in the tradition of Iona's founder, Adomnán combined influence in the public sphere with spiritual and intellectual activities.

On the spiritual and intellectual level, an outstanding achievement of his early abbacy was his writing of a work on the Holy Places. The arrival in Iona of a Gaulish bishop ship-wrecked in Britain en route home from the Holy Places led Adomnán to compile this record of the bishop's pilgrimage. However, the abbot does not simply record from dictation the testimony of the Gaulish bishop. Instead, in proper scholarly fashion, he checks the information about the Holy Places against that of authorities available to him. Adomnán's works reveal access to a well-stocked Iona library which included works by Jerome, Sulpicius Severus, and the so-called *Hegesippus*.[15]

Indeed, the latter text, and several other Latin works are in evidence also as sources for quite a different Iona composition from Adomnán's time, the Hymn *Altus Prosator*.[16] This impressive and learned work in Latin ranges in its subject-matter from the First Causes to the Last Judgement, dealing with the creation and fall, the seas and tides, hell and paradise, and the second coming. It echoes the strong scriptural base of the Columban learned tradition, while reminding us also of the *Amra's* witness to an interest in the science of natural phenomena. Indeed, the Iona intellectual milieu from Colum Cille's times particularly exemplifies the view that, in Irish learned circles, nature was assumed to be of interest in its own right, and an object of study well before there was access to external cosmographical materials such as those in the works of Isidore of Seville.[17] *De Locis Sanctis*, Adomnán's work on the Holy Places, moreover, combines a scholarly and devotional interest in the locations hallowed by Scripture with a lively curiosity about details of their contemporary surroundings – even, indeed, in the details of the return sea-journey of the pilgrim bishop. There is a strong sense of Iona's involvement both with the wider world of Christianity, and with the physical world in which it was situated.

This scholarly intellectual engagement, moreover, merges with an active commitment to the exercise of Christian influence in the secular and political spheres. This is conspicuously in evidence in Adomnán's public activities. In the year 697, the centenary year of the death of Colum Cille, the annals relate that Adomnán journeyed to Ireland and 'gave the Law of the Innocents to the people'.[18] A surviving text on this Law of Adomnán incorporates what appear to be its original provisions and its guarantor list. We see that the leading secular and ecclesiastical rulers, both from Ireland and from areas of Iona influence in Scotland, give assent to a Law to ensure the protection of non-combatants, women, children, and clerics from violence.[19] The Columban community under Adomnán thus takes the lead in public life, with a measure designed to bring about a more humane society. At the same time, the Law incorporates a system of enactment whereby the fines for its violation were to go to the community of its sponsor, Adomnán. There is, therefore, an evident Columban benefit in the Law of Adomnán, yet this should not detract from its importance as an ecclesiastical initiative in which leaders of church and state act jointly in the promotion of societal good.

As a churchman who was of royal blood, Adomnán had an evident and well-informed interest in the manner in which secular power operated. His second great literary composition, the *Vita Columbae* also witnesses to this interest. While I do not see a preoccupation with kingship as the primary theme of the *Vita*, particular episodes relating Colum Cille's associations with kings do express the Columban political outlook. Foremost was the view that the Uí Néill royal dynasty, kinsmen of Colum Cille and his successors, were entitled to 'the prerogative of monarchy over the kingdom of all Ireland'. The political reality of the seventh century indicates that such Uí Néill claims were far from being fully realized. We may speculate, however, on the extent to which the ambitions of these active, power-hungry rulers were being shaped, as well as articulated, by their learned ecclesiastical relatives. Even before Adomnán's time, the title 'king of the Irish' was granted in Iona sources to the Uí Néill king who died in 642.[20] Adomnán, however, uses his literary work not only to reiterate Uí Néill claims to power over all Ireland, but also to indicate that the successful acquisition and exercise of such power was dependent upon the action and approval of the Church.

It has been suggested that episodes in the *Vita Columbae* in which Colum Cille selects and consecrates kings have as their model the biblical depiction of Samuel and the scriptural texts of the Book of Kings.[21] There is no convincing historical evidence that Colum Cille played an active role either in the selection or inauguration of secular rulers, despite the evidence of the sources concerning his many associations with his royal relatives and neighbours. Adomnán's shaping of the saint's Samuel-like role serves the obvious hagiographical purpose of linking him with the great figures of Christendom. More specifically, however, the model of the holy man as king-maker seems to be the ideal paradigm of church-state relations envisaged by Adomnán and his community. There is support for strong over-kingship in Ireland, particularly by the relatives of the Columban abbots, the Uí Néill. The exercise of this power, however, was to be dependent on ecclesiastical overseeing of the selection of a Christian candidate, who was to be inaugurated, not by age-old native rites, but by unction of a churchman. As the Law of Adomnán indicates, the Columban model envisaged a society regulated by the co-operation of church and state, but with the secular power being legitimated and guided by the ecclesiastical.

While Irish and Columban sources thus witness to Adomnán's strong public involvement, from the north of England Bede's *Ecclesiastical History* illuminates another area of his life. Adomnán had made two journeys to Northumbria, and indeed, on one of these occasions he had presented a copy of his recently-completed book on the Holy Places to king Aldfrith. Bede, however, stresses that while in Northumbria, Adomnán had visited its churches, where it was impressed on him that he should unite with the universal church in observance, and abandon the Columban custom in which the community had persisted after the Synod of Whitby.[22] Adomnán did accept the arguments in favour of unity in observance of all churches, but Bede indicates that he failed to persuade his own community of Iona to do so. For Bede, the issue of conformity with Rome dominates his accounts of these times, but can we be sure that the issue equally dominated the many-faceted career of Adomnán? It would appear that Adomnán chose a novel way of explaining his stance by compiling a new life of his patron, Colum Cille. This he addressed both to his own community and to the Northumbrians.

A life of the saint had been compiled earlier in the seventh century in Iona by Cumméne, and Adomnán uses this work as a primary source. But while the earlier text appears to have been a memoir of Colum Cille compiled in, and for, his own Iona community, Adomnán's *Vita Columbae* sought to set the saint's life and work in a broader context. In effect, he wished to stress the harmonious conjunction of the universality and the particularity of Colum Cille's achievement. Drawing on the wide resources of Iona's library, and on his own scriptural learning, Adomnán shaped his sources about Colum Cille so that his subject's participation in the communion of holy men of Christendom was fully evident. The saint's healing of a broken hip-bone shows close affinity with a passage in the *Dialogues of Gregory the Great*. Like St. Germanus, Colum Cille is shown to have triumphed over contrary winds raised by druidic opponents. We see him draw water from a rock like Moses. In a miracle of raising from the dead, Colum Cille is revered as being at one in glory with the prophets Elijah and Elisha, and with the apostles Peter, Paul and John.

What we have here is literary highlighting of materials in accordance with hagiographical convention, to emphasise that the first abbot of Iona, in the manifestations of his sanctity, shared in the communal body of universal sainthood. He was a saint worthy of commemoration, not merely in Iona and Ireland, but throughout Christendom. Yet Adomnán was writing in Iona, and was conscious of the need to preserve the monastery's particular record of the founder, with all of its detail about the persons and places associated with his career. This Adomnán did by incorporating Cumméne's record of first-hand witnesses into the *Vita Columbae*.[23]

How does this literary composition reflect Adomnán's involvement in the debate over unity or diversity in ecclesiastical observances? Adomnán's life of his patron may be characterised as an eloquent sermon directed both at the Northumbrians, priding themselves on their Roman affiliation, and at his Columban brethren holding to their observances as the sign of their fidelity to their monastic forebears. Adomnán seeks a new perspective, one which focused on the central figure of Colum Cille, whose sanctity was above all dispute. Though the saint belonged to Iona, he belonged also to all of Christendom, and his community by recognising this, should not feel threatened by the prospect of uniting themselves in observance with the universal church. The Northumbrians, moreover, are reminded that sanctity is not a matter of keeping certain rules about Easter, but rather is a matter of divine affirmation. They owed their own Christianity to the Columban mission, and instead of focusing negatively on the observances of Iona, they should be mindful of the fact that Colum Cille was a saint worthy of comparison with the great holy men of Scripture and hagiography. It is interesting that at the close of Adomnán's text he adverts again to the often-cited matter of geographical peripherality. Adomnán says that though Colum Cille lived 'in this small and remote island of the Britannic ocean' he merited that his renown should extend not only throughout Ireland and Britain, but also that it should reach 'even as far as three-cornered Spain, and Gaul, and Italy situated beyond the Pennine Alps; also the Roman city itself, which is the chief of all cities'.[24] For the Iona abbot, the communion of saints was not defined by physical and political frontiers, and joining in observance with the rest of Western Christendom did not mean forsaking the ideals of Colum Cille.

It would appear that Adomnán's death in 704 came shortly after the completion of the *Vita Columbae*, too soon, it would appear, for his great work of advocacy to have had full effect. There is evidence of some subsequent dispute in Iona between those who sought unity in observance and those who sought to retain Columban particularity. By 716, however, the Roman Easter was fully accepted in Iona, and in the year 727, Adomnán's relics were brought to Ireland, and his Law renewed.[25] Thus, while Adomnán's tireless devotion to his monasticism within a short time had resulted in his acclamation as a saint, his legacy in public life also lived on. The Law of Adomnán was followed in the year 734 by the proclamation of the Law of Patrick, and in the period up to the year 842 the Annals record no less than thirty-three occasions on which Irish churches, in conjunction with their secular patrons, followed the Columban lead in enacting legal measures.[26] It would appear, however, that the Law of Adomnán held a particular position of importance as a measure of national (and indeed extra-national) application. The eighth-century Irish secular law tract *Críth Gablach* actually names the Law of Adomnán as an example of the type of ordinance to which it is proper for a king to pledge his people.[27]

The second half of the eighth century seems to mark a high point in the public influence of the community of Colum Cille in Ireland. The Annals show that each successive abbot of Iona travelled to Ireland, and proclaimed the *Lex Columcille*, 'The Law of Colum Cille', in conjunction with the Uí Néill king of Tara.[28] While we lack any detail about the provisions of this law, its enactment testifies further to alliance between the country's leading royal power, and what must be regarded as its premier ecclesiastical power, the Columban *familia*. We can reasonably infer that the aim was societal well-being, a continuation of the public-spirited legislation pioneered by Adomnán. While benefiting society, such legislation was also a potential source of material benefit for its sponsors. Moreover, the achievement of a more stable and equitable society would facilitate the promotion of the interests of both secular and ecclesiastical leaders.

Columban influence in the area of legislation is again in evidence in the eighth-century compilation of the *Collectio Canonum Hibernensis*, the joint author of which was Cú Chuimne of Iona, who died in the year 747. This Irish canon law collection sought to draw up a 'blue-print for all aspects of Christian living' and to legislate for the role of the church within the legal and political framework of a society which had not been within the ambit of Roman law.[29] Here we see the extent of the interaction between secular and ecclesiastical legal codes in Ireland, as canon lawyers took over concepts from native institutions, while contemporaneous secular law tracts bear the imprint of the churchmen who undoubtedly were involved in their redaction. The manner in which the Columban community was concerned at the highest level with the interaction of clerical and secular authorities clearly underlies Iona involvement in the legal activity of the period. The canon collection, for example, follows Adomnán's example in legislating for the 'ordination' of kings by churchmen.[30]

In late eighth-century Ireland, therefore, sources linked with the Columban *familia* show the church accommodating itself to its societal setting while at the same time exercising an influence over the manner in which social and political life were to be conducted. The model for secular and ecclesiastical governments which were both Irish and Christian seems to have owed not inconsiderably to the unique dynastic position of Colum Cille and his successors. Common kinship linked leaders of church and state and assisted in the creation of a mutual interest in the regulation of society. In a relatively peaceful and prosperous milieu, the interaction of secular and clerical magnates was readily accomplished. At a variety of levels, inheritance and innovation, native and Christian, vernacular and Latin, were fruitfully enmeshed. As the kind of society which Adomnán envisaged seemed to be in the process of evolving, harmony at the highest echelons of church and state may have deflected attention from potential problems. It would appear, for instance, that other monastic federations and secular leaders may have viewed the Columban model more in terms of success in the acquisition of power and property than in terms of the particular social and ideological contexts of which such were the by-products.

We can only speculate, however, on the kind of Irish society which might have resulted had the comparative stability of the early eighth century been maintained. But the final years of the century saw the beginning of the Viking incursions, which were to bring major changes to the Columban monastic *familia* in particular, as well as to Irish secular and ecclesiastical life in general. While the impact of the Vikings certainly cannot be held responsible for every development in Irish society in the succeeding century, we may point to certain specific influences. Viking sea-power hindered the link between Iona and Ireland, and dimished the influence of the successors of Colum Cille. In Ireland itself, churches sought secular patronage, and allowed the secularisation of their offices in return for much-needed protection. Potential problems in the eighth-century Columban church/state model now became an evident reality. Change already in progress was accelerated, as political leaders vied with each other and with the invaders for the power in Ireland which Colum Cille's community had sought for the Uí Néill. Churches became more involved in secular power-structures, but were unable to exercise influence over them. Ultimately, the fundamental structures of church and state survived, though changed, into the post-Viking era. However, the unique conditions of church/state relationships enjoyed by the eighth century Columban community were never again to be recreated.

Notes to Chapter 2

1. For a 'nativist' view, see Brendan Bradshaw, 'The Wild and Woolly West: Early Irish Christianity and Latin Orthodoxy', in W. J. Shields & Diana Wood ed., *The Churches, Ireland and the Irish* (Oxford, 1989), pp. 1–28. For other views see *passim* collections such as Próinséas Ní Chatháin and Michael Richter ed., *Ireland and Europe: The Early Church* (Stuttgart 1984); *Ireland and Christendom: The Bible and the Missions* (Stuttgart, 1987), Dorothy Whitelock, R. McKitterick, and D. Dumville, *Ireland in Early Medieval Europe* (Cambridge, 1982).
2. W. Stokes, 'The Bodleian Amra Choluimb Chille', *Revue Celtique* 20 (1899), 31–55, 132–83, 248–89, 400–37.
3. M. Herbert, *Iona, Kells and Derry: The History and Hagiography of the Monastic Familia of Columba* (hereafter *IKD*) (Oxford, 1988), pp. 9–12.
4. *Pace* Owen Chadwick, *John Cassian* (2nd ed., Cambridge, 1968), who states (pp. 148–9) that the transmission of Cassian to Ireland is 'not early'. See H. Mayr-Harting, *The Coming of Christianity to Anglo-Saxon England* (London, 1972), pp. 84–7 and E. James, 'Ireland and Western Gaul in the Merovingian period', in *Ireland in Early Medieval Europe*, pp. 362–86.
5. V. Hull ed. '*Apgitir Chrábaid*: The Alphabet of Piety', Celtica 8 (1968), 44–89; Pádraig P. Ó Néill, 'The date and authorship of *Apgitir Chrábaid*: some internal evidence', in *Ireland and Christendom*, pp. 203–215.
6. *Adomnán's Life of Columba* ed. & tr. A. O. Anderson & M. O. Anderson, revised by M. O. Anderson (Oxford, 1991).
7. *IKD*, pp. 12–26.
8. Fergus Kelly, 'A Poem in Praise of Columb Cille', *Ériu* 24 (1973), 1–34; 'Tiughraind Bhécáin', *Ériu* 26 (1975), 66–98.
9. *IKD* pp. 22–3.
10. *Bede's Ecclesiastical History of the English People,* ed. & tr. B. Colgrave and R. A. B. Mynors (Oxford, 1979), Book III, 3, 5.
11. *Cummian's Letter De Controversia Paschali and the De Ratione Computandi* ed. M. Walsh and D. Ó Cróinín (Toronto, 1988).
12. *Ibid.*, pp. 72–5.
13. *Bede's Ecclesiastical History* Book III, 3, 17, 22, 25. Mayr Harting, pp. 103–13.
14. *IKD*, pp. 44–8.
15. D. Meehan ed., *Adomnán's De Locis Sanctis* (Dublin, 1958).
16. These recent views on the date, origin, and sources I owe to Jane Stevenson's unpublished PhD dissertation on the *Altus Prosator* (University of Cambridge, 1986).
17. See Marina Smyth, 'Isidore of Seville and Early Irish Cosmography' *Cambridge Medieval Celtic Studies* 14 (1987), 102.
18. *The Annals of Ulster to AD 1131* ed. Seán MacAirt and Gearóid Mac Niocaill (Dublin 1983), (hereafter *AU*) at the year 697.
19. *Cáin Adomnáin: An Old-Irish Treatise on the Law of Adomnán*, ed. Kuno Meyer (Oxford 1905); See Máirín Ní Dhonnchadha, 'The Guarantor List of *Cáin Adomnáin*, 697', *Peritia 1* (1982), 178–215.
20. *IKD*, p. 52.
21. Michael J. Enright, *Iona, Tara and Soissons: The Origin of the Royal Anointing Ritual* (Berlin, New York, 1985), pp. 15–18.
22. *Ecclesiastical History*, Book V, 15, 21.
23. *IKD*, pp. 136–48.
24. Anderson (n. 6), pp. 232–3.
25. *IKD*, pp. 57–62.
26. See Kathleen Hughes, 'The Church and the World in Early Christian Ireland', *Irish Historical Studies* 13 (1962–3), 99–113 (pp. 101–104).
27. *Críth Gablach* ed. D. A. Binchy (Dublin, 1941), 38.
28. *AU* at the years 753, 757, 778.

29. H. Wasserschleben, *Die irische Kanonensammlung* (Leipzig, 1885). See Maurice
    Sheehy, 'The Bible and the *Collectio Canonum Hibernensis*', *Ireland and Christendom*,
    pp. 277–83; D. Ó Corráin, 'Irish law and Canon law'; *Ireland and Europe*, pp. 157–66;
    Enright, pp. 24–25, 44–8.
30. Enright, pp. 24–34.

3. THE CONTRIBUTION TO THE MAKING OF EUROPEAN CULTURE OF IRISH MONKS AND SCHOLARS IN MEDIEVAL TIMES

Gwenaël Le Duc

1. Introduction

The Irish contribution to European Culture is indeed a very wide and vast subject: I have to try and sum up nearly a thousand years of history.

First of all let us admit that whatever was Irish, I mean really, typically, and even *authentically* Irish, had little impact and influence. It was not worthless, certainly not, but apparently the Irish did not try to export it, or the others simply were not interested in it. This precision is essential, because what is thought to be essentially Irish, or what is nowadays important or essential in Irish culture could, in many but not in all respects, be left aside.

For instance: the poem about the scholar and his cat[1] which everyone knows, and which was written down, if not redacted, in Europe, on the continent, had very little impact, and actually was unknown before the last century. It is indeed a monument of early lyrical poetry, and a fine piece of poetry as well, but its impact was practically nil.

Irish institutions and laws also had very little impact. Anyway, they could not be exported to countries which already had a tradition of written law, under Roman influence. When we speak of architecture, or of coinage, or of pottery-making, nothing can be expected there as an influence, of course, since there was nothing. Irish art, though, is another matter I will have to consider.

The Irish language had no impact because it was never used on the continent, except by some Irish scribes, as a secret language.[2]

In fact, Ireland's contribution to European Culture is not what it could have been, or should have been. The position of Ireland as an island on the outskirts of Europe, far away from Rome and the Mediterranean, can explain a lot in that respect. The fact is that apart from a few settlements in Wales and Cornwall, the Irish never tried to gain *military* supremacy on the continent, that military supremacy which is so useful, if not essential for the spreading of an influence (see the Roman Empire and the spread of Latin). Ireland's contribution was mainly to acquire or receive a lot from the continent, select it, and afterwards to give back the

21

deposit – with interest, and I will deal here both in the deposit and in the interest.

I use evidence, and evidence is, unavoidably, detail. I cannot neglect it. But I will try to examine that detail and go beyond it, and thus suck the marrow out of many a bone to make my own broth. The problem with detail is that we very often cannot say what is known twice but definitely exceptional and what is isolated but highly significant. Here is an example:

Laon manuscript 444 is a Greek–Latin lexicon.[3] Was it a new thing? Apparently yes. Was it Irish? It was definitely copied on an old Irish exemplar. Was this exemplar brought to the continent by an Irishman? Perhaps. Copied by an Irishman? Certainly not. Corrected by an Irishman? Possible, but it is a moot point; rather a continental writer who could read Irish script. Was it used? The manuscript is clean. Any impact? Well, we cannot tell for sure.

The fact is however that the original manuscript, though lost, was Irish, since a few Old-Irish notes (mere binding indications) were copied together with the text, maybe because they were taken to be Greek. It was copied, but where is, or where was the original? Why was it copied and not given or bought? We do not know. The fact is that it is the earliest Greek–Latin lexicon we have on the continent, and that among the users certainly was John Scot, the first man to know Greek at the Carolingian court. But why did he not himself correct it? Why did someone else do so who was apparently a pupil of his? The fact is that John Scot was apparently at some time in the Carolingian court the only one who had some Greek.[4]

The importance of this manuscript however is clear: after John Scot, and after that manuscript was made, there was a new interest in Greek studies, and the coming of Byzantine scholars to the court certainly improved the knowledge of Greek in Northern France. In these later stages, if there is an Irish influence, or an Irish contribution, we are at pains to define it. Nevertheless, the Irish (or an Irishman) certainly were at the root of it.

John Scot[5] was not only a scholar in Greek, he was a theologian, and he was condemned as a heretic, therefore his writings had little impact – apparently: in fact, they had because, if only for the sake of contradicting him, it forced theologians to move along themselves, and thus he definitey contributed to the development of theological studies.

Now to sum it all up. The existence of one single manuscript is a fact; appreciating its impact is more difficult. The contribution of one single manuscript kept in one isolated and remote monastery could be an incident, a detail. Anyway, it did not and could not concern the majority of the population. After all, it is only very, very recently that the value of the Book of Kells could be appreciated by a number of people, and not merely by a few privileged individuals.

The situation is ambiguous. We tend to consider monasteries as closed units. They were, and they were not. They were so because monasteries usually are and remain severed from the world, and are not really concerned by its turmoils, and generally speaking they do not care much about the general level of education or culture in the country. Their aim is not actually culture or education. Therefore it is difficult to speak of them as cultural centers: they were not centers, merely points, small points on the map. If they had an influence, that was on other monasteries, far away at times, unlike towns with a strong influence on what is close, and a weak though real influence on what is far, within a certain area; or universities, which attract students from a definite area and spread them back again on a given zone which determines their influence.

At the same time, and this is why it is ambiguous, monks are usually stable in their monasteries, but Irish monks were not: they travelled, and travelled a lot. There were Irish pilgrims, forming a higher spiritual class, and also an intellectual class. A few scruffy individuals hiking along, maybe, beggars who were not welcome everywhere, but people who could share what could be shared with a benefit: knowledge.

Finally, and I will conclude my introduction here, the Breton bias. I am a Breton (and proud of it), so I might be slightly chauvinistic. Anyway it gives me a sort of privileged position, since I have mainly studied Irish influence in connection with Breton material. Apparently, the first place where Irish influence was felt, and where it was durably felt, was Brittany. In the tenth century, when monasteries were emptied at the Norman invasions, very often what the Bretons brought with them was Breton stuff, and very often that 'Breton stuff' was of Irish origin, with Wales or Anglo-Saxon England as possible and likely intermediaries. It is no coincidence that *scottus* can refer to an Irishman or to a Breton.[6]

I will more particularly insist on that aspect of things because it is still ill-studied, and more research will be necessary: to quote just one example, the first abbot of Bobbio was saint Columbanus, and he is (rightly) well known as the founder of the Irish monastery in Northern Italy. But his successor was a Breton[7] – and that made little difference for the future of the monastery.

2. The Three Main Contributions

The Irish contribution to European culture was not medicinal, or, thank God, military. It concerns three connected, even intertwined items: religion, culture and education.

Religion should not be underestimated: at a time when religion is severely declining and going far from our preoccupations, which become more and more materialistic, when profit has replaced religion, when differences in religion seem more important than religion or God himself, we might be tempted to forget its importance in Europe as it existed before we ourselves came into existence. But it was once part of everyday life, the sole beginning and end of everything, and the sole available explanation to everything and anything. The Irish contribution to religion in those dark times might seem minor to us; in fact it was essential.

The second contribution was of a cultural order. As I see it, the Irish contribution was essential to the survival of Latin. Latin indeed used to be *THE* language of Europe. It seems odd that nowadays we should be trying to build Europe in a political/economical way, because nowadays these are the things that matter. Indeed, in the Middle Ages, political and economical divisions were more numerous, and stronger, and quite unstable at that. Yet, in fact, in the Middle Ages, a so-called barbarous age, there existed a strong, real, actual community based on things such as one faith, one religion, and one learned language: Latin. Such elements of unity are nowadays much forgotten, preventing us perhaps from properly conceiving again that state of things which used to be and maybe is coming back again. The past teaches us a lesson here, if only because learning eventually outlives political passions and ignores frontiers.

Education, overlooked as it is by many budgets, seems secondary. In fact we must remember that someone who learns how to read needs something to read, and a teacher; if learning how to write, he needs to learn how to get a quill, how to sharpen it, how to make ink, how to make parchment, and he needs a teacher. The most important thing is that the Irish did a lot for the teaching of Latin, thus building up a dense net of relationships. Pupils do what they are taught to do by their teachers, and the Irish were the teachers, monasteries were schools; they had books. Now many Irish teachers (or their pupils) taught in royal courts, their pupils becoming kings, priests or bishops, or royal advisors. We cannot study the diplomacy of those times without stumbling on Irish names, even if those are not on treaties or charters.[8]

All this of course was under the roof of religion.

3. Religion

Of course, the Irish did not invent the Christian religion, evidently it was brought over here. But we then witness the following phenomenon: something imported that evolves, becomes different and is brought back to the continent, if not bettered, at least better than what it had become there.

However amazing it might seem, in the VIIIth–IXth centuries, the very text of the Gospels was practically unavailable.[9] When Charlemagne asked for the text of the Holy Mass to be established because he himself was not really sure of what was right, no one could find it and the text had to be brought over from Italy.[10] I am not sure, but this seems also to have been the case in Anglo-Saxon England, since they ordered gospel-books to be written for them in Brittany.[11]

In Brittany we owe the text of the Gospel to Ireland, though perhaps not only to Ireland. For 5 or 6 abbeys, we know over twenty Breton Gospels[12] before the year 1000 – and one psalter only (though the psalter was learned by rote and regularly recited). Why so? Simply because Brittany became a center for the production of Gospels for the benefit of other monasteries in which they had no text. I will also underline the fact that we have, both in Ireland and Brittany, and quite certainly in Wales and Cornwall as well (though I have no example to quote), smaller Gospels which must have been for individual use, or for use in smaller and poorer monasteries.

Let us consider these monasteries:

Monasticism spread in Ireland very easily. It is not very clear where 'Celtic' monasticism started first, maybe not in Ireland; but it is in Ireland anyway that it flourished to an unexpected point.[13] It did elsewhere as well, in particular Wales, Cornwall and Brittany, and also what is now Northern England and Scotland; but the fact is that when people travelled to get more knowledge, it is to Ireland that they went, perhaps because, as Michael Richter put it, 'Ireland was the most agreeable country to live in and to receive learning and instruction' in those troubled times.[14]

The first Irish monks who came to the continent were certainly not thinking of converting pagans: they did not come as missionaries, but as people looking for a separation from their own country in order to get closer to God. Nevertheless, they were not individuals or disorganised hordes looking for a cave for shelter. They had a rule and an ideal – and learning. This certainly is what made them welcome in several places, what led them to create more monasteries, for their example was contagious, and, as happens when religion is becoming lax, or weak, believers turn towards what offers them what looks to them as a truer religious practice; and the Irish monks offered that frame. One has to say that monasticism as it existed in Gaul was not of the best sort: monks married; had concubines; they had no books, and so on – maybe the very idea of what a monastery was, or should be like, was utterly forgotten.[15] The rule the Irish had however was not always a written rule, rather habits and regulations; obedience to the abbot being perhaps the only real rule.[16]

On the scholarly side, then, they had books and knowledge, but they were not deliberately spreading that knowledge – they had no sense of marketing. Nevertheless what they brought and kept there will be found later, diffused later, and that was potent. A detail: in Bobbio, some IVth-century mss (of Cicero's works) were found used for bindings:[17] they were not *that* concerned with lay matters.

These monasteries were schools – schools of religion, evidently, first of all, but also schools for Latin. In fact, in many cases, they were the only available schools, and for centuries all nobles, kings, priests of whom we hear as learned people were people trained in those schools, and they often finished or perfected their studies in Ireland. When they came back, I do not know if they had Irish, but they had Latin, and they had a wider notion of the world. I could not find many instances of Irish people mingling in European politics, but when we examine the history of diplomacy, or relationships between kings or bishops, we always stumble on Irish names, be it that of a master, be it that of a school, of a monastery, of a friend, of a message-carrier.[18] How could I sum it up?

In these international matters, I do not see Irish people having a prominent place, or a first role, but in teaching, they had a prominent place. Not in ecclesiastical matters, really, but in the teaching and study of the sacred language and texts. On top of this, like students who are more or less united by the fact that they have made their studies in the same place, Irish monks kept links between themselves, and so did their pupils, and the pupils of their pupils.

In Laon,[19] there is a manuscript of a work by Alcuin, and also of Bede. Both were Anglo-Saxons. Alcuin was trained in Ireland. The works of Bede were known on the continent by Irish intermediaries, and also Breton intermediaries, while, apparently, there is not one English manuscript among the old ones. If we follow the steps of the Laon mss, we have the work of Alcuin, an Anglo-Saxon trained in Ireland, who came to Tours, in France, and later became a teacher at Charlemagne's court, and became his biographer and the initiator of the reform of studies in the Carolingian period.

Well, that ms was copied by a Breton, where I do not know, but some aspects of the script are not Breton, and must come from an original written in Irish script.[20] It came to Laon at some time during the Xth century, and comes from a monastery founded by an Irishman and a friend, who was from Northumbria and had studied in Ireland. They founded the monastery of St. Vincent's in 961 with 12 monks from Fleury, where, in 960, Breton monks fleeing before the Vikings had taken refuge.[21]

Another ms., (Paris BN 12090), written in Brittany, contains glosses in Breton and Latin, some of them translated or adapted from Old Irish.[22] Everything remains within the family. On top of which, this is only what we know in reality: the truth is certainly more complex. The fact is however, that we find Bretons and Anglo-Saxons and Welsh monks here and there, but Irish everywhere, or they meet in monasteries founded by Irish monks, or using texts or manuscripts of Irish origins . . . and in their time, there are still Irish people in these places. They ate the same porridge.

It would take much time to describe the religious life in these monasteries, and it is not necessary. I think however that two points have to be considered because they were important contributions: penance and confession. For a modern Roman Catholic, going to confession is a normal act, and he would not think that he is in fact doing something quite modern. Nevertheless, originally, confession used to be public, and penance publicly given and performed. In Irish monasteries, and apparently in all Celtic monasteries, confession would be mutual, each monk confessing to his companion, called *animchara*, the 'friend of the soul'. The practice began with them, and spread.[23] After all, confessing sins in public is somewhat difficult, and the new practice certainly allowed thousands, if not millions of people to find relief in forgiveness. It is like finding a new medicine, not for bodies, but for souls.

After confession, penance. In early church discipline, penance used to be equal for all, whatever the sins, and could only be performed once, in a very stern way: ritual obligations like a place in the back of the church at mass, mourning garments, praying on knees, no conjugal practices, no military service, no trading, and worse, no communion. A bishop could temper this, but not much. In fact, it was perhaps too harsh to be really applied. Another type of penance developed in Celtic monasteries, which apparently never knew that type of penance, and invented a new one, where penance was given according to the sin. There was a law-like equivalence between the gravity of sin and the penance given. This gave rise to a new literature, the Penitentials.[24] To each sin its punishment, a certain number of years, or of weeks, fastings, and so on. Some penances were indeed quite severe, but there existed possibilities for commuting punishments. The practice was apparently imported onto the continent as early as the Vth century, perhaps in Brittany, the end of the VIth century, in Gaul, and this quickly gained ground without official opposal. Of course this was adapted and evolved over centuries, but once again penance as we know it (a certain number of prayers, and so on) has its origin on Irish ground. Was it influenced by Irish common law? I am not sure. Nevertheless, the redaction of laws and of penitentials have in common this constant care for gradation, foreseeing all possible cases, foreseeing difficulties in application, possible equivalences, and so on. I would hesitate to say that Irish Law had an influence on penitentials, but it is clear that many of these were redacted by people trained in law.

However: in the IXth century, so the (unpublished) life of saint Léry tells us, a priest was killed, the church treasure looted, and the local saint was called upon to denounce the murderer(s), but he would not. So they pulled down everything in the church: statues, books, garments, veils, called him a little old deaf man (which, if put into Breton, *is* offensive), and started fasting in cross-vigil for three days and three nights. The saint gave up, the murderers were caught and hanged. This does resemble traditional Irish law, but the practice must have come through ecclesiastical tradition.

One feature worth noting is that though most of these penitential texts come from Ireland, all are known through continental (several of them Breton) manuscripts,[25] which shows their success.

4. Education and Teaching
One of the particularities of the conversion of Ireland to Christianity is that it did not begin with the lower classes, or a few beggars or migrants, but that it started at the top, the very top, and in many respects it shows

that St. Patrick knew perfectly what he was doing; that he had a strategy to complement his faith.

In Ireland, the elites were converted first, not only the military, but also the intellectual elite, people who knew what knowledge was, what it was worth, and how necessary it was, even if it was for its own sake. St. Patrick had serious difficulties learning and writing Latin, which was a foreign language to him. But his followers, at least many of them, were already grammarians, if not linguists; not pupils, but respected teachers, and lawyers with a taste for subtlety – like all lawyers. People with a lore, and a capacity for memorising: changing religion was all right for them, but they demanded more than faith. They demanded the strong stuff. Consequently, at the very beginning of Christianity on the island, Ireland was like a sponge ready to mop up and absorb any sort of knowledge, and with the means to absorb it, willingly.

These learned groups in Ireland had a handicap, which eventually turned out to be an advantage: they did not all know Latin. Latin was the language of Christianity; the sacred language, the knowledge of which was indispensible for a believer to ensure his salvation. Latin was not really a problem as long as Christianity spread throughout the Roman Empire, where Latin had become the common language – even in Britain. Gildas Sapiens, though writing in Britain a hundred years after the Romans had left, could still be called a classical author. Latin was not the only language everywhere, nevertheless it had a dominant position, and was known everywhere. In Ireland, it was a foreign language (elsewhere people had it as a mother tongue, and could, for instance, listen to sermons in Latin) and it had to be learned first. They were eager to obtain books for elementary and advanced teaching, which were becoming scarcer and scarcer on the continent.

A young Roman had no need to learn Latin. What he had to learn was correct Latin, and the right way to pronounce it, in order to become elo-quent and thus gain access to the higher charges. After a few years spent studying the literary/correct language, he would learn rhetoric, compete in *declamationes*, and then give up school. For the plain people, teaching was not necessary. Later on, with the decline of Roman administration, and of Roman civilisation, schools became more scarce, rhetoric was no longer taught, books for the teaching and learning of Latin were kept for a while, then were forgotten or destroyed. At the same time, Latin was evolving into Late Latin, and various languages which at the time were not much more than degenerate Latin. In the VII–VIIIth centuries, Latin had become a dead language, while there were no schools, no books, no teachers to make things right again. In the Vth century already, Gregory of Tours wrote a History of the Franks. He apologises for the quality of his Latin, he is conscious that he is not writing proper Latin, but there is no way for him to improve or correct his Latin, no one to criticise or help him.[26]

In Ireland, the basics had to be learnt, and therefore taught. Very early therefore, they collected books for the learning of Latin, but without that self-confidence which the continentals had: these, even speaking degenerate latin, 'could manage'. An Irishman could not rely on his mother tongue for help. In fact, what books they got were made for the teaching of Latin, but not as a foreign language. Nevertheless, they made do with that, trying to get what knowledge of Latin they could.

On the continent, with the decline of paganism, quite a body of literature was condemned by the Church, and was not preserved: authors were banned, books destroyed, literature being reduced to the Bible, the Gospels, the writings of the Fathers. Cicero, Horatius, etc., were forgotten. Only one author escaped: Virgilius, because he was mistakenly considered a prophet, and because his works were abundantly quoted by authorities such as Donatus, and St. Jerome. In Ireland, on the contrary, such authors were welcome inasmuch as they could help to learn Latin. On the continent what turned the Church against these writings was the pagan elements of them. In Ireland, paganism was of a different sort, and this did not arouse as much hostility.

Since they had to learn the language as a foreign one, the Irish developed new types of grammar, as complements of the existing ones.[27] A native needs no grammar to speak his own language, but it is necessary, at least helpful for a foreign language. Now in monasteries the learning of Latin (and often learning by rote) began quite early at the age of twelve, but instead of stopping at the age of 20, it would endure: learning Latin was not reserved for children, it was also necessary for adults, and while a Roman would not study grammar any more when he had become an adult, an Irishman would have to if he wanted to ensure his salvation. Grammar then could not stay at an elementary level. Thus they ensured the teaching of Latin, and therefore of grammar. Of course, they had kept, and they transmitted, grammars from antiquity, which served as books of reference. But they invented new grammars, and new grammatical approaches. Roman grammars were made for natives, and eventually they were rather descriptions of the basic facts of language, a study of exceptions, at times lists of things 'not to say' rather than grammars. They were analytical, not describing the functioning of the language.

Irish grammarians had a more synthetic approach, looking for more general rules governing not only words but their relationships within the sentence, the connexion of sentences, trying to sort out the serious problems they had with relative sentences for instance. The functioning of the relative pronoun is something hard to master when there is nothing of the sort in the native tongue, and so is subordination, and so is the peculiar order of words, the splitting of word-groups. The Irish apparently were the first to elaborate a method for analysing sentences and their relationships. The method passed on to the Anglo-Saxons, the Brittons and the Bretons. When I was young and learned (or tried to learn) Latin, what we did was the same thing: in a poem, try to connect the noun and the adjective that went with it, where is the verb and the end of the sentence, connect subject and verb, pronoun and verb, verb and adverb. That type of analysis was in fact initiated long ago by the first Christians who had to learn Latin. The method has known many variations, but it is basically, the same.

The result was that at the beginning of the IXth century – the time of Charlemagne, when Latin was a foreign language for everyone – the Irish (and thanks to them, the Anglo-Saxons and the Bretons) were nearly the only ones equipped to deal with the problem. This, maybe, prevented Latin from sinking into oblivion; and allowed it to become or remain the language for communication in Europe during the Middle-Ages and afterwards.

One of the best ways to learn a language is certainly to speak it, but we have no record of how they spoke Latin, so I might be wiser to leave it aside. Another way is to write. Certainly that was part of the training. Therefore the Irish wrote, that is, they created texts. I am not speaking of literature actually, merely of commentaries.[28] On the continent, at the same time, we just wonder how many individuals were still able to write: in a few places, there were people who would redact charters, but using models and formulae, nothing original at all. Others were able to sign their names, but we can wonder if they could actually do more than that. At the same time, maybe out of intellectual laziness or excess rigorousness, original writing had become impossible, and mere copying had become increasingly difficult.[29] The Irish would leave no stone unturned, every word in the Bible and Gospel would be examined, studied and commented upon. On the continent, what the fathers had written had become the sole possible commentaries. Nothing beside it was admitted, or even conceived. As a consequence, in the VII–VIIIth centuries, the Irish were nearly the only ones who still composed in Latin, however surprising it might seem.

We cannot say that the Irish invented writing, and the specifically Irish script, the Ogham script, has not been used on the continent to my knowledge. It was used by the Picts in Scotland, some inscriptions are known in Wales and Cornwall, but it seems to have been limited to Irish communities, and perhaps to be derived from Latin script. It must be noted that the Romans did not use abbreviations, except for common names, or for inscriptions, but that in manuscripts, no word was abbreviated, except, for reasons of respect and not of economy, the names of God ($\overline{DS}$ = DEUS) and Jesus (I$\overline{H}$S). That practice meant much space, and was expensive, all the more since they would then write in capital letters. But now once again we meet the phenomenon: the Irish inherit something, change it or improve it, and give it back.

The Irish inherited that script but, since they had the need to write a lot, since they had to write schoolbooks, since they had manuscripts for individual use, which had to be economical, they developed three important features:

a minuscule script, where letters were actually smaller. On top of this, writing was 'compressed'. I am not talking of course of the majestic lettering of the book of Kells, but of the writing of very humble manuscripts. Less legible perhaps for the beginner, but a definite economy.

a full range of combinations (ligatures) allowing letters to be written in a shorter space (perhaps under Greek influence): si, st, ns, nt, and the like.

a full set of abbreviations, some of them quite obscure actually, but quite efficient, derived from Tironian notes, that is a kind of Roman shorthand.

That was a curiosity, of course, but the fact is that it allowed texts to be written in between one half and one quarter of the space that was previously needed (e.g. mía = misericordia, $\hat{g}$ = igitur). When we consider that one book at the time could represent 200 leaves, that is 50 sheep, we could say that it would cost the price of a car nowadays. That was no mean saving. Such an invention was welcome in many respects, but if many abbreviations and symbols were lost in the transfer, because they were in fact quite obscure, the ideas were kept. Even after the Carolingian reform, which changed the shape of letters towards more legibility, as we know them today, much of the system was kept. Even at the beginning of this century the Papal Chancellery still used some of these abbreviations.

The Irish were not behind every scribe, but they had actually brought something. I am glad and proud to say that the Bretons certainly contributed much to the spreading of this new way of writing, because they had it before the others. That, in some respects, was as important as the discovery of printing, or the invention of the typewriter: the cost of knowledge, the cost of books, was seriously diminished, and was within the reach of a greater number of people, even of individuals. To give an idea of what a library could be like in the Xth century: when the Normans looted the cathedral of Nantes, they took hostages on an island off the coast. Then, during the night, they drank one drop too many, quarrelled, and in the turmoil one man escaped at low tide, carrying on his back the whole cathedral library:[30] books were scarce and precious.

It seems to me that this development was possible because the Irish gave more priority to a very peculiar writing instrument: the quill, the goose feather. Surprising? not really: reeds used to be the most common instrument for writing in the Roman world, and they are in use very late. In Ireland, reeds, especially the right sort which I have never seen over here, were scarce, and perhaps unavailable, while goose (or swan) feathers were quite available. In a way, the Irish had no choice but to use imported reeds (they imported ink) or local feathers. Not an Irish invention of course, but anyway they used quills long before others, and since I have tried both, I can say that the Irish did much for the pleasure of writing! That instrument allowed for more suppleness especially in curves, and longer drawing. It is essential for what I would call *elegant* rather than *stiff* writing.

The writing they developed thanks to that instrument was quite peculiar, and highly characteristic, and it is plain that the writing used by Anglo-Saxons down to the Norman conquest was a writing taught by Irishmen. Actually it went further than writing. The first mission sent to England by S. Gregory in Kent in 597, the very year Colum Cille died, brought many volumes written in normal Roman uncial – but these seem to have had no influence whatsoever. Now in 634, when Oswald, who had been educated at Iona in an Irish community, became king of Northumbria, he called several Irish monks to help him. One of them, Aidan, founded the Abbey of Lindisfarne, the influence of which was felt as far away as Wessex. English writing, and the writing of English began at Lindisfarne. This is how the English came to write, Latin first of all, then their own language with Latin letters.[31]

At the end of the IXth century, King Alfred gathered in his court scholars from Wales (among them his biographer Asser), Gaul, Ireland and Brittany, who all kept coming and going.[32] His grandson Æthelstan was educated there: he sheltered Matuedoi, King of Brittany, whose son Alan became Æthelstan's godson, and also Louis IV, a future King of France . . . later, after Alan had reconquered his country from the Vikings, Brittany enjoyed peace with France for a good while: once again, the Irish played an early and apparently minor role, not appearing in the end and therefore too easily forgotten.

4. Culture

Let us distinguish native and classical cultures.

Was there an impact of native Irish literature? Apparently not that early. The main contribution of Irish literature to European literature was the voyage of saint Brendan, but it was much later than the period I am considering. The legend however was known in Brittany in the IXth century,[33] but it is only in the XIth century that the story was known elsewhere. Commentators of medieval literature occasionally refer to Irish literature (cf. for instance the Graal and the Cauldron of Plenty), but these are tales: we do not really know their origin and their dates: in fact, we do not know how these travelled, if their origin is Irish or not, or Irish through Latin, Welsh, or something else. Parallels are often possible, not unfrequent, and instructive, but ascribing an Irish origin to these is prejudice rather than demonstrable truth.

It is often assumed that all classical literature known on the continent had been brought by the Irish, who had been hoarding it while the whole of Europe was ablaze. A nice cliché, but far from truth, in fact.

What 'cultural stuff' the Irish got or had access to was got from ecclesiastical sources, and what they had, had already been filtered, excluding classical literature. It is true that in the early times of Christianity, many churchmen on the continent had a good classical training, but this was frowned upon, and usually discarded or forgotten when entering a monastery or religious life, and not transmitted or taught. Such literature was rejected because it was pagan, licentious, and anyway useless since clarity is preferable to flowery or turgid style in preaching.

What the Irish could get was quite limited therefore, to Christian material, plus a few authors that escaped, among them Virgilius. However, even in this case, maybe they did not possess the whole text, only quotations. They were certainly eager to possess more, but could not lay their hands on everything. Even if they had not whole texts, they had much to say about what they had, often reduced to crumbs of knowledge detached from the works of Pliny, for instance. We have a Breton manuscript of Virgilius (Berne 167), with Old Breton glosses, and a lot of notes in the margins, some of them referring to the cult of Pagan Gods in Ireland – nothing to do with Virgilius, of course, but there must have been an Irishman on the line all the same.

A good instance of this is the work of Isidore of Seville, which was a sort of compendium of all available knowledge of the time, drawn from pagan sources, but filtered and classified so that such matters could be made accessible to all. That book can be said to be the Encyclopedia of the Middle Ages. Though composed in Spain, it came to Ireland very early, and it is from Ireland, and not from Spain, that it was brought to Gaul, and Northern France. There is in Laon library a manuscript of it, with glosses in Old-Irish – and according to Pr. Bishoff's notes there exist three similar mss. written near Mainz, in Germany; there worked an Irishman called or nicknamed Probus, who gave mss. to the library of Rheims Cathedral.[34] In a way therefore, if they did not bring the whole of classical literature to Europe, they nevertheless seriously contributed to its understanding: they created a thirst for knowledge, prepared readers, they knew where books were and managed to obtain the texts.

It has been too quickly said that all classical knowledge on the continent had come from Ireland. In fact, what the Irish had and brought were religious texts, not even classical texts, plus quite a number of extracts, excerpts, notes, quotations from classical authors. It is rather as if they were the only ones with dictionaries. The fact is that they made classics understandable to people who had forgotten the language: in Laon library, most of the early collecting of books was made by Martinus, one of John Scot's (best) pupils.[35]

5. Art

The influence of Irish art is a more complex subject to deal with. First, it would be necessary to define Irish art. It can be quite simple to define it as a harmonious combination of native pre-Celtic element with Celtic elements, and foreign elements which can be traced up to the Scandinavian countries and the Mediterranean, and even further afield. That is to say, eventually, that though the originality of Irish art is patent, and though its native quality, if I may say so, is not contested, when we come to study the detail and not the whole, one motif and not a whole page, issues of foreign borrowing and native invention become more ambiguous.

Two examples will be enough: one of the great crosses of Monasterboice is evidently Irish. But if we study it panel after panel, the Irishness of each is not always that 'pure'. One of the panels of interlacing at least has a Roman model.[36] No one will doubt the Irishness of the decoration of such manuscripts as the Book of Kells, or the Book of Durrow. Nevertheless, the same thing happens: if we separate things, we come to the conclusion that Irish art is in fact a unique and harmonious combination of the motifs from several decorative abstract arts.

At the same time, when we try and study the influence of Irish art on the continent, and what influence it could have had, the problem becomes even more complicated. For instance, interlacing, or animals treated as interlacing. This was originally a feature of Germanic art; with variants from Austria, Scandinavia, Merovingian France. It was brought to Ireland, and there brought to a higher point of perfection and complexity. When it came back to the continent, very often under simpler forms maybe, or in the hands of inexperienced people, this complexity disappeared, and it declined together with the local native forms of decoration.

Another problem: if there was an influence, how was it exerted? It seems that the greatest monuments did not leave the country other than for England, and apparently exceptional works of art like the Gospels were not brought to the continent. What was brought was certainly closer to personal handbooks, with less elaborate decoration. I will therefore remain on the safe side. What they seem to have brought was a new concept of decoration. Decoration was not unknown, but it was, and appeared secondary. They showed that decoration could exist for itself. Instead of a wee letter with some colour on it, a gigantic letter. They certainly contributed to the development of abstract art outside a few decorative borders. One of their contributions seems to me that they had a technique which allowed a higher quality and complexity for decoration. They knew how to construe interlacing with a ruler and a pair of compasses on a manuscript. Even if we are at pains to describe how this was brought about, regularity and symmetry in interlacing certainly was an Irish import since it was unknown to Germanic art.

A parenthesis must be opened here as regards Breton art in the higher Middle Ages, because here we have something which owes more to Irish art and less to others, at least down to the Xth century. What is perhaps the earliest known Breton gospel for instance shows definite affinities with Irish art, and filiation is not deniable. The manuscript, known as the St. Gatien's Gospels, is a very pregnant and useful example.[37] The text it contains is anterior to the revision of the text by Saint Hieronimus, that is in fact an archaïc text, which must have come from Northern Africa to Ireland very early, and was later copied by a Breton in Brittany. This illustrates the early relationships of Ireland with the Mediterranean, and the debt of Brittany towards the Irish for the knowledge of the Gospel. It was done by a man called Holcundus, of whom we know nothing, and it has been neglected because it was (wrongly) attributed to St. Hilarius of Poitiers, because it was in Tours until quite recently, and classified as Irish.

In fact, we find elements which must have accompanied the text before it came to Ireland: a Carpet-Page which is a Coptic feature, which has known a certain success in Irish art: art for its own sake. On the top and lower part, two animals with crude interlacing have been interpreted as camels facing each other. In the margins, we find two sorts of abstract decoration: interlacing and goemetric patterns. The interesting point here is the way it was traced: the man who did that had a ruler, which he used elsewhere to draw lines. He might have had compasses. Nevertheless, he did not use them for drawings. This might lead us to think that in Brittany, they had models but no technique. Breton interlacing is usually made that way, quite crudely, clumsily, but at the same time without hesitation or mistake, as if the artist had carefully prepared and repeated his drawing before he put it onto parchment.

Another feature which had come to Brittany from Irish art, or from Coptic art through Ireland, is the degree of abstraction even in realistic subjects. They simply were not interested in realism. This is a feature which must have been partly inherited from early Celtic art, this technique of dividing a subject into separate surfaces which were motifs in themselves. In Irish art, the Southampton Psalter, which is an early manuscript, seems to me the best case to allow for comparison.[38] Once again, though, however clumsy it might look, we have the same feature: use of ruler or compasses for everything except the drawing, which is carefully repeated in advance. What we have is not a crude imitation, but a deliberate rendering tending towards abstraction.

Unfortunately, with the coming of the Normans everything will be swept away, dispersed, and will be forgotten. The only thing which will remain out of all this maybe was the courage to use full pages for decoration, or to give ample decoration to an initial letter, also perhaps the technique for drawing them with a ruler and compasses. In fact, we have to wait for the beginning of this century, the progress of photography, scholarly work, and nationalism to appreciate the real influence of Irish art on the Continent, as *the* Celtic art on the one hand, as an abstract art on the other. Before that, it would have been considered as crude and barbarian, not art anyway. But now, as originally, it is admired, used, imitated, copied, profitable, but not yet equalled.

7. Conclusion

The Irish contribution to the culture(s) of Europe was not gigantic, but only, if we obstinately speak in terms of size, of quantity and not of quality, because the quality was there. They did not fill up empty libraries to the brim, though they did found libraries, enrich already existing libraries, and give them the means to enrich themselves, if only by communicating exemplars, that is, books which could be copied, or by knowing where and how those could be got. More important, they often shook the dust off the old stuff, and brought a waft of fresh air which often was a strong breeze. They rocked the boat (for fun or by mistake, often more than they themselves thought).

After the collapse of the Roman Empire, and the crash of Rome, they shared and saved spirituality and the knowledge that goes with it.

- They kept up the flame of learning during the dark ages, by offering a repository for manuscripts, but also as a center for teaching and knowledge, without which manuscripts are just food for mice.

- They provided a spiritual backbone, a practical sound guidance at a time when Europe might have crashed back into barbarity.

The real, tangible Irish element is often punctual (like glosses, or interlacing), often filtered when it comes to our notice, or is transmitted through others; facts are often odd, or mingled, mixed up: Ireland has a glamour which Anglo-Saxon England, Wales and Brittany do not have, consequently the presence of an 'insular element' in a manuscript is often ascribed to Ireland or Irish scholars. Now if it is wrong (after all, I know at least one case of a Breton transcribing an Old-Irish gloss), once this ascription has been written, it can be taken for granted for quite a while. But, whatever the fire or the blaze, the spark that started it is often Irish even if the fuel was not.

So, even if the Irish contribution to European culture does not seem enormous in terms of quantity, it was enormous for the time, and it also was enormous in terms of quality and efficiency.

As regards religion, they brought back to life a declining or forgotten ideal, practical solutions, and ensured solidity. In culture, their contribution has been overestimated, but they allowed for the preservation of classical culture. In education, they increased efficiency, while through their pupils they did contribute to the making of peace, perhaps also to the future making of Europe. Their contribution in art is more difficult to appreciate, but it is clear in Breton art, also perhaps in techniques, though it is rather in our century that old Irish art has a real undoubted impact. Last but not least, they contributed to wit and did something to save our world from dullness; but to illustrate that would require another and a very different lecture.

Indeed, the Irish contribution was not the sole one, but it often provoked, or caused, or gathered more contributions. It was not gigantic, but it was crucial, and without it, we can wonder if there would have been Latin (once *the* language of Europe), and even religion. Certainly we would have been poorer. Anyway, in all senses of the word, it was generous. Thank you for it.

Notes to Chapter 3

1. Various editions and translations exist, among them Gerard Murphy, ed., *Early Irish Lyrics: Eighth to Twelfth Century* (Oxford 1956), p. 2–3.

2. Cf. n.18 below.

3. The manuscript has never been entirely edited, unfortunately, apart from extracts; for the quire signatures, in Stokes and Strachan, *Thesaurus Paleohibernicus* (Dublin, D.I.A.S., 1975), II, p. 507 and *Revue Celtique* 25, p. 377. For the ms., John J. Contreni, *The Cathedral School of Laon from 850 to 930, its Manuscripts and Masters*, Münchener Beiträge zur Mediävistik und Renaissance-Forschung 29 (München 1978), full ref. in index p. 204. Also Kenney, *The Sources for the Early History of Ireland* (Dublin 1979), pp. 589–591.

4. Contreni, *op. cit.,* p. 81–94.

5. Literature about Johannes Scotus Eriugena is bulky – access to it should be easier with Kenney, *The Sources for the Early History of Ireland*, p. 569 ff., and more recently *Jean Scot Érigène et l'histoire de la Philosophie*, Laon, 7–12 juillet 1975, Colloques internationaux du C.N.R.S., n° 561 (Paris 1977).

6. Léon Fleuriot, 'Les très anciennes lois bretonnes, leur date, leur texte', in *Landévennec et le Monachisme breton dans le Haut Moyen-Age, Actes du Colloque du 15ᵉᵐᵉ centenaire de l'Abbaye de Landévennec, 25–26–27 avril 1985,* pp. 65–84, esp. p. 70–71.

7. He was named Uuorgust; Fleuriot, 'Le "saint" breton *Winniau* et le pénitentiel dit "de Finnian", *Etudes Celtiques* XV/2, pp. 607–614; pp. 608–609 list the various Bretons known to have been companions of S. Columbanus.

8. Jean-Michel Picard, 'Church and politics in the seventh century: The Irish exile of King Dagobert II', in J.-M. Picard ed., *Ireland and Northern France, A.D. 600–850* (Dublin 1991), pp. 27–52.

9. Pierre Riché, 'Les Monastères hiberno-francs en Gaule du Nord, VII°–VIII° siècle', op. cit., pp. 21–26.

10. Archdale A. King, *Liturgies anciennes* (Paris 1961), pp. 140–144.

11. David N. Dumville, 'L'écriture des Scribes bretons au dixième siècle', in *Mélanges Fleuriot* (Saint-Brieuc/Rennes 1992), pp. 129–139.

12. J.-L. Deuffic, 'La production manuscrite des scriptoria bretons (VIII°–XI° s.)', *Actes du Colloque de Landévennec* (cf. n.6), pp. 289–321.

13. Olivier Loyer, *Les Chrétientés celtiques* (Paris 1965).

14. Michael Richter, 'The English Link in Hiberno-Frankish relations in the seventh century', in J.-M. Picard ed., *Ireland and Northern France*, pp. 95–118, p. 100.

15. Loyer, *op. cit.,* p. 48.

16. Loyer, *op. cit.,* p. 39–40.

17. Lowe, *Codices Latini Antiquiores.* Cf. Riché, *Ecoles*, p. 45.

18. Cf. J.-M. Picard, ed., *Ireland and Northern France*, pp. 21–52, 95–142.

19. This ms. is n.448.

20. More precisely: the final ligature -nt (minuscule) is traced with four and not three strokes. It is not a Breton ligature: it was imitated.

21. *Gallia Christiana*, t. IX, col. 600. The founder, Maccalan, an Irishman, was helped by Cadroen, from Northumbria, trained in Ireland.

22. These have been studied by P.-Y. Lambert in *Etudes Celtiques*, 22, pp. 205–224; 23, pp. 81–128; 24, pp. 285–308. His remarks, dense and documented as they are, foretell more discoveries in that field.

23. Cyrille Vogel, '*Les Libri Paenitentiales*', Typologie des sources du Moyen-Age Occidental, fasc. 27 (Brepols 1978).

24. Cf. n.23, and for these texts the fresh edition made by L. Bieler, *The Irish Penitentials* (Dublin, D.I.A.S., 1963). I would not hold for an Irish origin for all these texts.

25. *Ibid.*, p. 20–24.

26. Gregory of Tours, *Historia Francorum*, VI, 9.

27. P. Riché, *Ecoles et enseignement dans le Haut-Moyen-Age.* (Paris 1989), pp. 41–42, 89–92.

28. A glimpse of this can be had from Martin McNamara, M.C.S., *Biblical Studies, The Medieval Irish Contribution*. Proceedings of the Irish Biblical Association, n°1 (Dublin 1976).
29. Riché, *Ecoles et enseignement dans le Haut Moyen Age*, p. 45; the book sets the Irish contribution against its wider background, and deserves attention.
30. The anecdote is told by the Chronicle of Nantes, P. Merlet, *La Chronique de Nantes, 570 environ – 1049, publiée avec une introduction et des notes*, Collection de textes pour servir à l'étude et à l'enseignement de l'histoire (Paris 1896), p. 19–20.
31. Fernard Mossé, *Manuel de l'anglais du Moyen-Age*, Bibliothèque de Philologie germanique, VIII (Paris 1950), §8–9, pp. 27–29.
32. W. H. Stevenson, *Asser's Life of King Alfred* (Oxford 1959), §76 1.22, p. 60.
33. It forms the beginning of the *Life of Saint Malo* by Bili; Gw. Le Duc ed., *Vie de Saint Malo, évêque d'Alet, version écrite par le diacre Bili, fin du IX° siècle*, Les Dossiers du Ce. R.A.A., n°B, 1979, pp. 31–83.
34. ms. 477. These notes are kept in manuscript form in the Laon Town Library.
35. About whom see Contreni, *op. cit.*, pp. 95–134.
36. One of the panels on this Monasterboice cross is identical with a pattern on a sarcophagus in saint Sabina's church, in Rome.
37. ms. 1587, Nouvelles Acquisitions Latines, Bibliothèque Nationale.
38. A reproduction of these pages can be found in Françoise Henry, *Irish Art*, London (Methuen 1967), plates 45 and 48.

4. 'TALES OF THE TIMES OF OLD' – THE LEGACY OF MACPHERSON'S OSSIAN

Fiona Stafford

Let me begin with a birth. It took place in Ireland on 16th November, 1854, and though not directly connected with the subject of this lecture, is a good illustration of the often unrecognised influence of Macpherson's *Ossian*. It is not the child who interests me today, but his name: Oscar. Nowadays, the name Oscar may conjure up associations of wit, elegance, aesthetics and even decadence – largely as a consequence of this child's eventual career and personality – but for William and Jane Wilde, choosing a Christian name for their second son in the 1850s, 'Oscar' had very different connotations. In a letter to a friend, written only a week after the birth, Jane Wilde described her big, bouncing boy and announced:

> He is to be called Oscar Fingal Wilde. Is not that grand, misty, and Ossianic?

For Lady Wilde, the names Oscar and Fingal evoked the great heroes of early Irish legend; they were the Celtic equivalents of Achilles or Jason, and the choice undoubtedly reflected her passionate nationalism. What is interesting from my point of view, however, is that her carefully chosen 'Irish' names are evidently derived from the Scottish versions of the old myths, which had been familiar to every educated person since the mid eighteenth century, when James Macpherson's *Ossian* burst on an unsuspecting Europe.

For it was in Macpherson's 'translations' of the Gaelic ballads of the Scottish Highlands that the traditional heroes of the Fionn and the Ulster cycles were transformed into the 'grand, misty, Ossianic' images of Romantic readers such as Jane Wilde. Through Macpherson's phenomenally popular work, Oscar, Oisin, Cuchullain, Dermid and the rest were lifted from a living oral culture to become fixed in an essentially literary, printed tradition, where they exerted a powerful influence on late-eighteenth and nineteenth-century perceptions of 'the Celt'. Had it not been for Macpherson, Oscar Wilde's second name might well have been Fin MacCool rather than Fingal. What is more probable, however, is that he would not have been named from Irish legend at all. And this is the question I would like to address: was Macpherson a falsifier of the Irish tradition, or a vital channel for the survival of Celtic culture?

Despite Macpherson's popularity and massive influence on European culture, it has always been fashionable in scholarly circles to dismiss his work as unimportant, untalented and, above all, untrue. From Dr Johnson to Lord Dacre, the line of redoubtable English critics stands firm: all asserting, with varying degrees of evidence and expertise, that Macpherson was an ambitious opportunist, his *Poems of Ossian*, fake. And even among those better equipped to judge Macpherson's enterprise, the accusations of malpractice have been furious and frequent. Indeed, it has often been Gaelic scholars who have found the anglicised Ossian most infuriating – not because they assume that Macpherson concocted the entire world of Fingal and the Fiana, but because they recognise the vestiges of genuine tradition and see Macpherson as a distorter of Celtic genius. A brief extract from the preface to Kenneth Jackson's fine *Celtic Miscellany* will illustrate this point:

> Since the time when Macpherson exploited Celtic sources to provide a public eager for Romantic material with what they wanted, it has been the fashion to think of the Celtic mind as something mysterious, magical, filled with dark broodings over a mighty past; and the Irish, Welsh, and the rest as a people who by right of birth alone were in some strange way in direct contact with a mystical supernatural twilight world which they would rarely reveal to the outsider. The so-called 'Celtic Revival' of the end of the last century did much to foster this preposterous idea. A group of writers, approaching the Celtic literatures (about which they usually knew very little, since most of them could not read the languages at all) with a variety of the above prejudice conditioned by the pre-Raphaelite and Aesthetic movements and their own individual turns of mind, were responsible for the still widely held belief that they are full of mournful, languishing, mysterious melancholy, of the dim 'Celtic Twilight' (Yeats' term), or else of an intolerable whimsicality and sentimentality. Although scholars have long known, and all educated people really acquainted with the Celtic literatures now know, that this is a gross misrepresentation, the opinion is still widely held; and for instance a Welshman can hardly publish a book of the most realistic and cynical short stories without some reviewer tracing in them the evidences of 'Celtic mysticism' or the like.

Although this comment dates from 1951, I think the perception of the 'Celtic mind', to which Professor Jackson objected so strongly, is still very much alive. (When I asked a group of English students what the word 'Celt' suggested to them, I received puzzled silences followed by an uncertain list of harps, crosses, mountains, spirits and general mistiness).

It is significant that Kenneth Jackson should trace this false image of Celtic literature as mournful, misty and melancholic through the late-nineteenth-century Revivalists and straight to James Macpherson, who he sees as an 'exploiter' with an eye to the growing reading public of eighteenth–century Europe. But although I think he is right about the source, it seems to me that the process through which this image developed is rather more complicated.

It is also worth noting that Jackson's own *Miscellany* is explicitly presented to counter Macpherson's mists and mysticism, thus making it an example of the influence of *Ossian*, which has often worked not in the obvious way of fostering imitations, but in the opposite direction of stimulating fresh interest in the genuine Gaelic tradition. As Clare O'Halloran pointed out in a recent article on the Irish response to Macpherson's *Ossian*,

> Historians and literary critics have, for the most part, failed to appreciate the importance of Macpherson as a catalyst in Irish cultural development, confining themselves mainly to the damaging influence which his 'spurious and bardic sentimentality' had on Matthew Arnold's stereotyping of the Celt in the second half of the nineteenth century.

She is arguing that however annoying Irish scholars may have found what they saw as Macpherson's misappropriation of their culture, this very irritation has served as a 'catalyst in Irish cultural development' – stimulating new research and therefore appreciation of a native tradition that might otherwise have been neglected or even lost.

Before attempting to assess Macpherson's legacy, however, and his role as either preserver or destroyer of Celtic tradition, it is useful to consider the man himself and his translations/compositions. For although he was a household name in the eighteenth century, and his work was regarded by the foremost critics of the Romantic period as being comparable to Homer, Dante or the Bible, he is rather less familiar today. The news that Napoleon took a copy of *The Poems of Ossian* with him on his campaigns is generally greeted with a blank expression – for *Ossian* is no longer news . . . But this neglect is fairly recent, and the knowledge that Macpherson's characters were used in an advertising campaign for BL Scotch Whisky in 1923 is a good indication of the general familiarity with *Ossian* that persisted until well into this century. But no one should feel embarrassed to admit their ignorance of Ossian these days. My own work was after all the result of coming across frequent references to Ossian in English Romantic literature and being very uncertain as to who or what Ossian might be (even the entries in reputable literary Guides or Companions are not always entirely satisfactory on the subject of Macpherson!).

What people often don't recognise when coming to Macpherson for the first time, is his own passionate identification with the Celts. He is frequently grouped with Chatterton, who *did* invent the mediaeval Rowley and his poetry, or with Thomas Gray whose poem, 'The Bard', is an imaginative reconstruction of the words of a Welsh bard. The difference is that the so-called 'primitive' poetry of Chatterton and Gray was based on antiquarian researches, while for Macpherson the *Poems of Ossian* represented the living tradition of his own native community. Although his interest in publishing the Highland poems was undoubtedly influenced by the broader cultural influences that were also inspiring Gray and

Chatterton, Macpherson's primary motivation appears to have been a deep personal interest in a culture that had survived for centuries, but now seemed threatened with imminent extinction.

James Macpherson was born near Kingussie in the Central Highlands of Scotland in 1736. It was a gaelic-speaking area and he would have been brought up like any other member of the close-knit rural community, living on the family farm, surrounded by blood relations and familiar with all the local legends and stories from his earliest days. The common Gaelic inheritance of Ireland and the Scottish Highlands and Islands meant that ballads relating to Fionn, Oscar and Oisin were current throughout Inverness-shire, and it is easy to imagine the young Macpherson imbibing the stories at the hearth of his old neighbour, and well-known local story-teller, Finlay Macpherson of Lyneberack. Through the long winter nights in eighteenth-century Badenoch, story-telling and poetry recitals were popular social events, as the eminent nineteenth-century collector of West Highland Tales, J. F. Campbell of Islay recorded:

> During the recitation of these tales, the emotions of the reciters are occasionally very strongly excited, and so also are those of the listeners, almost shedding tears at one time, and giving way to loud laughter at another. A good many of them firmly believe in the extravagance of these stories.
>
> They speak of the Ossianic heroes with as much feeling, sympathy, and belief in their existence and reality as the readers of the newspapers do of the exploits of the British army in the Crimea.

Far from being a matter of antiquarian research for Macpherson, knowledge of the Highland legends was part of his upbringing, and he lived in a country where mountains, streams and caves were named after the Celtic heroes.

What is curious, however, is that Macpherson should have chosen to translate, or convey the old tales into English, and in a form specifically adapted to the taste of the polite reading public. After all, the poems and stories had been around for centuries and no one before had felt the need to communicate them beyond the Highland line.

The reasons behind Macpherson's decision must always be open to a degree of speculation, but there are various factors that might reasonably be assumed to have exerted some influence. If you visit Macpherson's birthplace today, you will not find a blue plaque with his name on it, and indeed the exact site of his parent's house is not known. What you can still see, however, are two impressive monuments which reveal a great deal about the man. One is Macpherson's own country house, Balavil, which he had built according to a design by Robert Adam when he returned to the Highlands in the 1780s, a wealthy and famous literary figure and by then a Member of Parliament. It is an ostentatious construction, in the neoclassical style, and as such reveals much of Macpherson's personal taste and self-image. The other monument is the ruins of Ruthven Barracks which, though less personal in significance, must have exercised considerable power over the imagination of the young James Macpherson.

Ruthven Barracks was built in the 1720s as part of the Government campaign to bring order to the Highlands after the 1715 Rising. It was part of the great network of roads and bridges built by General Wade to reduce the possibility of further insurrection and to allow for the swift movement of troops in mountainous areas. From his earliest days, then, Macpherson's image of home must have included the presence of soldiers, stationed within a mile of his father's farm to check movement among his own extended family. But if this political aspect caused resentment among the locals, the very existence of the road and the military presence was emphasising the possibility of a life beyond Badenoch. And for a boy of Macpherson's character, this must have been significant.

If Macpherson's early childhood was spent under the shadow of what might be perceived as an occupational army, however, his teenage years saw the aftermath of the Forty-Five. Though too young to take up arms, James would have seen his Chief and close relation, Ewan Macpherson of Cluny join forces with the army of Charles Edward Stuart on the march south. He must have seen Ruthven Barracks sacked by the Jacobites early in 1746 and left to blaze as the Prince marched on to Inverness. Soon afterwards, he may well have seen the relics of the Stuart army, fleeing from their disastrous defeat at Culloden, rally at Ruthven before dispersing for ever.

With defeat came disgrace for Clan Macpherson, as Cluny Castle was burned and much of the community destroyed by Cumberland's victorious troops. In the summer of 1746, Charles Edward Stuart was himself in hiding in Badenoch, along with Cameron of Lochiel, Cluny Macpherson and a handful of supporters. Although the Prince rapidly escaped to France, Cluny remained a fugitive in his own territory for nine years, while the British army maintained an intensive search for the rebel leader.

Between the ages of nine and eighteen, then, James Macpherson saw his home and family under constant threat of violence and repression, while the local culture suffered a series of deliberate blows. After 1746, the tartan plaid was banned and no Highlander allowed to carry arms or play the bagpipes. The estates of prominent rebel chiefs (including Cluny) were forfeited to the Crown, while the ancient systems of ward-holding and heritable jurisdiction were abolished. Such measures came on top of the earlier moves to open communications in Northern Scotland and to encourage the use of English rather than Gaelic. In the light of such developments, it is not surprising that James Macpherson should have perceived his native culture as being in danger of extinction, and thus his subsequent efforts to preserve the disappearing remnants of the oral tradition should be seen in the contemporary context.

Macpherson's collection of the old heroic poetry was, at least in part, an attempt to repair the damage sustained as a result of the Forty-Five.

But if the aftermath of the Rebellion heightened Macpherson's awareness of the vulnerability of his culture, I think it also made him conscious that the depressed rural community could offer little scope for a young man of his talents. His Adam mansion reveals an interest not only in the material side of life but also in impressing others, and Badenoch had few opportunities for fulfilling such ambitions. Fortunately for Macpherson, his intellectual abilities won him a place at the University of Aberdeen in 1752, an experience which was to prove as important to his subsequent literary work as his early life in the Highlands. It is, after all, unusual to become fully conscious of the peculiarities of one's home until one has lived elsewhere.

To summarise an entire degree course in a matter of minutes would be neither easy nor helpful, so I will merely attempt to outline the aspects of Macpherson's university education that seem particularly relevant to the development of his interests in Celtic culture. The most important feature of the arts degree was probably the general emphasis on the classics as the foundation of all knowledge; and while this may seem paradoxical, in that Greek and Latin are often seen as the antithesis of Celtic culture, the Aberdonian veneration for antiquity and serious interest in the development of society from its origins must have had an effect.

From all the literature of the classical world, it was Homeric Greece that particularly aroused enthusiasm, largely due to the extensive influence of Thomas Blackwell. His most famous work, *The Enquiry into the Life and Writings of Homer*, 1735, had portrayed Homer as a wandering bard, gaining inspiration for his magnificent poetry from the volatile society of early Greece and from the legends and tales of the local oral culture. The literary qualities admired by Blackwell were those of passion, wildness, energy, simplicity and natural genius, which he saw reflected in the highly metaphorical language of the Homeric epic. It was a very different sort of classical model from those imitated by Dryden and Pope and the so-called 'Augustan Age', and reflects the changing tastes of the mid eighteenth century on the road to Romanticism.

A similar enthusiasm for the 'primitive' can be discerned in other favourite Aberdonian texts. While Macpherson was an undergraduate, his third year tutor, William Duncan, published a very impressive translation of *Caesar's Commentaries* which displays a similar fascination with pre-civilised societies. Though apparently designed to present Caesar as a model for the Prince of Wales, Duncan's introductory essay reveals his own interest in the Germans and the Gauls. The enemies of Rome seemed to embody all the strength, austerity, courage and simplicity that disappeared in the materialistic society of the 'civilised' Romans, so despite the admiration for Imperial expansion, Duncan showed a contradictory awareness that the Roman conquests 'proved their Ruin, and they sunk under the weight of their own greatness'. The parallels with modern life were not difficult to work out, and it is clear that by the 1750s, Rome was being associated with not only Augustan power, but also the decline and fall of Empire.

Despite a progressive education policy at Aberdeen, with the usual aims of improving society through higher education, the ideals presented to the students were those of Homeric Greece, Sparta, Germany and Gaul. It is interesting to consider how Highland students would respond to such lectures, especially any concerned with the Gauls (i.e. Celts). Many of the characteristics of early society praised by Blackwell and Duncan as a result of their work on classical texts would, after all, have been familiar since birth. The ancient bard, for example, whose social role is discussed by Blackwell and Caesar, would not have seemed strange to someone from the Highlands where until very recently, the bard had been a recognisable and important figure in the community. The related tradition of oral poetry would have been equally familiar, while Caesar's image of Gallic society divided into small groups under a powerful leader and functioning according to family ties rather than financial obligations had much in common with the clan system.

At the same time, however, the notion of defeat is never far away. Indeed, Caesar appears to have emphasised the wildness and strength of the North European tribes largely in order to make his ultimate victory seem the more impressive. The image of the Celt that emerges from Caesar's *Commentaries* is that of the primitive hero – noble, wild, energetic, but doomed. It is the Dying Gaul, an image immortalised in classical sculpture, and one that must have struck a special chord for any Highlander who had witnessed the aftermath of the Jacobite Rebellion.

The classical image of the Dying Gaul sheds interesting light on Macpherson's perception of the Celt. Although he was being encouraged to admire the primitive virtues of such peoples as the Spartans or the Gauls, he must also have been conscious that his tutors' enthusiasm was based on their own sense of difference. As Caesar found, it is easy to praise a foreign people once they no longer provide any real threat. For Macpherson, however, the situation was rather more complicated, since he could probably identify more easily with the descriptions of the Gauls than the Romans. While his classical education was opening his eyes to the value of things he had always taken for granted, then, it must also have made him aware that in the eyes of those born outside the Highlands, he might himself appear as some sort of barbarian.

Emerging from University, we thus find Macpherson perceiving his home in a very different light from when he left. On the one hand, he could see new value in many aspects of Highland society, but on the other was a feeling that he must prove himself in the 'civilised' world. Throughout Macpherson's life there is evidence of his personal desire to prove himself a gentleman, and an accompanying sensitivity to the insults of those such as Johnson (who described him as a 'Ruffian') or David

Hume (who suggested he should 'travel among the Chickisaws and Cherokees, in order to train him and civilise him').

When Macpherson finished his studies, he returned to Ruthven to become the teacher at his own village school. By now Cluny had escaped to France, leaving the community depressed psychologically as well as economically – and none more so than James Macpherson. It was at this stage that he began to collect the local ballads and stories relating to Oisin and the Fiana. Presumably the collection was partly an attempt to stave off boredom, but it nevertheless suggests a new realisation of the importance of early poetry and the oral tradition. This might also have been stimulated by the publication in 1756 of the first translation of a heroic poem from the Gaelic, which Jerome Stone had published in *The Scots Magazine*. But what should be stressed at this stage, is that Macpherson's motivation was purely personal, and that he had no intention of publishing the verses he collected, nor indeed, of 'cashing in'.

After a few months at the school, he became tutor to the Grahams of Balgowan and in the autumn of 1759, accompanied the family to Moffat Spa. While he was there, a momentous meeting occurred. It took place on the bowling green between James Macpherson, (still only twenty-two, tall, unknown and rather awkward) John Home and Alexander Carlyle (both thirty-something, urbane, famous and socially gifted). According to various accounts, Home had a long-standing curiosity about gaelic poetry and so when he came across a young man who was both a native speaker and a 'good classical scholar' (Home's term), he was determined to get something translated. Macpherson, curiously enough, was very reluctant to comply, but eventually agreed to translate a short piece which he produced a couple of days later. I will include a few lines to give you a taste of his first foray into the Ossianic:

> He fell as the moon in a storm; as the sun from the midst of his course, when clouds rise from the waste of the waves, when the blackness of the storm inwraps the rocks of Ardannider. I, like an ancient oak on Morven, I moulder alone in my place. The blast hath lopped my branches away; and I tremble at the winds of the north. Prince of the warriors, Oscur, my son! shall I see thee no more!

It is in many ways typical, in that Macpherson uses recognisable characters from the gaelic tradition and draws on his native landscapes for the imagery, but is not making a literal translation of any surviving poem.

Home and Carlyle were delighted with the results of their cajoling and hurried back to Edinburgh with a handful of similar pieces. Macpherson was then summoned and, with due 'encouragement' from the Edinburgh literati – including among others, Hugh Blair, Adam Ferguson, David Dalrymple, Lord Elibank, David Hume – he published a small collection of *Fragments of Ancient Poetry, collected in the Highlands of Scotland*.

It is difficult now to imagine the degree of excitement roused by this little pamphlet, but if you read the letters that started to fly between the principal writers and antiquarians of the day, you begin to get an idea. Thomas Gray, for example, admitted to having 'gone mad about them', and it is interesting to see which aspects of Macpherson's work struck him most forcibly. The lines he quotes are these:

> Ghosts ride on the tempest tonight;
> Sweet is their voice between the gusts of wind;
> Their songs are of other worlds!

It was not the swash-buckling Celtic warriors that appealed to Gray, but the spirit world and the misty mountains. Already one sees the beginnings of the 'other-worldly' Celt which scholars such as Kenneth Jackson have found so annoying: it emerges not from Macpherson's text alone, but from what his readers found there.

North of the Border, it was not the poetic quality of these Fragments that excited many people, but rather the promise of a Scottish epic. In the preface (written by Blair), the poems are introduced as 'episodes of a greater work which related to the wars of Fingal', a work which is explicitly described as an 'epic poem'. Suddenly it seemed that Britain was to have its own Homer, in the shape of the ancient Highland bard, Ossian. In the competition for cultural supremacy that had been going on since the 1707 Union, it looked as if Scotland had a hidden ace.

The idea of the Highland epic obviously came from Macpherson. David Hume, for example, wrote to Adam Smith describing the old surgeon in Lochaber, whom Macpherson insisted knew the entire epic by heart. While it is possible to intepret such conversations as careful manipulation on Macpherson's part, it is important to remember that at Aberdeen he had learned that, on the basis of the Homeric example, the natural form for early heroic poetry was the epic. It therefore seemed logical that the stories and poems current in the Highlands were the broken remains of a much older and more complete work.

Whatever Macpherson's motives, the promise of a Scottish Homer proved irresistible to the Select Society, who seem to have viewed it as a literary find on a par with the archaeological discoveries at Herculaneum. The knowledge that the poetry survived mainly in the memories of old men, however, gave the task of recovery an added urgency and so in August 1760, the Edinburgh intellectuals put their hands in their pockets and despatched Macpherson to the Highlands and Islands in search of the epic.

When he returned several weeks later, he was laden with old manuscripts and jottings taken from the lips of poetry reciters, which all had to be collated in order to 'recover' the lost epic of the Highlands. That the final work was to owe as much to Macpherson's imagination as to the materials he had gathered is partly due to his character, but is also consequent on the pressure he was under and the preconceived ideas which he shared with his patrons as to the nature of early poetry.

By the end of 1761, the Scottish *Iliad* was ready for the press and appeared under the title, *Fingal: An Ancient Epic Poem in six books,*

together with several other poems, by Ossian the Son of Fingal. Since time
is limited, I will not comment on the content of the book here, but merely
draw attention to the title-page, which embodies Macpherson's complicated attitude towards Celtic culture and helps explain some of the influence of *Ossian.* The format is that of a classical translation, complete with
a Virgilian tag to elevate the Celtic epic to the level of the *Aeneid.* In the
centre of the engraving is the rhapsodic bard, reminiscent of eighteenth-
century portrayals of Homer. He is surrounded by Celtic motifs – the
Irish harp, the oak tree, the mountain, rocks and river – but the overall
image is of a stage-set rather than a real landscape. Gazing at the bard is
the thinly draped figure of Malvina whose pose is that of the classical god-
dess rather than of the Highland lass, while the ghostly warriors in the
clouds seem largely decorative, rather than threatening or tragic. And
similarly with his text; Macpherson drew on his native culture for material, but refashioned it according to prevailing aesthetic tastes thus providing images of the Celt, rather than genuine Celtic poetry.

Macpherson's poems were massively successful, not only in Scotland
but throughout Europe and America. In London, for example, one finds
Mr and Mrs Sheridan (parents of R.B.) using *Ossian* as an emotional
thermometer by which to assess the sensibilities of their guests. *Fingal*
was also received warmly in Paris and by 1763, the first translation by the
Italian Melchior Cesarotti was sweeping across Europe. In Germany,
Herder seized on the poems of Ossian to support his own theories of folk
culture, while numerous creative writers turned to Macpherson for new
inspiration. The most famous example is Goethe, whose temperamental
hero, Werther, whips himself into a frenzy by reading Ossian before
shooting himself and apparently encouraging a wave of suicides. By the
1790s, *Ossian* had been published in America, inspiring a number of dramatic productions and continuing to influence writers such as Cooper,
Whitman and Longfellow until well into the nineteenth century. Even in
England where people were perhaps most reluctant to acknowledge
Scottish genius, Macpherson's influence was extraordinary. As new
editions poured from the press, so the imitations poured from
Macpherson's readers, and almost every one of the major Romantic
poets drew on *Ossian* at some point. Coleridge even planned an opera
based on 'Carthon' but, like so many of his grand schemes, it never got
further than his notebook.

But what was it that people found in *Ossian*? The answer is probably
quite simple – they have always found what they were looking for. It may
seem odd that the same text can have provided images of heroism, action
and adventure for some readers, while others were moved by the sweet
tales of love, the chivalric ideals, the sensibility of the heroes or the sublime landscapes. What stimulated philosophical ideas on the progress of
society in some was little more than emotional escapism to others, and
this, perhaps, is the secret of Macpherson's success. On one level *Ossian*
is a historical blockbuster suited to eighteenth-century tastes, with all the

sex, violence and supernatural ingredients that so often feature in the genre. But the knowledge that readers as sophisticated as Coleridge, Goethe and Hazlitt should also respond so positively suggests that there is more to *Ossian* than sensationalism.

An important aspect of Macpherson's work is the very insubstantial quality of the texts. The mistiness that was to displease Kenneth Jackson had great appeal for Romantic readers, who felt free to create their own worlds, using hints from Macpherson. The text is built up of impressions – stones, rocks, ruined trees, streams and storms – from which disembodied voices emerge from time to time. There is a strongly elegiac tone, but no clear idea of what is being lamented, or by whom. Since so many of the characters appear only for a few pages before dissolving again, the overriding impression is not of a straight narrative with distinct episodes, but of a strange, intangible landscape filled with half-developed figures in similar states of despair and longing. This is also accentuated by the device of the narrator, Ossian, who is ultimately the most prominent character, if only because all the heroes of his songs are dead.

The mixed responses to Macpherson's vague Highland world are demonstrated by the various paintings on Ossianic themes that have survived. Napoleon, for example, seems to have seen Ossian not as the poet of defeat, but as an ancient Gallic bard, inspiring military ambition through his evocation of great heroes. At Malmaison, paintings by both Gerard and Girodet illustrate this martial element, its contemporary relevance emphasised by the extraordinary 'Apotheosis of Napoleon's Generals' which depicts Ossian embracing the Imperial army. In the same collection, however, is Ingres' 'Dream of Ossian', which is much more static in design, and portrays the bard's melancholy rather than his anger. Ingres' painting is classical rather than Gothic in inspiration and can be seen perhaps as an early nineteenth-century version of 'The Dying Gaul'. It is also marked by a profusion of nude women which, though perhaps surprising in the Highland setting, had been a common feature in Ossianic iconography since the appearance of the first edition. Angelica Kauffman's, 'Trenmor and Inibaca', 1773, for example, had been neither misty, militaristic nor melancholic, but depicted a moment of Ossianic titillation, as Inibaca reveals her sex to a startled Trenmor.

For J. M. W. Turner, painting 'Fingal's Cave' in 1832 in the wake of a host of Romantic readings of *Ossian*, the human dimension of the myth had been subsumed into a bright haze, which contrasts with the dark steamship in the foreground and the sinking sun on the horizon. The nineteenth-century perception of the Celts as a semi-magical people, a Romantic alternative to their own industrial society, but always associated with sunsets, twilights and death is already well-developed.

The misty, other-worldly image of the Celt thus had as much to do with what Macpherson's readers created in response to his work, as with his own texts. In late eighteenth and early nineteenth century Europe, the need for an alternative to the polite, urban society of the Enlightenment was very real. As anxieties about the corruption and decay of Western civilisation grew, so the Rousseauan ideal of the Noble Savage began to gain ground. *Ossian* was the perfect text, because it had all the virtues of the 'natural' (i.e. uncorrupted) age, but none of the inconvenient barbarity that so often seemed to accompany 'primitive' people. As Hugh Blair observed,

> In Ossian we find the fire and the enthusiasm of the most early times, combined with an amazing degree of regularity and art. We find tenderness, and even delicacy of sentiment greatly predominant over fierceness and barbarity. Our hearts are melted with the softest feelings, and at the same time elevated with the highest ideas of magnanimity, generosity and true heroism.

Nor was it merely the happy combination of primitive and refined virtues. From the 1750s, there was a growing taste for wild scenery to thrill and terrify readers with ideas of vastness and 'the Sublime'. Macpherson's Highland scenes, with their storms and ghosts were thus the perfect embodiment of Burkean aesthetics, and by 1817, when John Martin painted 'The Bard', the association between the figure of the Celtic Bard and a 'sublime' mountain setting was well established.

For the late eighteenth-century, *Ossian* was somehow very necessary, psychologically. If the Celts hadn't existed, it would have been necessary to invent them, but that is of course what many critics assumed Macpherson had done. Once again, however, the objections to *Ossian* reveal as much about the cultural preoccupations of the assailants as the positive responses reveal of the enthusiasts.

Almost as soon as the *Fragments* appeared, so did the doubts as to whether they were genuine. Even Gray, who was so 'extasié' about the poetry, found it hard to believe that such poems could have survived intact from the third century. Indeed, it seems to have been his prejudice against contemporary Scots alone that made him accept the authenticity of *Ossian*: 'I will have them antique, for I never knew a Scotchman of my own time that could read, much less write poetry; and such poetry too!' (Anyone familiar with Johnson's *Journey to the Western Islands* will remember similar prejudices colouring any discussion of *Ossian*.)

It was from Ireland, however, that the more informed criticisms were to emerge, from men such as Ferdinando Warner, Charles O'Conor and Sylvester O'Halloran, who seem to have objected not to the poetry, but to Macpherson's presentation of himself as a Celtic expert. Briefly the Irish objections can be summed up as follows;

1. That Macpherson handled his sources too freely, taking unjustified liberties with the form and the names.

2. That he confused the Fionn and Ulster cycles to make Fingal and Cuchullain contemporaries – an error all the more unforgivable for someone so proud of his historical credentials.

3. That he appropriated Irish heroes onto Scottish soil and refused to accept that the Scots were originally inhabitants of Ireland.

Although there is considerable justification for much of the Irish attack, it is worth remembering the conditions under which Macpherson was working. The manuscripts he collected are extremely difficult to decipher and for someone working without the guidance of an established tradition of gaelic scholarship, largely inaccessible. By the eighteenth century, there was also a considerable divergence between the oral tradition of the Highlands and the more literary culture of Ireland, which may account for some of Macpherson's 'liberties', including the mixing of distinct ballad cycles. What seemed intolerably anachronistic to an Irish scholar such as O'Conor was probably nothing more than a reflection of what Macpherson had heard since his childhood, in poems where Fingal and Cuchullian could appear together for the purposes of a good story.

Macpherson's refusal to see Fingal as Irish, too, is probably due in part to the common gaelic inheritance and, since the heroic names are common throughout the landscape of the Highlands, it perhaps seemed reasonable to assert a Scottish origin for the Scots. But here, of course, Macpherson's native pride must have influenced his interpretations of early history, for the Ossianic poems are very much a personal myth of origin and the Scottishness of the Celtic past would have been important. It is also significant, that this particular criticism has seemed important only to Irish scholars, who have perhaps been influenced by similar preoccupations.

My purpose, however, is not to defend Macpherson, but merely to show that any assessment of his contribution to the culture of Europe is complicated firstly by the controversial nature of his work and secondly by the response of readers, whose judgements have so often said more about the reader than the text. And so – what is Macpherson's contribution to European culture? Perhaps a few points can be made in conclusion.

From a purely antiquarian point of view, Macpherson deserves credit for saving a number of invaluable manuscripts, most notably the *Book of the Dean of Lismore*, which is the finest surviving collection of mediaeval gaelic poetry. Given the reported fate of various similar manuscripts at the same time (one thinks of Lachlan MacMhuirich's description of an old collection being cut up to make tailor's measures, or the Douay manuscript which provided kindling for several days) there can be no doubt that Macpherson's collection and the general recognition he effected, that such books were worth preserving, is of the highest importance.

As mentioned earlier, he has also served as an important 'catalyst' for Celtic researches. The arguments over the authenticity of *Ossian* produced some of the finest work on gaelic poetry, including J. F. Campbell of Islay's monumental *Popular Tales of the West Highlands* and *Leabhar na Feinne*.

More difficult and debatable, however, is his raising of the Celt in European consciousness. I have spoken briefly of the extraordinary vogue for Ossian in the eighteenth and nineteenth centuries, but in addition to the direct influence was the part played by Macpherson in altering the entire perception of Celtic culture in modern Europe. The image of the Highlands, for example, changes decisively at this period, from being perceived as a terrifying, inhospitable region full of illiterate barbarians, to become the romantic, Northern Arcadia favoured by Queen Victoria for her summer holidays. Although the change is not due to Macpherson alone, his work was nevertheless an important factor in the creation of the new, post-Jacobite myth. Let us consider Wordsworth's most famous Scottish poem, 'The Solitary Reaper':

Behold her, single in the field,
Yon solitary Highland lass!
Reaping and singing by herself;
Stop here, or gently pass!
Alone she cuts, and binds the grain,
And sings a melancholy strain;
O listen! for the Vale profound
Is overflowing with the sound.

No Nightingale did ever chaunt
So sweetly to reposing bands
Of Travellers in some shady haunt,
Among Arabian Sands:
No sweeter voice was ever heard
In spring-time from the Cuckoo-bird,
Breaking the silence of the seas
Among the farthest Hebrides.
Will no one tell me what she sings?
Perhaps the plaintive numbers flow
For old, unhappy, far-off things,
And battles long ago:
Or is it some more humble lay,
Familiar matter of today?
Some natural sorrow, loss, or pain,
That has been, and may be again!

Whate'er the theme, the Maiden sang
As if her song could have no ending;
I saw her singing at her work,
And o'er the sickle bending;
I listened till I had my fill:
And, as I mounted up the hill,
The music in my heart I bore,
Long after it was heard no more.

Here we have the Romantic Celt: solitary, melancholic, but nevertheless a natural poet, singing more sweetly than the nightingale. But the Celt is also strange and beyond communication. The songs are in an unfamiliar tongue, suggestive of 'old, unhappy, far-off things, And battles long ago' (in other words, of Ossian). They are also under threat. For it is the masculine, English observer who absorbs them and continues up the hill, while the sweet voice of the feminine Celt is 'heard no more'.

Wordsworth's 'Solitary Reaper' looks forward to Matthew Arnold's perception of the Celt, which appeared almost a century after Macpherson's original publication. In his famous lectures on *The Study of Celtic Literature*, Arnold argued for the development of Celtic studies in Britain. His very emphasis on *study*, however, re-inforced the existing sense of the Celt as an Other – remote, wild, admirable in many ways, but basically alien to nineteenth-century society.

The qualities admired by Arnold owe much to the image that had its seeds in *Ossian* and had grown up through a century of Romantic mythmaking, the key words being style, melancholy, passion, natural magic, sentimentality, sensibility and, of course, defeat. For despite Arnold's enthusiasm for the Celt, the entire lecture is written from the view-point of the Saxon, who may be less spirited, less artistic and less emotional but is nevertheless, in his own eyes at least, the winner in this post-Darwinian interpretation of struggling races. And this, I think, is important.

When James Macpherson describes the disappearance of Fingal's race, he is really dealing with the devastation of his own culture, and attempting to create a memorial to something that he sees as vanishing for ever. It is a highly personal attempt to come to terms with the problem of loss – a form of exorcism. But instead of portraying a victorious, non-Celtic army as being responsible for Fingal's defeat, Macpherson makes the causes of Ossian's grief mysterious. What emerges is a general sense of social decline, of the inevitable degeneration from a perfect state. The loss of Fingal is thus a secularised Fall, and the succeeding society is unquestionably inferior to that which it replaces.

For Arnold, matters were very different, and each of the racial qualities he appears to celebrate have the subtext 'ineffectual', or 'unable to survive'. In the context of the 1860s, a political agenda is not difficult to discern:

> And as in material civilisation he has been ineffectual, so has the Celt been ineffectual in politics. This colossal, impetuous, adventurous wanderer, the Titan of the early world, who in primitive times fills so large a place on earth's scene, dwindles and dwindles as history goes on, and at last is shrunk to what we now see him. For ages and ages the world has been constantly slipping, ever more and more out of the Celt's grasp. 'They went forth to the war,' Ossian says most truly, 'but they always fell'.

As usual, *Ossian* is harnessed in the service of a theory. Just as eighteenth-century philosophers had used *Ossian* as evidence of whatever their pet theory on the progress of society might be, so Arnold uses the text to support his own views on the Celts, which were coloured by both the new evolutionary concepts of progress as a racial struggle, and his own line on the 'Irish Question'.

If Matthew Arnold believed that Macpherson 'had the proud distinction of having brought this soul of Celtic genius into contact with the genius of the nations of modern Europe, and enriched all our poetry by it', he was himself contributing to the myth of the Celtic Twilight through his own interpretation of Macpherson's work. For, just as Macpherson had drawn on existing myths to create his work, so the Romantic myth of Ossian resulted from the combination of Macpherson's text and a host of subsequent poems, novels, plays, paintings and musical interpretations.

Should Macpherson be seen as an important preserver of Celtic culture? As virtually rescuing the heroic tradition of the Scottish Highlands from the verge of extinction? Or was he rather collaborating with its defeat, by refashioning the native art into alien forms, under the dictatorship of the dominant English culture? Any judgement on these points will probably depend largely on the person making the assessment. Personally, I find the question resistant to solution, but then, that says a lot about me.

5. PROTESTANT CHRISTIANITY AS A SOURCE OF DEMOCRATIC FREEDOMS

John Barkley

Over forty years ago at a Sunday School examination a brother minister told me how he had examined a young boy, aged about eleven, who couldn't answer a single question, so he said to him 'but aren't you a Christian', to receive the answer, 'No, I'm a presbyterian from Garmany's Grove'. 'I'm a presbyterian from Garmany's Grove'. Here was his identity. Here was the centre of his life. Now if you have never experienced being on the top of Mullyash mountain with the rain teeming down and a bitter east wind in the dark of the moon on a winter's night you couldn't know what the lad meant. 'I'm a presbyterian from Garmany's Grove'. There was the root of his identity and the core of his culture.

'Identity' and 'culture' are terms which cannot be understood in abstract. They may be discussed, but to be understood they have to be rooted. Let me, therefore, use a general term and describe 'culture' as 'a way of life'. When a student at Magee College, Derry, one of the books I had to read was W. P. Paterson's *Rule of Faith*. One sentence in it stood out then and does so still: 'The value of a religion depends upon the truth and sufficiency of its idea of God'. The same is true of a culture. A culture can be enriched or degraded by changes in its character, its aims or methods, its leaders, or its environment. A culture is not static. It is alive. It can develop and grow, or it can decline.

The changes and institutions in the sixteenth century may be studied from many angles. They affected the whole of Europe from Poland to Ireland and from Scandinavia to Italy. In various degrees the reforming movement affected all. In our approach we must not dissociate Reformed theological doctrine from its social effects, for example, Luther's doctrine of the priesthood of all believers formed a theological foundation for belief in the equality of every citizen before the law and his peers.

Historians are familiar with the achievements of Martin Luther and the hopes and failure of Cardinal Contarini. Let us rather look at the movement in Swiss cities like Zurich, Geneva, and Constance, and Imperial free cities like Strasbourg, Nürnberg, and Lübeck in Germany.

Let us take Zurich as an example. Huldrych Zwingli was born on New

Years' Day in 1484 at the village of Wildhaus, and was educated at Basle, Berne, and the University of Vienna. He was a brilliant scholar, became a distinguished humanist, and corresponded with Erasmus, the greatest scholar in Europe. He also studied Greek and copied out in his own hand the Pauline epistles. Ordained a priest in 1506, he was called in 1519 to the Gross Munster, Zurich. His study of the *New Testament* had opened his eyes and for some ten years he had preached from Scripture. This he continued to do. Indeed, in his theology the central doctrine was that Scripture alone was the norm and test of Christian doctrine and life. His scriptural preaching raised a number of issues so Zwingli called for a public discussion. The town council consented and fixed 23 January, 1523, as the date.

Some six hundred interested parties crowded into the Town Hall. In the centre was Zwingli and his friends with his folio volumes of the NT in Greek, the OT in Hebrew, and the Latin *Vulgate,* faced by the representatives of the Bishop of Constance. The latter's case was badly put. Two further disputations followed, but the papal cause never recovered. Zurich adopted the reform. The centrality of Scripture and the democratic procedure in the proceedings should be noted. This procedure was followed in city after city – Geneva, Constance, Berne, Strasbourg, Nürnberg, Ulm, Rostock, and others.

The case of Zurich illustrates that the reforming movement was a gradual period of non-revolutionary development. First, there was evangelical Biblical preaching, then the formation of a popular following, and finally, there was eventual government sanction. It was an orderly and natural pattern of change, not violent political revolt. The preachers were not revolutionaries, and the civil authority and people acted democratically. At the same time, the Protestant preachers must not be regarded as isolated from the circles of political power, for example, there was the relation of Spalatin as an intermediary between Luther and Frederick the Wise, Elector of Saxony, or the close relationship of Philip of Hesse with Melanchthon, Bucer, and Zwingli.

On the fatal field of Kappel in 1531 Zwingli, who was present as a chaplain, was cut down as he ministered to a dying man and finished off as he lay wounded. When his body was recognised it was treated with great indignity. With his death the leadership of Swiss Protestantism passed from Zurich. Into the vacant place stepped Geneva under the leadership of John Calvin.

At the end of the fifteenth century the bishopric of Geneva had been a perk of the House of Savoy. The maladministration of John the Bastard (1513–22) was such that the citizens rebelled and drove him out. Duke Charles II of Savoy attacked Geneva in 1525 and the new bishop Pierre de la Baume cast in his lot with the Duke against the Genevese. So the people repudiated the authority of the Bishop, the Duke, and his representative. Now the city was governed by the General Council; the Little Council of 25; and the Council of 200. The General Council consisted of

1 in 10 of the entire population; the Little Council of the four syndics of each of the last two years, the treasurer, and 16 others nominated by the Council of 200, which consisted of the Little Council and 175 others chosen by it. It was the Council of 200 which on 21 May, 1536, decreed 'to live in this holy evangelical law and word of God, as it has been announced to us'.

All this had happened before Calvin ever set foot in Geneva. Within two years he was expelled from the city and went to Strasbourg (1538–41). In 1541 he was not only asked but begged to return.

Two features of Calvinistic theology are relevant here. During the Middle Ages the Church was defined in terms of the hierarchy very similar to the words of Pope Pius X in the encyclical *Vehementer nos* '. . . the masses . . . have no right other than that of letting themselves be led, and following their pastors as a docile flock'.

In the Reformed tradition the Church is always defined in terms of 'the people of God'. The latter is certainly a more democratic statement.

While the Lutheran and Anglican traditions retained a hierarchical structure, the Reformed tradition did not. Bucer and Calvin on the basis of the *New Testament* held the ordained ministry to be, not an office, but for the service of the Gospel. The minister was called by God to proclaim the Gospel and celebrate the Sacraments. They believed in parity of ministers, and the moderator of a Church Court was *primus inter pares*. In every Church Court the laity was entitled to be represented, and the Lord of the Manor was on a par with a farm labourer. Government in the Reformed Church was a living example under God and His Word, of democratic principle.

The second feature of the Reformed tradition to which I refer is its concept of 'spirituality'. Calvin's view, based on Scripture, differed greatly from that of the Middle Ages, as found, for example, in Thomas à Kempis. No longer was it to enter a monastery and become 'a religious'. The world – its cities and towns, its market-places, its shops and homes – is the 'arena' of spirituality. It was not 'escape' from the world. The world had to become obedient to God. God had to be served in the world. Consequently Calvin as well as being a great theologian was also a great social reformer – railings were ordered for balconies for the safety of children, no fires allowed in rooms where there were no chimneys, latrines were to be provided in houses where there were none, streets were to be kept clean and refuse collected, manufacture of cloth introduced to provide work for the unemployed, a scheme was proposed for cheaper heating of houses, the hospitals reorganised, meetings arranged with politicians to prevent war, provision of a police and 'night watch' to maintain good order, building and repairing the city walls. Admittedly his regime in a harsh age was harsh according to present day standards, but it was far more humane than it is generally depicted. In all these reforms the people had a responsibility. Calvin was only one person in the Councils of the city.

Some consider the beginnings of toleration to commence with the *cujus regio ejus religio* (Whoever rules, his religion), of the Religious Peace of Augsburg in 1555. To me this is questionable. All it ever meant was conform or get out; for example, if a subject of Ducal Saxony became a Lutheran or a subject of Electoral Saxony became a Roman Catholic he had to leave the territory. Further it was only a Lutheran/Roman political agreement. The Reformed were not included. The Lutherans did not recognise them as co-religionists until 1647, and the Romans until 1964.

At the same time, you did have symptoms of tolerance in the existence of refugee congregations. There were English, Dutch, and Italian congregations in Geneva; there were English and Walloon congregations in Frankfurt; you had Dutch and French congregations in Strasbourg; you had English and Italian congregations in Emden; and you had Dutch and Walloon congregations in London, all within the Reformed tradition; all approved by the civil authority. Their existence witnessed to recognition of a measure of freedom of conscience.

In France there was the Edict of Nantes in 1598 giving a measure of freedom of conscience to the Huguenots. It was revoked in 1685. Many fled and a considerable number found refuge in Ireland.

Experience of the Anglican Establishment in Ireland meant that Irish Presbyterianism held the principle of the separation of Church and State. The reformers held both Kirk and civil authority were ordinances of God, and that life was to be lived in conformity with the Gospel. On the continent there was considerable concern and controversy on this relationship and the lines of demarcation. Acceptance of a concept of ecclesiastical pluralism lay in the future.

Ulster Scots would have agreed with Andrew Melville that in 'Chryst Jesus' Kingdom the Kirk . . . King James the Saxt is . . . nocht a king, nor a lord, nor a heid, bot a member'.

Roman Catholics will know that the Council of Trent consisted of three series of meetings, 1545–46, 1551–52, and 1562–63. The first two dealt with Lutheranism, but the third with Calvinism. The Lutheran movement was limited mainly to Germany and Scandinavia, and the Anglican to the British Isles, whereas Calvinism had become an international movement extending from Hungary and Poland to Scotland and from the Netherlands to Italy.

Today this world-wide community is linked together in the World Alliance of Reformed Churches consisting of 72,000,000 members in 173 Presbyterian or Reformed Churches in 86 different countries, with headquarters in Geneva. Its General Council – a non-legislative body, recognising the autonomy of each of the individual churches in decision-making – meets in various parts of the world approximately every five years. I am proud to say that the Presbyterian Church in Ireland played a major role in its foundation, and that each member-church has democratic freedom.

The first letter I received inviting me to this conference expressed an interest in 'the ethos and culture the Scots-Irish took to America . . . and in its religious origins in particular'. To this let us now turn.

Let us begin by looking at the life of a young man, born in Ramelton in 1657. In his home Grace would have been said before every meal. There would have been family prayers every day. In them he would have heard the Bible read. It would have been revered as the Word of God. He also would have learned to pray. He would have been taught in his home, in church, and school that the Gospel of God's love demanded from him and all men a response. He tells how at fifteen years of age 'through a godly schoolmaster' he was converted. The building to which the family went each Lord's Day was not called a 'church', but a 'meetinghouse', emphasising the *New Testament* truth that the Church is 'the people of God', 'the body of Christ', not the building. Here he was baptised with water 'in the name of the Father, and of the Son, and of the Holy Ghost'. Here he heard the exposition of the Word by the Rev. Thomas Drummond. Here he would take his place at the long table in the aisle, covered with a white linen cloth and partake of the body and blood of Christ. Here he would hear of the wider church in Europe and the Americas. Some days the preacher would be a stranger. Mr. Drummond was in prison. He would see his father as a man of significance taking part in decision-making with other men at the Kirk. He would feel the wind and the rain, and see the fields, the mountains and the sea. This was the core of Francis Makemie's culture. This was the centre of his identity. While all might not respond this was true of all members of the Reformed Church, whether in Ireland, Scotland, France, Hungary, or elsewhere. This was the core. Every other identity of nation, party, school or family, must be subservient to this. A culture, as we have said, is not static. It must be alive, able to develop and grow.

Here he heard God's call to become a Christian minister. Education was impossible in Ireland for a presbyterian so he enrolled in the University of Glasgow, 'Franciscus Makemius Scoto-Hyburnus'. This meant walking from Ramelton to Donaghadee, crossing to Port Patrick, walking to Glasgow, and at the end of the session retracing his steps. Learning among presbyterians was highly valued. As a student he was under the care of the Presbytery of Laggan by whom he was licensed, and in 1652 ordained *sine titulo* to go to Maryland where he arrived in 1683.

A man cannot be separated from his upbringing and environment. So he knew the drudgery and hazards of farming. Born within twenty years of the 1641 rebellion and within ten of Cromwell's campaign he would have heard many stories about atrocities, the Lagganeers, and the Restoration ejections. No doubt such things influenced him. But there was one other. He would hear about this, if not in his home, later at Presbytery meetings.

The Presbytery of Laggan, Co. Donegal, as early as 1673, complained that marriages conducted by its ministers were being regarded as 'fornication'.[1] Even though the universal practice of the Reformed Church that marriage be solemnised *in facie ecclesiae* and the procedure of the Church of Scotland was followed, some went to the bishop or rector to be married to avoid the *obloquium* or scandal that followed marriage in their own Church.

In 1702, the Rev. John McBride (Belfast) in his *Vindication of Marriages as solemnised by Presbyterians* complains of episcopal attacks on presbyterian marriages and condemns the episcopal clergy for demanding and taking fees in respect of marriages they declared to be invalid (see part iv).

In 1713, the Rev. James Kirkpatrick (Belfast) in his *Loyalty of Presbyterians* declares that 'extreme provocation' was given 'by numerous and violent prosecutions in the spiritual courts of many of untainted reputation who are libelled and prosecuted as fornicators merely for cohabiting with their own wives, whom they had married according to the Presbyterian way' (p. 507).

Under the *Sacramental Test Act* (1704),[2] which was not repealed until 1780,[3] presbyterians could not enter parliament, hold any office under the crown, enter the teaching or legal professions, and suffered other disabilities. Having dealt with this, Dr David Kennedy, St. Malachy's College, Belfast, in *Outline of Irish History* continues, 'More galling perhaps than these restrictions was the fact that the presbyterian minister had no status in the eyes of the law. The Catholic priest was regarded as an enemy of the State but the State recognised that he was validly ordained and that he could validly administer the Sacraments. But before the law the presbyterian minister was only a layman unless he had been ordained by a bishop. Consequently the marriages he performed were not valid and children of such marriages would not be regarded as legitimate. For the greater part of the century Presbyterians, like Catholics, were second-class citizens'. (p. 101).

Apart from a section in a *Bill of Indemnity* in 1737,[4] it was chiefly owing to the influence of the Volunteers that presbyterian ministers were enabled by an Act in 1782[5] to marry their own members and not until 1845[6] in spite of episcopal interference and opposition that the Government introduced a Bill to remove this stigma. Note that 1782 and 1845 were after the American *Declaration of Independence* (1776). Today the done thing is to play down the religious aspect and base the whole reason for the eighteenth century emigration on economic and social issues. Consequently it was necessary to give an illustration of the religious aspect that is beyond dispute. This is not to deny that there were economic and social issues, but no amount of revisionism can completely annul the religious. Suppression, real or imagined, colours one's outlook – and in this instance it was real and harsh.

Following the Flight of the Earls the almost destitute and uninhabited Laggan countryside came to be largely populated by Scots. While there had been an uneasy peace, the coming of John Leslie in 1632 and John Bramhall in 1634[7] to be bishops of Raphoe and Derry respectively, completely altered the situation.

In 1619, Robert Pont, grandson of John Knox, the Scottish reformer, had been 'denizated' as a 'preacher of the Word of God'; and it is generally accepted that he ministered at Ramelton. In 1639, he was 'obliged to flee from Ireland, owing to his opposition to the *Black Oath*', a political measure requiring everyone over sixteen to swear 'on their knees' and 'upon the Four Evangelists . . . that they would never oppose any of the King's commands, and that they would abjure and renounce the Government'.[8] Leslie administered this in the Laggan. Mrs Pont remained behind her husband. Leslie had her arrested and imprisoned for three years in Dublin because she had 'attended unlawful religious assemblies'. Though the bishop was held to have run into *praemunire*, no redress was received.[9] Further illustration is unnecessary.

To quell the rebellion of 1641, a Scottish army under General Robert Munro was sent to Ireland. Having restored a measure of order the responsibility of reorganising the church fell to the chaplains. They formed a Presbytery at Carrickfergus on 10 June, 1642.[10] Petitions for assistance poured in from many areas, that from the Laggan in 1646 stating that 'the whole country was void of ministers, except one, Mr Robert Cunningham', Taboyn.[11] Presbyterianism recovered somewhat, but it was in a precarious situation. In 1643, the Scots Estates and the English Parliament entered into the *Solemn League and Covenant* in opposition to the despotism of Charles I.[12] While the Ulster Scots were also opposed to the despotic claims of Charles they denounced without equivocation his execution.[13] Cromwell, therefore, having suppressed the rebellion made the signing of the *Engagement Oath* obligatory, binding those who signed 'to renounce the pretended title of Charles Stewart, and the whole line of King James, and to be faithful to the Commonwealth'. All the ministers in the Laggan refused and were ejected.[14] Indeed, all but five presbyterian ministers in Ireland were driven out of their pulpits by soldiers, imprisoned, or had to flee to Scotland.

It was not intended that only the ministers should suffer. At a Council of War in 1653 an act was passed 'to transplant a certain number of such persons (that is, leading presbyterians) . . . into the provinces of Leinster and Munster'.[15] The enforcement of this proved impossible. Both this act and the *Engagement Act* were political measures, but by them presbyterianism was decimated. Thanks to the intervention of the Lord Deputy, Henry Cromwell, in 1654 it was able to recover and by 1659 there were five presbyteries with about eighty congregations.

At the Restoration prelacy was restored, and all presbyterian ministers were required to conform. All thirteen in the Laggan were ejected.[16] The total ejected from their pulpits was 64.

The years 1661–65 saw the enactment of the *Clarendon Code*,[17] and in 1664 Leslie of Raphoe was responsible for four presbyterian ministers –

John Hart (Taboyn), William Semple (Letterkenny), Thomas Drummond (Ramelton), and Adam White (Fannet) – being imprisoned for continuing to exercise the office of the ministry and refusing to appear before the Bishop's Court. On a petition to the Lord Lieutenant, their case was heard before the King's Bench and later the Court of Chancery, in both of which it was opposed by the bishop. After an imprisonment of six years they were released 'by order of the king'.[18]

During the years 1662–90, the General Synod of Ulster never met and Presbyteries only clandestinely. Presbyterian worship was, for the most part, proscribed, and the doors of some of their Meetinghouses nailed up.

Makemie's American career illustrates his cultural background.[19] It is Biblically based. There is a moral standard in both private and public life. His controversies with George Keith (a presbyterian turned zealous Quaker, turned aggressive and militant anglican) show him to be a Calvinist in the Dortian and Westminster connotation of that term.[20] He deplored the division between anglicanism and presbyterianism but rejected prelacy as a Church-Order.[21] Opposing the efforts to establish the Church of England by law he organised in 1706 the first Presbytery probably on the basis of his Laggan experience. He rejects Erastianism completely.

In December Makemie and John Hampton, from Burt, who was t become in 1716 moderator of the first Presbyterian Synod, visited Ne. York. On Sunday 19 January 1707, Makemie conducted a Service in th home of William Jackson[22] and Hampton preached at Newtown, Lor Island. On the Thursday they were arrested and brought before Lo Cornbury where he charged them with preaching without a licence. Th were handed over to the High Sheriff and taken to his house 'as the pla of their confinement', where they were held until 11 March, forty-six days. The charge against Hampton was dropped, but Makemie was remanded for trial on 3 June.[23] The case turned on the issue that 'there can be no law unless there has been promulgation'. Makemie was acquitted, even so Cornbury ordered him to pay the costs of his prosecution, £83.7.6.

'When Francis Makemie stood before Lord Cornbury in New York', writes C. M. Drury, 'and fought the first great battle for religious toleration on American soil he did not stand as a solitary individual. In the unseen background were such men as Thomas Drummond, John Hart, Robert Campbell, and William Trail'.[24] What was it that put it in his soul to defy Lord Cornbury? Why was Makemie prepared to go to prison for the sake of religious liberty? Such a stand is not the luxuriant growth of a hot-house plant, but rather the harvest of years of bitter experience. He was faithful to his cultural heritage. 'The acquittal of Makemie', says Anderson '. . . paved the way for freedom of religion in all of the colonies in America'.[25] Without denigrating the contribution of others, such as the Dutch Reformed Church, the Society of Friends, John Witherspoon in New Jersey, it may be said that the Laggan made a notable contribution to the cause of religious liberty, eventually enshrined in the *Bill of Rights*, 15 December, 1791: 'Congress shall make no law respecting the establishment of religion, or prohibiting the free exercise thereof'. This freedom of religion was welcomed by Irish emigrants to America following the Famine in the mid-nineteenth century.

During his early years in America because of the number of emigrants from the Laggan, Makemie was well informed concerning the civil war in England and events in Ulster, such as the Break of Dromore, Tyrconnell's campaign, Derry, Enniskillen, the Boyne and Aughrim. Tyrconnell's track record as Lord Deputy was well known. His campaign following the Break of Dromore spared 'neither age nor sex' and put 'all to the sword without mercy', all unable to escape fleeing to Enniskillen or Derry. Derry stood at the end of a campaign of slaughter, so the city was crowded with refugees when it was called upon to surrender. The assurances of James II and Tyrconnell carried no conviction. The evidence of Tyrconnell's campaign was clear. There was no evidence that to admit would not continue in massacre. So James' terms were rejected, and a siege, which lasted fifteen weeks began. For about a decade after the Revolution Settlement presbyterians were able to act as burgers, but then were removed from their seats as anyone entering First Derry Presbyterian Church should know from the first Memorial Tablet to meet his eye. These events as well as the revocation of the *Edict of Nantes* in 1685, and the *Sacramental Test Act* (1704), referred to above, were all known to Makemie and no doubt influenced his actions in harmony with his culture and identity. These events all pre-date Makemie's New York stand for religious liberty.

The trickle of emigration at the end of the seventeenth century became a flood in the eighteenth, especially from 1718 onwards. This did not simply consist of individuals, but of whole families and communities. Between 1680 and 1775, more than one hundred and eighty presbyterian ministers emigrated. Meeting in Derry it may be noted that according to F. D. Stewart's *Fasti of the American Presbyterian Church*, three of those who were accompanied by large numbers of their congregations had lived through the Siege – James McGregor, Thomas Craghead, and Matthew Clark. While assessments of the total number varies, the generally accepted figure is around 250,000. In every case the cultural background would have been identical with that of Makemie outlined here.

Some years ago, when doing a bit of research in the Presbyterian Historical Society in Philadelphia, I came across a pamphlet entitled *Brewed in Scotland, Bottled in Ireland, and Uncorked in America*. While it only dealt with one aspect of the Ulster Scot culture, religious liberty, it neatly sums up what I am about to say.

Let us look at a family in Downpatrick and the grandparents' home in Saintfield. Here again the culture was the same with one difference. Both were manses. Francis, son of John Hutcheson, minister of Downpatrick, was born at Drumalig in 1694 and when he was eight years old went to live there with his grandfather Alexander Hutcheson, minister of Saintfield, who had been minister there from 1657, evicted in 1663, installed in Capel Street, Dublin, in 1690, and returned to Saintfield two years later. Here Francis, who was to become a scholar of European reputation, received his early education. In 1711 Francis matriculated at the University of Glasgow, being described as 'Scotus Hibernus'. He graduated Master of Arts in 1713 and entered the theological department where John Simpson was professor of Divinity. While his father had been a calvinist of the seventeenth century school with its primacy of law – law, law broken, grace – under Simpson's influence Francis was closer to Calvin – grace, grace lost, grace restored. After conducting an Academy in Dublin (1721–1729) he was appointed Professor of Moral Philosophy in Glasgow. Limitation of time prevents discussion of his career. Suffice it to say he proved to be 'an apostle of the Enlightenment', and that while not the founder of the Scottish Common Sense School of Philosophy he was its forerunner. Throughout the rest of the century this was the dominant School in all the Scottish Universities – Reid (Aberdeen), Young (St. Andrews), and Stewart and Stevenson (Edinburgh). The influence of this may be grasped from the fact that of the 350 presbyterian ministers ordained in Ireland in these years, 322 were educated in Glasgow and Edinburgh. This makes it necessary to summarize Hutcheson's philosophy underlying social policy

(i) Political philosophy begins as a part of moral philosophy which deals with God's moral law.[26]

(ii) Man is created by God with external and internal senses, of which the highest is 'the moral sense', and with the ability to reason.[27]

(iii) The criterion of right action is its tendency to promote the general welfare of Mankind.[28]

(iv) Man's passions and affections are a 'trustee' for society.[29]

(v) Civil society necessarily implies a 'compact' by which men agree among themselves to live in society and give over to some person or council the right to decide controversies, to compel obedience, and to direct the whole body towards the common good.[30]

(vi) Civil society is a body of free men united under one government for their common interest, thus 'the common interest of the whole people is the end of all civil polity'.[31]

(vii) The authority of the sovereign people, 'that all power is vested in, and consequently derived from the people, that magistrates and rulers are their trustees and servants, and at all times answerable to them'.[32]

(viii) Religious liberty and pluralism within a structured society.[33]

Why is this important? Because in another Donegal family, this time at Leck, a son studied under Hutcheson, became a presbyterian minister, and emigrated to America. His name was Francis Alison.[34] He became Vice-Provost of the College of Philadelphia (1752–79), and lectured on moral philosophy. A typescript of his lectures is extant and a comparison shows that he follows Hutcheson item by item and often verbatim. Among his students were two who signed the *Declaration of Independence*, four members of the Continental Congress, 11 who held government office in the States of Pennsylvania, Delaware, and North and South Carolina, two members of the Constitutional Convention, and five members of the House and Senate of the United States Congress, one of them being Charles Thompson, 'the perpetual secretary' of the Continental Congress.

This philosophy was also taught in the College of New Jersey by a Scot, John Witherspoon, one of the signatories to the *Declaration of Independence*. In his classes were nine members of the Constitutional Convention – the most distinguished being James Madison, fourth President of the United States. While this element of the Ulster Scot culture received recognition in America, it remained a latent force in Ireland because of the disabilities imposed by the *Sacramental Test Act*, which was not repealed until 1780. This may be seen in the speeches by Ulster Scots at the Volunteers' meeting in Dungannon in 1782 demanding the independence of the Irish parliament and the relaxing of the Penal Laws against Roman Catholics.[35] And similarly at the Ulster Reform Convention in 1793 demanding parliamentary reform and Roman Catholic emancipation.[36] Indeed, these speeches are paralleled in the proceedings of the Synod of Ulster. 'The Address to the King's Most Excellent Majesty' in 1782 says:

> ... As Irishmen ... we trust the desire of your Majesty ... to promote the happiness of all your subjects will be perfected, that every species of persecution for Religious opinions will be done away, when every equally good subject will be equally cherished and protected by the State ...[37]

In 1793 the Synod 'however unwilling to obtrude their Political sentiments on the attention of the Publick ... feel themselves called upon' to issue a Declaration:

> That as members of Civil Society they deem it not inconsistent with their Public character to join ... in expressing their opinion, That a Reform in the Representation of the Commons House of Parliament, is Essentially necessary to the Perfection of the Constitution, and the security and Maintenance of Public Liberty ... And finally, it is their earnest Prayer ... That Intolerance of every kind may be trodden under foot; and every equally good subject, shall be equally cherished and protected by the State.[38]

To this has to be added the fact that every Presbytery in the Synod, with one exception, voted in favour of Catholic Emancipation.

Following the *Declaration of Independence* the Ulster-Scot culture again played a role. The American *Declaration* did not establish a British/American relationship, but thirteen British/State relationships. The only body in which all thirteen States were represented was the Synod of the Presbyterian Church. It with its independent and democratic principles served as a model for the Federal Constitution.[40]

I have tried up to this point to avoid personal comment. Let me now attempt a summary. The culture and identity of the Ulster Scot is firmly rooted in the worship and obedience to God in Christ. This is the core. All other identities, whether of nationality, political party, school of thought, are subservient to the core identity. History, generally speaking, has depicted him as a man of integrity, honest and hard-working; opposed to dictatorship in Church and State. He is pioneering in spirit and radical in thought; and in the main, when given the opportunity, an upholder of freedom, justice and human rights. At times, he has failed. Men and women, being what they are, culture and identity can be tarnished. On the other hand, they can be enriched.

Permit me a Biblical reference which is the one absolute in the culture of the Ulster Scot? God declared to Israel, 'I am your God'. This demanded the response of obedience. But, on occasion, Israel did erect and worship 'a golden calf'. It is possible to make a golden calf for: Irish or British; Republic or Ulster; Orange or Green; Nationalist or Unionist; Derry or Londonderry. In fact you can even with Catholic or Protestant make a golden calf. If any aspect of an identity today demands amoral action, murder hatred, deceit, false-witness, the end can only be enmity, the loss of community, division and sectarianism and corruption of our true identity as human beings. The core identity alone can enable us to achieve harmony and gain true community.

Notes to Chapter 5

1. MS Laggan Minutes 1673–74.
2. 2 Anne c.6.
3. 19 & 20 Geo III c.6.
4. II Geo II c.10.
5. 21 & 22 Geo III c. 25.
6. 7 & 8 Vict c.81.
7. J. M. Barkley, 'Some Scottish Bishops and Ministers in the Irish Church, 1605–35' in *Reformation and Revolution*, edit. Duncan Shaw, pp. 150–153, 142.
8. The reference is to the *National Covenant*, 1638.
9. *Jour of Hse of Commons Ire* i pp. 379, 453–55.
10. P. Adair, *True Narrative of the Rise and Progress of the Presbyterian Church in Ireland*, edit. W. D. Killen, pp. 92–93.
11. *ibid* pp. 128–130.
12. *ibid* pp. 103, 106, 115, 143, 144, 213, 230.
13. J. S. Reid, *History of the Presbyterian Church in Ireland* ii, p. 151.
14. Reid, i, p. 247, n. 29.
15. Reid, ii, pp. 177–82, 471. The list in the Brit. Mus. contains 260 names.
16. Reid, ii, pp. 253–55 gives a list of those ejected.
17. 13 Chas II c.1. 22 Chas II c.1. 17 Chas II c.2.
18. *CalSPIre* 1660–62 pp. 203–204. Reid, ii. p. 287.
19. J. M. Barkley, *Francis Makemie*. R. S. Schlenther, *The Life and Writings of Francis Mackemie*, pp. 13–15.
20. J. Makemie: *An Answer to George Keith's Libel.*
21. J. Makemie: *Truths in a True Light.*
22. J. Makemie: *A Good Conversation.*
23. J. Makemie: *Narrative of a New and Unusual Imprisonment.*
24. C. M. Drury, 'Francis Makemie: Prophet of Religious Freedom' in *Prophetic Realism*, p. 15.
25. C. A. Anderson, 'Makemie's Struggle for Religious Freedom'. Typescript in Pres Hist Soc Philadelphia p. 2.
26. *Inquiry Concerning Moral Good and Evil*; *System of Moral Philosophy*, iii.
27. *Essay on the Nature and Conduct of the Passions and Affections*, i: and as above.
28. *Inquiry Concerning Moral Good and Evil*, iii.
29. *Essay.*
30. *System*, iii. 212–16; 220–21.
31. *System*, iii. 277.
32. *System*, iii, 266; iii 221, 227, 229, 233.
33. *System*, ii, 44–46.
34. J. M. Barkley, *Francis Hutcheson*, pp. 10–13. F. D. Stewart: *Fasti of the American Presbyterian Church.*
35. R. B. McDowell, *Irish Public Opinion, 1750–1800.* p. 61.
36. *ibid* pp. 189–90.
37. *Records of the General Synod of Ulster* III p. 46.
38. *ibid* III pp. 156–157.
39. *ibid* III p. 397. *Northern Whig* 24 April 1829.
40. R. B. Morris, *Framing the Federal Constitution.*

6. ABSENTEE LANDLORDS AND SQUATTERS' RIGHTS: THE SCOTS-IRISH BACKCOUNTRY AND THE AMERICAN REVOLUTION

Marilyn J. Westerkamp

When I first agreed to address this question of the Scots-Irish influence on the American Revolution, it was with some trepidation. To begin with I, personally, am not a political historian. I don't like studying war and diplomacy; I'm not really interested in politicians and governments. I am, in fact, a religious and cultural historian. I enjoy examining churches and theology, clergy and conversions. Give me Presbyterians and Catholics, not Democrats and Republicans. But then, this is a false distinction. As I tell my students about the seventeenth century, and we know this has held in Ireland up through the last twenty years, the religious is political.

Even more frustrating, the Scots-Irish promised to be extraordinarily difficult to study. Their presence on the British colonial political landscape was difficult to discern. They fought Indians, routed Anglican preachers, constantly moved from place to place. Excepting a few ministers, they did not write elegant revolutionary treatises, either before, during, or after the American revolution; they did not engage in learned debates. Following in the footsteps of their ancestors in Ireland, they appeared to live life on their own terms, and live it to the fullest – a brand of eighteenth-century existentialists.

Andrew Stewart, for example, was thoroughly unimpressed with the character of his fellow Scottish countrymen in early seventeenth-century Ulster: 'From Scotland came many, and from England not a few, yet all of them generally from the scum of both nations, who, for debt, or breaking and fleeing from justice, or seeking shelter, came hither, hoping to be without fear of man's justice in a land where there was nothing, or but little, as yet of the fear of God.' The noted minister Robert Blair, pastor among the early Ulster Scottish tenantry, was kinder, perhaps, but still sceptical: 'Albeit Divine Providence sent over some worthy persons for birth, education, and parts, yet the most part were such as [were driven by] either poverty, scandalous lives, or at the best, an adventurous seeking of better accommodation . . .'[1]

True, that was in the early days, but the people grew in stature, embraced moral principles and political responsibilities, and they

brought an idealistic political vision to the North American colonies.
Perhaps. In 1768 Charles Woodmason said that:

> They are very Poor – owing to their extreme Indolence . . .
> They delight in their present low, lazy, sluttish,
> heathenish, hellish Life, and seem not desirous of
> changing it. Both Men and Women will do any thing to
> come at Liquor, Cloaths, furniture, &c. &c. rather than
> work for it – Hence their many Vices – their gross
> Licentiousness, Wantonness, Lasciviousness, Rudeness,
> Lewdness, and Profligacy they will commit the grossest
> Enormities, before my face, and laught at all
> Admonitions.[2]

Of course, I find it very difficult to trust the opinion of an Anglican
minister on the behavior of Scots-Irish Presbyterians, particularly a
man who cannot understand the economic need and cultural importance of distilling one's own whiskey and peach brandy. However, be
that as it may, the Scots-Irish just don't come across well in the documents.

This all doesn't mean that the Scots-Irish didn't have political opinions,
it simply means that it is more difficult to discover them. Nevertheless,
having studied the Scots-Irish from a cultural perspective, I would like to
propose considering the problem of ideas from another direction. I'd like
to talk about ideas in terms of practice, people's behavior as a primary
manifestation of their ideas. When the Presbyterians all brought their
dogs to the Anglican preacher's sermon and then set the dogs howling
and fighting in the midst of it, I have some idea of their opinion of Mr
Charles Woodmason. So too, when, in 1763, 250 backcountry residents
marched on Philadelphia demanding that the government provide military protection on the frontier, they are writing political theory with
actions.

In fact, I would go even further. I believe that sometimes behavior or
activity influences, or even constructs from scratch, the political ideas of
a community. When one considers the hostile social situation and
uninviting natural environment that awaited the pioneering newcomers,
first in Ulster and, later, in the North American colonies, the extraordinary difficulties of day-to-day survival must have brought about many
'unthinking' decisions.[3] The Scots-Irish did what they needed to do and
then explained and justified their actions. From such an uninspired ideological source, the struggles of daily life, came their commitment to radical egalitarianism and democratic self-determination.

Despite the lack of respect that contemporaries paid them, the Scots-
Irish were of central importance to both the Irish and North American
colonization movements. They represent par excellence a transitional
colonial population, neither colonizer nor colonized, but the disempowered tenants and instruments (though perhaps not unwilling) of the

imperial rulers. In colonial studies such groups have often been identified with the imperial authority and the dominant, hegemonic culture, yet the group's members had very little political power and no legitimated authority. Such people often considered themselves to be colonized, under the complete control of an oppressive ruling elite. In fact they are neither dominant nor completely oppressed. They hold an undefined, insecure middling position of critical importance to the development of a colonial society, but one that is frequently unrecognized in writings on colonialism. As the title of this paper suggests, they were, in fact, unofficially authorized squatters. From this doubtful status, they would fight for the power to determine their own destiny.

I have deliberately employed the language of squatters for two reasons. First, many of the Scots-Irish were, in fact, squatters in North America, holding questionable tenure of their land. Having failed to file legal ownership documents, or unable to afford the purchase price, or refusing to pay quitrents to the proprietor, the Scots-Irish often established their ownership of land through brute force and dogged determination. As Gregory Nobles has argued, the pioneers took a rather Lockean approach to land, ignoring proprietors' claims for the same reasons that colonizers ignored natives' claims, because the land was wasting unimproved. The frontiersmen established their ownership by squatting, possessing and farming the land.[4] Throughout this process, the losers were the government and the native Americans as the Scots-Irish proved willing and able to fight both for their own claims.

Beyond this, as unofficial agents of colonization, the Scots-Irish held the unenviable position of favored but disempowered tenants: a sort of squatter status. This was certainly true in Ulster; that status was explicitly established in terms of public policy (erratic, unpredictable persecution by the Anglican Bishops) and the realities of land ownership (or should I say non-ownership). It was also, during the eighteenth century, true in fact (though not in theory) for the North American colonies. Supposedly, the Scots-Irish had equal access to wealth and power in the colonies. Yet their Irishness earned the derision of the educated, 'cultured' English elite who controlled access to the pathways of power, and their lack of economic resources rendered them unable to breach the established citadels of power as other non-English newcomers had done. In addition, the lateness of their arrival, combined with scant financial resources, forced them to seek land in the west, far distant from the east coast power base and seats of government. They couldn't even be heard, much less get involved.

However, at the same time that they were alternatively encroached upon and ignored by the dominant culture and government, they had become the willing instruments of that oppressive government against native peoples, first the native Irish and later, with the skills learned in colonizing Ireland, the native Americans. Constantly on the move, the restless Scots-Irish pushed the frontier ever westward; they acquired land, built their farm, and then sold it in order to search the west for even greater opportunities. Because they were able to challenge the native peoples and wrest control of the land, because, essentially, they did the colonizers' dirty work, they were grudgingly, unofficially tolerated by the governments.

Amidst this grudging toleration, the Scots-Irish were destined to find their political voice. But how does a disempowered, excluded people find a voice? Where are lessons of political challenge and activism learned if a people are excluded from politics? It's not that the Scottish tenantry of northern Ireland weren't interested in secular affairs. Surely the problems of land ownership and lease renewals, fair judgments, taxation, and governmental restrictions on behavior, especially religious affiliation, constantly engaged their attention in the effort to accommodate their lives to the requirements. But in Ireland the tenantry had no legitimate impact on civil decisions; after the passage of the Test Act in 1704, they were not allowed to participate in the public/political world, even at the local level. Many, in fact, ended up formally expressing their opinion in the one way left untouched, with their feet: by emigrating to North America. (An expression, incidentally, that affected and worried the Anglo-Irish government.)

Although the seventeenth century had been difficult for the Scots-Irish in terms of economic restrictions and religious persecution, the eighteenth century got worse. Parliamentary legislation subordinated the interests of the Irish textile industry to those of England's manufacturers. Landlords finally able to renegotiate all those ninety-nine year leases shortened the terms to twenty-one, or even seven years and tripled or quadrupled the rents. Finally, a series of droughts and bad harvests sparked the massive migration. In 1717–1718, the first group of ships left the Ulster region for North America. Initially they came to New England, but found the Puritans inhospitable. Thus ten years later when, after worse droughts, migrants tried again, they found Pennsylvania, the 'Best Poor Man's Country'.[5]

These settlers landed primarily in two places: Philadelphia/Newcastle and Charleston, South Carolina. Most arrivals soon headed for the nearest available land, the western frontier, or backcountry. Shipowners attracted passengers with claims that in America there was much land, little or no rent, no taxes, and no tithes. As one minister wrote back to Ireland in 1737, 'tell all the poor folk of ye place that God has opened a door for their deliverance ... for here all that a man works for is his own; and there are no revenue hounds to take it from us here ... no one to take away yer Corn, yer potatoes, yer Lint or yer Eggs'.[6] Reports came that 'all men are there upon a levell and that it is a good poor mans Country, where there are noe oppressions of any kind whatsoever', while one promoter reported that 'There is Servants come her out of Ereland, and have serv'd their Time here, who are not Justices of the Piece [sic] . . .'[7]

Between 1720 and 1774, between 150,000 and 200,000 Ulster emigrants arrived in the colonies. By 1790, the Scots-Irish represented 10% of the American population, 15% of the inhabitants of Pennsylvania, and almost 20% in South Carolina.[8]

Just as most of these migrants had bitterly resented the treatment they had received in Ireland, they continued in their resentment when the British passed the Proclamation of 1763 prohibiting settlers from moving west of the Appalachian Mountains. Some backcountry settlers already lived there; were they expected to leave? Others hoped to improve their condition on the new, uncolonized land. These new arrivals especially resented the domination of the English inhabitants who controlled the eastern regions of the colonies and, therefore, the provincial assemblies. And they proclaimed their resentment with a resounding fury, finally earning representation and building for themselves a recognized, legitimate power base. How did they do this? To return to my initial question: how does an historically disenfranchised people find a voice? Where are lessons of political challenge and activism learned if a people are excluded from government and political participation?

Perhaps, in the end, I am the right person to explore this subject, for I have a ready answer here. I would argue that the primary forum for early Scots-Irish political activity was the relatively small world of Presbyterian politics, for they could and did exercise extensive power within the Presbyterian Church. Fascinated by a political process that granted the lowly lay person, as well as the clergyman, some authority and decision-making power, the Scots-Irish engaged in Presbyterian politics with gusto, perhaps inflating the importance of theological and polity issues as they spread their wings in synodical debate and presbyterial courts. Here they learned the rhetoric of persuasion and the machinations of politics as they manipulated church and clergy to achieve their goals. Having demonstrated intense interest and skills in politics itself, they brought these lessons to British colonial politics, rationalizing in Presbyterian language their invasion of civil politics and demand for squatters' rights.

Among the earliest lesson learned was the overriding importance of money. Financial compensation was, for American and Irish Presbyterian ministers, a primary problem. Ministers were dependent upon voluntary contributions from congregants in order to survive. Very few Irish congregations were supported by landlords, so that the middling-lower class status of the congregations added to the salary problems. Scotland's clergy did not have this problem because they were supported by tithes. In Ireland, congregants also paid tithes, but these monies supported the Anglican Church. Thus a people whose economic situation rendered them less able to pay were saddled with the support of two ministers. So too, throughout the Atlantic colonies, Presbyterian ministers' salaries, as well as building maintenance and congregational expenses, were all provided by voluntary contribution.

During the late seventeenth and early eighteenth centuries, I have identified 123 Irish congregations in dispute with either their ministers or the hierarchy – about 40% of the total.[9] Most of these disputes involved salary deficiencies. Of course many congregations were simply unable to pay what was asked. In most cases, however, there are hints, if not open accusations, that portray a discontented laity bringing charges and deliberately not paying salaries. In 1713, the people of Killrachts claimed poverty, but they were outraged that pastor Robert Neilson demanded his stipend, 'a very great ground of that people's dissatisfaction'. In the end, Neilson asked to leave, he was permitted to do so, and the congregation's debt was *reduced* to 78 pounds, or three years salary, out of regard to the 'people's good', not upon any fault proved against him. Later the debt was further reduced to 60 pounds, but Neilson was to stay until the money was paid. With that incentive, the people raised 60 pounds in one year.[10]

A faction of the tri-part congregation at Omagh had similar success. Those who lived in Tiermond were unhappy and wanted their own church; they said the charge at Omagh was too much for one minister. While the people in Cappy were paid up, and those in Drumra were a bit behind, the residents of Tiermond had not contributed for several years. They claimed they were too poor. The delinquents were publicly denounced; they were summoned before the presbytery; they were denied their seats in the meetinghouse; they were denied the Lord's Supper. Finally, they were promised permission to start a congregation at Tiermond if they paid up the entire debt; they did so within six months.[11]

In North America, the presbyterian records though scant, record several financial disputes between minister and congregation. In 1732, Pastor John Thomson of Pennsylvania complained that he had not been paid for several years, and he wanted release from his congregation. That this was a refusal to pay rather than poverty was reflected in Thomson's reference to 'discouragements' and the presbytery's own report that the people were divided. In fact, 16 of the 43 families had refused to subscribe his call and pay their dues. Thomson was released and the congregation never did pay what they owed.[12]

While Pennsylvania appeared to have some of the most obstreperous, defiant lay persons, this attitude was reflected elsewhere. In 1726 the Presbyterians living at New London, Delaware, left the congregation at Elk River and built themselves a new meetinghouse. Then they asked the presbytery for a preacher. The presbytery, fearing that there would be inadequate financial support for the minister at Elk River, criticized the separators and told them to return. The people abused the presbytery in papers addressed to the Synod, which upheld the presbytery's decision and censured the people. The next year, the synod noted that since the people were 'constantly and firmly resolved not to be reconciled . . . by Reason of Feuds and Differences', the synod would permit them to separate. However, the meetinghouse had to be moved at least six miles from any other meetinghouse. Rather than move the meetinghouse, the congregation called a minister. Three years later, the synod finally acquiesced. New London could remain where it had stood, independent, for the previous seven years.[13]

While these represented passive tools of resistance, congregants were certainly capable of direct action. The Scots-Irish learned how to manipulate political processes with great success. In Ulster, the best known example is probably the subscription controversy: the 1720s debate as to whether ministers should be required to subscribe to the Westminster Confession. While every one believed that the Confession was the most perfect of creeds, some ministers complained that forced subscription smacked of inquisition. The Subscribers said that those refusing to subscribe were heretics.

Although the clergy generally controlled judicature procedures, it was the laity who raised and re-raised this question, finally establishing their own criterion, subscription, as *the* criterion for orthodoxy. Every year the clergy peaceably resolved the question, presbyteries made concessions, and every year the laity raised it again. An elder brought charges against four ministers on the basis of an anonymous pamphlet; many people stopped all converse with those who refused to subscribe; vacant congregations refused to have such clergy in their pulpits. In 1725 the synod gathered all the 'nonsubscribers' into the Presbytery of Antrim and the following year threw them out. That vote noted a large majority favoring division. Yet the clergy were tied 36–36, with 42 ministers (35%) abstaining, afraid of alienating their congregations. That large majority must have been entirely laymen.[14]

This controlling behavior was repeated in less than twenty years on the other side of the ocean. The issue was no longer subscription but support of the massive emotional revivalism of the Great Awakening. Congregations used whatever power they could muster or manipulate to bring pastors to support the revival or chastise them for failing to do so. In 1740 one congregation brought charges against Pastor Samuel Black, including seeking after his stipend, complaining of fatigue during pastoral visits (apparently ministers were not permitted to get tired), little regard to the promotion of family piety, immoral conduct, intemperance, lying, and sowing sedition. The accusations of immoral conduct, particularly intemperance to which Black confessed, seemed well-founded. But a second look reveals Black's antagonism toward the revival. Black had 'lied' when he initially condemned field preaching, then accepted it, then expressed renewed distrust. He had 'sown sedition' when he censured congregants who supported revivals. He was charged with 'seeming to oppose the work of God appearing in the land'. The presbytery exonerated Black and condemned the way that the laity had brought the charges: they displayed much malice, both in their eagerness to present copious oral and written evidence and in their failure to bring these charges of immorality until this moment. When the congregation did not succeed in offically removing Samuel Black, they voted with their feet, seceding from that presbytery and joining a pro-revival one.[15]

Sometimes the issue was of less cosmic importance. Sometimes the people simply 'turned on' their leader and got rid of him. In May 1737 Thomas Creaghead refused to give his wife communion even though she had been given a token. When challenged after the service, he claimed that indeed she was a sinner: her sin had been committed the night before, it was between the two of them, and he could not in good conscience give her the sacrament. (The exact nature of her sin was not recorded.) The congregation was scandalized. Creaghead had made a mockery of the Lord's Supper; he was guilty of sacrilege. Creaghead was brought before the presbytery on these charges, and during the hearings his family problems were worked out. He admitted his error and paid a hefty penance of 6 months suspension. After he had been restored to the ministry, the congregation warned the presbytery that they would not allow him in their pulpit. The presbytery bowed to their demands; there was no discussion and no recrimination. He was gone.[16]

This was power. This was an authority that the laity had claimed and fought for, an authority that supported the extreme anti-clericalism of these congregations. When reading the institutional records, one can almost hear the complaints against indolent, immoral clerics and feel the resentment against intellectualizing ministers who think they know more than the common layman. Why should any one respect an unsympathetic clergyman simply because of his learning and ordination? On the harsh frontier, where a meager living was wrested from uncultivated land that was wrested from understandably hostile natives, the clerics' credentials of learning, trial, and ordination were indeed unimpressive.

Of course the Scots-Irish were not doubtful of clerical leadership only. They lifted a sceptical eyebrow at all those who asserted the right to rule. That the Pennsylvania proprietor should receive quitrents when the freeholders did all the work on the land seemed absurd, especially when the proprietor had no means of forcing payment. That the South Carolina Assembly should receive taxes when it provided no services was grossly unfair, so, often taxes and quitrents were not paid. That any planter, merchant or lawyer in the east had even the slightest knowledge of and ability to govern the west seemed to have been doubted by everyone on the frontier. For the Scots-Irish pioneer, the relative merits of wealth, rank, an English birth, even land ownership were undoubtedly lower than ordination and a university degree.

But this is a negative philosophy, this scepticism about English authority, this rejection of deference and social hierarchies. The Scots-Irish were not preoccupied with disobedience for its own sake (even though they did a fair amount of that as well). No, initially they acted when their needs were not being served by the government. By the middle of the eighteenth century, the backcountry, usually led by the Scots-Irish, was sending out tentative questions to the eastern colony governments. In the beginning, frontiersmen were unhappy with the material circumstances of their lives: lawlessness on the frontier; the poor condition of the roads by which they got produce to market; the high prices charged by merchants for imported goods; the growing scarcity of land; the governments' refusal to negotiate with the Indians for more land; and the failure of the governments to protect the western settlers from the Indian attacks that followed settlers' attempts to acquire land themselves.

I say that initially they were unhappy with the conditions of their lives, because what happened was that the backcountry residents first tried to have their grievances redressed through the normal, non-threatening channels of petition to the colonial governments. When the requests were more or less ignored, the populace engaged in political action, sometimes violence. As they confronted the governments, the cause of discontent and the resulting goals of the confrontation also changed. The people came to realize that their grievances were not being addressed because *they* were not represented within the government.

They learned that the governments were dominated by residents of the eastern counties who were, in fact, grossly overrepresented. They also learned that the interests of the assembly happened to coincide with the self-interest of the easterners. (Of course this would not surprise good Calvinists who always expect the worst of human nature.) In other words, backcountry residents learned that not only was the government unsuccessful in accomplishing the tasks necessary to govern the frontier, but that the very process of government was unfair. Just like the absentee landlords of old, the easterners governed the unrepresented residents of the west in order to satisfy their own designs. The backcountry residents soon began to grieve not only the difficult conditions of their lives, but also the attitudes and structures that excluded them from participation in the government and denied them all access to power.

The anti-clericalism of the early eighteenth century became transformed into anti-authoritarianism generally. Denouncing the ruling classes as incompetent as well as unjust, the deference that had been grudgingly paid to the upper classes completely disappeared. In its place rose a radical egalitarianism that denied the superiority of any class, whether by wealth or birth. There also rose a determination of the westerners to govern themselves, to participate fully within the government. After all, they argued, they could see the problems on the frontier better than anyone in the east or in England; more to the point, they had some pretty clear ideas on how to deal with these problems.

In this struggle lay the central role that the Scots-Irish played in the American Revolution. For decades, when historians wrote of the American Revolution, they were discussing the resistance movement against England which resulted in the end of British imperial control of thirteen of the North American colonies and the creation of a new, independent nation, the United States. The anti-English sentiment, sowed deep in the hearts of the oppressed Scots-Irish contributed to that cause. However, in the last thrity years or so, historians have begun writing of not only the revolution for home rule, but the revolution against rulers at home: the rising challenge of the middling classes, the artisans, and the hinterlands farmers against the cultural, economic, and political domination of the eastern merchants and planters. In this struggle against deference to birth, to virtue, and to wealth, a struggle that saw the backcountry fighting the dominance of the eastern settlers, the Scots-Irish took a leading part. Not only did they have opinions; they had some ideas about how to get their opinions across.

Residents on the Pennsylvania frontier had long been dissatisfied with the colonial government. Severely underrepresented in the Assembly through inequitable apportionment that favored the three eastern counties, western inhabitants' resentment crystalized around the colony's Indian policy. The Quaker-dominated assembly had long favored peace through treaties and trade, sending missionaries among those willing to entertain them, while westerners wanted the colony to open more land to settlement. Constantly pushing the frontier further, squatting on Indian lands, the Scots-Irish settlers throughout the 1750s and early 1760s suffered extensive repercussions, particularly during the Seven Years War, and asked for military protection. However, the Pennsylvania Assembly, holding the frontier partly responsible for its own problems, was reluctant to raise a militia.

The crisis came in 1763, when Pontiac, a war chief among the Ottawas, led a pan-Indian movement among the nations of the Great Lakes region. The natives attacked British forts all along the frontier. During that summer alone they killed at least 2,000 people in settlements throughout western Pennsylvania and Virginia. Settlers now wanted revenge and, it must be added, they still hoped the government would open more land to settlement. In the end, the Indians would be unable to take the major forts and the uprising would end in 1766, but long before that would happen, the 'riotous and murderous Irish Presbyterians' would find their own revenge in the massacre of a peaceful village of Christian Indians at Conestoga.[17] The Assembly proved unwilling, perhaps unable, to protect its western residents, and 250 armed frontiersmen, the 'Paxton Boys', marched on Philadelphia, demanding military protection against future Indian attacks (which they had provoked) and, incidentally, more equitable apportionment for representation. Benjamin Franklin met the frontiersmen at Lancaster, and, despite the flourish of militaristic strength, the Paxton Boys presented their petition in an orderly fashion and returned home. The Assembly began to consider seriously the defensive/military needs of the colony, heralding the beginning of the end of the Quaker/Anglican domination of the legislature.

The South, too, saw more than its share of conflict over class and deference: here between the English society and culture of the low country planters and the rough and ready society of the backcountry, dominated by Scots-Irish and Scottish settlers. Eastern planters, having established fairly stable plantations that produced a cash crop with African slave labor, dominated the colonial assemblies. They used their wealth, influence, and power to create legal and economic systems that would protect the planters' property (land and labor), increase the profitability of the plantation economy, share the financial burden with the west to ensure that their own taxes were kept low, and maintain their positions of authority in the government. The problems of the west – costs of marketing crops, problems in transport, lack of access to the judiciary headquartered in the east, the physical safety of the frontier residents, the uncertainty of Indian relations – concerned the assemblies very little.

Westerners worried not only about the threat of native peoples, but also about uncontrolled, roaming bandits. They were being pressured economically by eastern-based Scottish merchants who had extended considerable credit to the debt-ridden farmers, and they lacked the eastern planters' financial cushion of vast tracts of land under cultivation. Lawyers had recently appeared in these countries, insinuating themselves into positions of influence and interfering with the people's access to power. Corrupt officials appointed through the patronage of the assembly charged oppressive fees, while the inequities of the tax system became more apparent as the taxes themselves became less bearable. Those who would organize as 'Regulators' described themselves as 'industrious peasants,' exploited by merchants and 'damned lawyers who practised numberless . . . devilish devices to rob you of your livings.' Their leader spoke out against 'clerks, lawyers, or Scotch merchants . . . whose interests jar with the interest of the public good'.[18]

'Regulatory' movements formed first in North Carolina, in 1768, and, less than a year later, in South Carolina. Initially, backcountry residents engaged in basic, frontier, vigilante justice – closing down courts, preventing the collection of taxes, suppressing the bands of outlaws, and burning down the homes of unsympathetic officials. In North Carolina, this mob violence/resistance lasted for three years, until the royal governor, along with the assembly, mobilized the colony's militia. The primary confrontation occurred at Alamance River in 1771 where the militia easily defeated the rag-tag, ill-equipped Regulators. The South Carolina backcountry organized a similar Regulator movement when the assembly proved unable or unwilling to locate and control the bandits on the frontier. As the organized vigilantes grew more violent and less discriminating, some inhabitants petitioned the colonial assembly for courts and legitimate law enforcement so that such vigilante justice would not be necessary. Here, with the possibility of compromise, the governor avoided military force. Instead, the provincial assembly granted the needs of justice and created judicial circuits (though not county courts) for the western counties. Of course, by resolving one complaint, the assembly managed to do nothing about the others.

Although the South Carolina movement seemed more successful (their leaders were not tried, convicted, and executed, as in North Carolina), both movements in fact experienced similar levels of failure and success. On the one hand, western counties continued underrepresented in the assembly; the planters still predominated numerically by means of unjust apportionment structures. Also, the tax structure remained unfair, with the backcountry paying far more than its share for systems and governments that primarily benefitted the east. In such ways, the eastern power blocs in both colonies kept their western counties dependent and subordinate. On the other hand, the Regulator movements served to organize and raise consciousness. These farmers rarely deferred for the sake of deference, and the Regulator riots, and the unsatisfactory official response, reminded the frontiersmen of the indifference, if not downright hostility, of the eastern planters and reinforced their own animosity to the political leadership. It is not surprising that when the Carolina assemblies sought the support of the west in their resistance against England, westerners would demand access to political power and an equitable distribution of offices, representatives, and taxes as a condition of their participation. The people of Mecklenburg County, in western North Carolina, for example, 'instructed their delegates to the state constitutional convention of 1776 to "oppose everything that leans to aristocracy or power in the hands of the rich and chief men exercised to the oppression of the poor".'[19]

Upon declaring independence from Great Britain, the thirteen colonies found themselves states organized into an ad hoc nation governed by an ad hoc Congress at war with one of the strongest powers in the western world. Each state took on the task of rebuilding its own government even as the Continental Congress of the United States gave it a try. Although in the five years preceding independence the royal governors had systematically disassembled the provincial governments, the reorganizing task was not as formidable as one might have suspected.

The actual process of organizing the resistance had involved the construction of committees of correspondence. These committees had gathered the people around the cause of resistance, closing courts, blocking tax collections, interfering with customs officers, designing and implementing symbolic protests, and enforcing, sometimes with great brutality, non-importation agreements. These committees also corresponded, hence their name, with those of other colonies, maintaining an efficient system of political communication. Finally, they had sponsored the election of representatives to popular, extralegal assemblies that would rule the colonies in the absence of a legitimated popular government and in spite of the royal governors' prerogatives and interdictions. These committees also worked to ensure enlistment in and the equipage of a military force. The recruitment and participation of the Scots-Irish in the resistance organization pushed the committees of Pennsylvania and the

Carolinas in directions far more radical than the colony-wide eastern-based national leadership wanted.

In the wake of the Regulator Movements, southern backcountry frontiersmen were reluctant to join the patriot-resistance cause. Many western residents, particularly those from Germany and the Scottish Highlands, believed that the English government would provide greater service and protection than independent provincial governments. The Scots-Irish, always wary and distrustful of the British, were inclined to remain neutral, although many in the end fought for independence. In addition to the British, the Scots-Irish distrusted the Indians, and they feared that an Indian/British alliance destructive to frontier interests would be formed. In several ways, it seems as if backcountry residents joined one side because they disliked the other.[20]

However, through their support for the patriot cause, westerners gained concessions in several colonies: the extension of the courts into the western counties, an expansion of local control at the expense of the state, the realignment of districts to ensure equitable representation in the state assembly, the broadening of the franchise generally, and more equitable tax schedules. All across the states, the electorates were expanded. South Carolina radically expanded the representation of the western counties, and in Georgia and Pennsylvania, property qualifications were removed altogether. And almost every state included a constitutional bill of rights designed to protect individual liberties against state encroachment.

Probably the most amazing transformation occurred in Pennsylvania. There the regular Assembly members had been extremely reluctant to support the resistance movement, with individual representatives to the national Continental Congress often abstaining from key votes, and in several cases voting against independence altogether in 1776. Outraged and disgusted by the feet-dragging of the established leadership, the populace, represented by the radical committee, threw out most of the old governors and elected a new collection to draw up the new Pennsylvania's Constitution. This state constitutional convention incorporated the few radical members of the elite, but it was drawn primarily from the ranks of tradesmen, artisans, and farmers. Not surprisingly, a hefty proportion were Scots-Irish who, for the first time, found themselves at the center of power.

This convention drafted and ratified the most radical, egalitarian constitution created in this era. The legislature was to have only one house, with representatives whose terms were strictly limited, only four years of every seven. This convention was the only state convention to see no need for an elite, 'more virtuous', upper house, for all people, they believed, were equally likely to be virtuous and just. The check necessary for the legislature would be applied by the people themselves, for all sessions were open to public view. These representatives would be chosen by an electorate of all free men over twenty-one who had joined the militia, paid taxes, and lived in Pennsylvania for at least one year. These guidelines meant that as many as 90% of the free men in western areas could vote. Representation was apportioned strictly by population, vastly increasing the representation from Philadelphia and the west, approaching the simple one-man/one-vote formulation. Moreover, this assembly would be elected annually so that members would be more responsive to the desires and will of the people. These elections were, in fact, hotly contested. Unlike elections of the previous decade, where men of 'virtue' were returned to office year after year by a respectful electorate, slates of candidates would be elected in or out according to their position on political questions. Candidates were expected to vote on major issues as their constituencies requested.[21]

The Scots-Irish, along with other westerners and middling-class urban dwellers, were certainly moving to the center of power, but this movement stopped abruptly. After the war had ended, those favoring popular politics and strong local governments held sway. But by the middle of the 1780s, the new nation's economy was near collapse. Soldiers had not been paid; military suppliers had not be recompensed; foreign loans remained unpaid; and securities held by citizens were believed irredeemable. The holders of those securities were naturally concerned, but so was the general populace. Merchants and major land owners decided that in order to stabilize the economy and the political process, local autonomy would have to be sacrificed and governmental control returned to the elite. Pennsylvanians sponsored a new constitutional convention that replaced the radical experiment with the old 'government by the propertied elite' model. Representation was still more equally distributed than it had been, and many could still vote. But the egalitarian respect and popular safeguards were gone.

The nation followed suit only two years later. Between 1776 and 1786 the government had swung between nationalists, advocating a strong, centralized government, and antinationalists, favouring local autonomy and states' rights. By 1786 the nationalists had raised hue and cry against the fragmented, powerless nature of the Confederation government overseen by the antinationalists. In 1787 the nationalists succeeded in calling a convention, presumably to amend the current government charter, the Articles of Confederation. In fact, the convention, with, we believe now, full premeditation on the part of the central participants, completely scrapped the Articles and drafted a new constitution that placed most authority into the hands of a centralized power, strengthening this federal system at the expense of states' rights. As the new United States held its first elections in 1788, it did seem as if the high expectations of self determinism and protection of liberties so important to artisans and farmers, both Scots-Irish and others, had given way to the interests of the virtuous, that is, the propertied, elite who would rule for the common, that is, the property's good.

Of course, the story does not end here. In order to convince states to ratify the constitution, the writers had to promise that one of the first orders of business would be passage and ratification of a national Bill of Rights. These ten amendments would protect individuals' liberties against federal encroachment, thus restraining the tyrannical potential of the powerful rulers. Moreover, the 'virtuous elite' soon discovered that they could not agree upon public policy, and an increasingly bitter competition flourished between two unofficial political parties. But unofficial or not, party politics were party politics, and both the strong government advocates, Federalists, and the state autonomy advocates, Democratic-Republicans, competed in the only pathway open to parties – electioneering. Representatives could be expected to legislate according to the desires of their constituents, and those who did not risked losing their position in the next election. As each party worked to gear its program and appeal to the common-man electorate, egalitarian ideals and the promotion of self-determination returned to the center of American political discourse. Within thirty years, three-fourths of all states enjoyed universal white manhood suffrage. A man's ability and right to choose the representative who would best speak for his interests again became the primary ideal of party politics in the United States.

What truly fascinates me is the fact that popular religion was rejuvenated by this populist political conversation. There rose a new religious emphasis upon individual conscience and choice, spiritual equality, and the call of ordinary, uneducated men (sometimes women, sometimes African American men and women) to the ministry of God. This appeal was spread through open air speeches and the popular press, both methods begun in the early eighteenth-century revival meetings, encouraged by politicians in the 1790s, and flourishing, again, among the popular churches. The Scots-Irish were numerous among these new evangelicals, be they Baptists, Methodists, or the old Presbyterians. Not surprisingly, evangelical churches swept through the western states, moving with the frontier, and gathering new members. What goes around comes around, and by 1820 the ideals and methods of evangelical religion and popular politics were functioning in symbiosis, together reinforcing an egalitarian sensibility and recognizing the potential power of the people.[22]

Uneducated laymen; squatters; religionists of an undefined status; farmers with an uneasy tenure on the land: these "squatters' " claims to rights represented a concept of rights grounded in their spiritual estates, in their working and living on the land. These rights were not *granted* through legal machinations and political enfranchisement, they were not *granted* by churches or constitutions. These rights were presumed, taken. Scots-Irish Presbyterians did not request a hearing; they exhibited their strength, made their case, and demanded response. Scots-Irish frontiersmen did not beg recognition and redress; they proclaimed their presence and demanded accountability. Surely if any radical ethic emerged from the American Revolution, it was this: ordinary people, generally unnoticed, or ignored, or deliberately disempowered by the ruling elites, stood up, announced themselves, and claimed their rights as inherent in their humanity. When the rulers became convinced that this was true; when the rulers came to wonder whether all men might have been created equal, that personal rights and liberties were inherent in the human condition; when the rulers then shifted political power over to the populace; when rulers had to shift power to the populace in order to maintain their own position, a revolution had indeed begun.

Notes to Chapter 6

1. Andrew Stewart, 'History of the Church of Ireland,' in Patrick Adair, *A True Narrative . . . of the Presbyterian Church in Ireland (1623–1670)*, with introd. and notes by W. D. Killen (Belfast: C. Aitchison, 1866), p. 317; Robert Blair, *The Life of Mr. Robert Blair . . . His Autobiography from 1593–1636*, ed. Thomas McCrie (Edinburgh: Wodrow Society, 1848), p. 57.
2. Charles Woodmason, *The Carolina Backcountry on the Eve the Revolution: The Journal and Other Writings of Charles Woodmason*, ed. Richard J. Hooker (Chapel Hill: Univ. of North Carolina Press, 1953), p. 60.
3. A term used in another context by Winthrop D. Jordan, *White Over Black: American Attitudes Toward the Negro, 1550–1812* (New York, Norton, 1968). Here Jordan describes the origins of slavery in the British colonies as an 'Unthinking Decision'. As he lays out the dynamics of this development, and its relationship to racism, he reveals in broader terms the ability of economic circumstances and behavioral responses to affect ideology.
4. Gregory H. Nobles, 'Breaking into the Backcountry: New Approaches to the Early American Frontier, 1750–1800', *William and Mary Quarterly* **46** (1989), pp. 654–655.
5. Christopher Sauer, 'An Early Description of Pennsylvania: Letter of Christopher Sauer written in 1724 . . .' ed. Rayner W. Kelsey, trans. Adolph Gether, *Pennsylvania Magazine of History and Biography* **45** (1921), p. 249.
6. As quoted in James A. Henretta and Gregory H. Nobles, *Evolution and Revolution: American Society, 1600–1820* (Lexington, Mass.: D.C. Heath, 1987), p. 120.
7. Ezekiel Stewart to Michael Ward, 25 March 1729, Public Record Office of Northern Ireland, D2092/1/3; Letter by James Murray, *Pennsylvania Gazette*, 3 November 1737.
8. Kerby A. Miller, *Emigrants and Exiles: Ireland and the Irish Exodus to North America* (New York: Oxford Univ. Press, 1985), pp. 137–168; R. J. Dickson, *Ulster Emigration to Colonial America, 1718–1775* (London: Routledge & Kegan Paul, 1966); Thomas L. Purvis, 'The European Ancestry of the United States Population, 1790', *William and Mary Quarterly,* **41** (1984).
9. My figures come from my own research in manuscript records at the Public Record Office of Northern Ireland, manuscripts held by the Presbyterian Historical Society, Belfast, and *Records of the General Synod of Ulster, 1692–1820*, 3 vols. (Belfast: John Reid and Co., 1898). See my *Triumph of the Laity: Scots-Irish Piety and the Great Awakening* (New York: Oxford Univ. Press, 1988).
10. *Records of the General Synod of Ulster*, 1713, **1**, 302–304; 1714, **1**, 338.
11. Minutes of the Presbytery of Strabane, Ireland, 25 December 1717–17 February 1720, Presbyterian Historial Society, Belfast.
12. Records of the Presbytery of Donegal, North America, 1732–33, Presbyterian Historical Society, Philadelphia.
13. *Minutes of the Presbyterian Church in America, 1706–1788*, ed. Guy S. Klett (Philadelphia: Presbyterian Historical Society, 1976), 1727–1731.
14. *Records of the General Synod of Ulster, 1720–1726*, **1**, 521–2: 109; *Narrative of the Proceedings of Seven General Synods . . . in which they issued a Synodical Breach* (Belfast: James Blow, 1727).
15. Records of the Presbytery of Donegal, North America, September–November 1740.
16. *Ibid.,* May 1735–October 1737.
17. Frank J. Cavaioli, 'A Profile of the Paxton Boys: Murderers of the Conestoga Indians', *Journal of the Lancaster County Historical Society,* **87** (1983), p. 81.
18. As quoted in Henretta and Noles, *Evolution and Revolution*, p. 121.
19. *Ibid.,* p. 123.
20. This idea of 'negative-reference group-behavior' defining positions during the independence movement is laid out in Richard R. Beeman, 'The Political Response to Social Conflict in the southern Backcountry', in Ronald Hoffman *et al.*, ed, *Uncivil War:*

The Southern Backcountry during the American Revolution (Charlottesville, VA, 1985), pp. 230–231. See also Rachel N. Klein, 'Frontier Planters and the American Revolution: The South Carolina Backcountry, 1775–1782', in *Uncivil War*, pp. 37–69.

21. Richard Alan Ryerson, *The Revolution is Now Begun: The Radical Committees of Philadelphia, 1765–1776* (Philadelphia, 1978), 252–253, n. 13.

22. Nathan O. Hatch, *The Democratization of American Christianity* (New Haven, 1989) provides a brilliant interpretation of this interplay of religion and popular politics.

7. PRESBYTERIAN COMMUNITIES, TRANSATLANTIC VISIONS AND THE ULSTER REVIVAL OF 1859

Stewart J. Brown

In the summer of 1859, a religious revival swept through the Protestant communities of Ulster, affecting tens of thousands and representing perhaps the most significant event in the province – certainly in terms of numbers involved – between the Rising of 1798 and the Home Rule crisis of 1886. The Ulster revival had its origins in the revival movement which had spread through much of the United States during the previous year, and it was brought to Ulster through the strenuous efforts of Presbyterian clergymen, who believed it would strengthen Calvinist orthodoxy and restore Irish Presbyterianism to an imagined seventeenth-century 'golden age'.[1] The dramatic events of the Ulster revival, especially the prostrations and charismatic episodes, attracted international interest, and the movement spread to Scotland, Wales and England, where it renewed and transformed the British evangelical movement, ushering in over a decade of intense evangelical activity which brought the rapid expansion of the YMCA, the emergence of the Salvation Army and the Moody and Sankey campaign of 1873–75. In 1859, Ulster briefly formed the centre of a transatlantic revival movement. It was, in the hyperbole of one Ulster revival leader, 'lifted up to the gaze of universal Christendom', to form a beacon to evangelical Protestantism 'even to the ends of the earth'.[2]

For many years neglected by historians of modern Ireland, the Ulster revival of 1859 has recently attracted serious scholarly interest. The ecclesiastical historian, Finlay Holmes, has viewed the revival as the culmination of the Irish Evangelical movement beginning in the 1820s and associated with the conservative Calvinist leadership of Henry Cooke. For the social historian of religion, Peter Brooke, the revival marked a major stage in the breakdown of the traditional communal organisation of Ulster Presbyterianism. The social historian, Peter Gibbon, has explored the revival as an emotional response of rural labourers and new factory workers to the social dislocations associated with rapid industrialisation and urbanisation during the 1850s.[3] The revival has also been the subject of a thorough and balanced article by the social historian of religion, Myrtle Hill, who has offered an overview of the movement in light of these new historical interpretations and 'modern sociological approaches to the study of revivalism'.[4]

This essay will explore the Ulster revival of 1859 with particular attention to the Presbyterian Church and to the larger transatlantic connection – viewing the Ulster movement as a link between revivalism in America and Britain. In this, it will draw on the recent work of the American historians, Marilyn Westerkamp, Ned Landsman and Leigh Schmidt, who have traced the influence of Scots and Scots-Irish Presbyterian piety – especially as reflected and preserved in the communion occasions – on the development of American revivalism.[5] The essay will also be concerned with the tensions between the communal and individualistic aspects of the Ulster revival – how on the one hand, supporters of the revival were concerned to restore and preserve traditional Presbyterian communities, while on the other hand, the revival stirred intense personal fears and aspirations, that encouraged highly individualistic responses. As Peter Brooke has argued, the Ulster revival formed a transition between seventeenth-century notions of the covenanted community and the nineteenth-century ethos of religious voluntaryism and individualism.[6]

I

The Scots-Irish Calvinist communities of the north of Ireland had played a significant role in the development of Protestant revivalism in the north Atlantic world. From their arrival in Ulster as part of the early seventeenth-century plantation, the early Scots settlers had perceived themselves as a covenanted community, a godly band, representing God's order in an unruly country. Confronted by a rugged countryside and a hostile Irish population dispossessed of their former lands, these Scots frontiersmen had found strength in the idea of the covenant, which they had brought with them from their homes in the southwest of Scotland.[7] Their covenanting identity was strengthened in the Six-Mile-Water Revival which began near Antrim town in 1625 and profoundly affected the Scots settlements between 1625 and 1633 – 'taming the lawlessness of the early settlers and transforming them into a race of sober and God-fearing men'.[8] From the mid seventeenth century, the Scots-Irish communities also periodically renewed their covenanting identity through the rituals of the communion occasion – the annual or biannual communion held in each congregation, to which neighbouring congregations were invited to come to celebrate, and neighbouring Presbyterian clergymen would assist with preaching and serving the elements. These Presbyterian communion occasions developed into corporate rituals – lasting three or four days and attracting hundreds of participants, who would confess and repent their sins, reconcile themselves with their neighbours, and renew the sense of covenant with God. The communions became the means of periodically purifying communities of pent-up anger and aggression, of converting young persons and bringing them into the community of the faithful, and of providing a degree of assurance of salvation.[9] They represented, in the words of Marilyn Westerkamp, 'the ritualised experience of community conversion' through which 'the people found themselves able to return their community to God and once again find the spiritual peace of the common bond'.[10]

This communal, conversionist piety, preserved in the rituals of the communion occasion, was carried across to the Middle colonies of North America by Scots and Scots-Irish Presbyterian immigrants.[11] In North America, Scots-Irish Presbyterian communities exercised a powerful influence on both the First Great Awakening of 1730–60 and the Second Great Awakening of 1800–30, religious movements which in significant ways helped to shape the identity for the new American nation. The First Great Awakening strengthened the role of the laity and spread an emotional, conversionist piety through the colonies, helping to define a sense of common Christian mission. The Second Great Awakening, affecting mainly the dispersed communities along the western frontier of the new Republic, was characterised by camp meetings – largely a development of the Presbyterian communion occasion – which frequently became scenes of physical prostrations and convulsions under the influence of intense emotional preaching.

During the Second Great Awakening, American revivalism moved in new directions, becoming less oriented to preserving the purity and corporate discipline of traditional religious communities, and more concerned with converting individuals. This was reflected in the waning of the Presbyterian communion occasions, which had largely ceased in the United States by the 1840s.[12] Many American Protestants also departed from the Calvinist view that the season of revival was a mystery, known only to an inscrutable God, and that Christians could do nothing to assist or hasten the coming of revivals. In the 1830s the celebrated revivalist Charles G. Finney began employing 'new measures' – prayer meetings, direct conversionist preaching, gospel songs and the 'anxious bench' for the nearly converted – as means to prepare communities for revival.[13] Finney's new measures were soon being emulated by other preachers. While Finney and the new measure revivalists continued to seek the transformation of communities, they placed increasing emphasis on achieving individual conversions through a direct, personalised preaching. With the spread of the new measures, American revivalism became increasingly emotional and non-denominational. In their confidence that Christians could prepare for the revivals that would renew the nation's religious identity and mission, the new measure revivalists reflected the optimism of the young American republic. There was also a drift away from the confessional statements and Calvinist orthodoxy that had defined traditional religious communities, and a growing emphasis on personal conversion and individual freedom to accept Christ.[14]

Late in 1857, the cities of the eastern seaboard of the United States began to experience a series of revivals, associated largely with prayer meetings conducted among businessmen in the financial districts. The prayer meetings and revivalist fervour were largely a response to the severe commercial crisis of 1857. Distressed by the economic stagnation and experiencing guilt over sharp and amoral business practices, many businessmen felt compelled to confess their sins and turn to prayer – in the belief that if they returned to the faith of their fathers God would restore them to prosperity. Other factors also contributed to the spread of the movement. Disputes over slavery had led to schisms in the major Protestant denominations during the 1830s and 1840s, and were threatening the unity of the nation-state. Continued immigration, especially during and after the Irish famine of 1845–49, was changing the religious and ethnic composition of the nation. Between 1800 and 1860, the Roman Catholic Church had grown from 50,000 to some two million members, and had become the largest single denomination in the United States, raising nativist fears about the Protestant character of the nation.[15] The new measures of the professional revivalists, including active preparation for the coming of revival through prayer meetings, special addresses and the distribution of tracts, contributed to the rapid spread of the revival. Moving from the eastern coastal cities across the midwest and south, the revival of 1857–58 brought widespread interdenominational co-operation and claimed perhaps a million converts across the country.[16] The movement differed significantly from previous revivals in the American experience. First, it was based mainly on the prayer meeting and lay participation, rather than on the personalities and influence of certain charismatic preachers. Secondly, it was more an urban than a rural movement, gaining considerable support among urban business and professional classes which had not previously shown much interest in revivalism. Thirdly, it was almost entirely free of the 'physical manifestations', the prostrations, convulsions and trances that had accompanied previous American revivals, especially the camp meetings of the Second Awakening.[17]

II

Early in 1858, reports of the American revival began reaching Ireland, where they were received with intense interest by Irish evangelicals, especially those within the Presbyterian Church in Ireland. Although Ulster Presbyterians had not experienced a major revival since the events at Six-Mile-Water in the early seventeenth century, Presbyterian evangelicals now directed attention to the historic connections of Irish and American Protestantism and to the benefits the American revival was bringing to its people. On learning of the American movement, for example, the Presbytery of Omagh sent a deputation to address each congregation within its bounds on the need for a revival.[18] At its annual meeting in July 1858 in Derry, the General Assembly of the Presbyterian Church devoted attention to the American revival – with the moderator, John Johnston of Tullylish, calling on ministers to 'pray that the Spirit may be poured out upon us as plenteously as upon the Churches of America with which we hold so many interesting associations'.[19] The Assembly held a special conference on the American revival, with four leading ministers delivering addresses on revival themes, and it agreed to send a deputation of two ministers, Professor William Gibson of the Assembly College and the Revd William McClure, to visit the scenes of revival in America. The Assembly also sent a pastoral letter to all members of the Church, calling on them to pray and prepare for a religious awakening for the whole of Ireland.[20]

This interest in the American revival came largely from the conservative evangelical wing of the Irish Presbyterian Church, which had gained a firm control over the Church during the 1820s. For most of the eighteenth century, the dominant mood of Irish Presbyterianism had been rational and intellectual, with emphasis on moral duty, liberty of conscience and freedom from the authority of confessional statements. Eighteenth-century Presbyterian clergymen had been the moral and intellectual leaders of their largely self-contained communities, and many had been attracted to a republican ideology, emphasising a disinterested civic virtue, religious toleration and stoic reserve. However, following the defeat of the United Irishmen in 1798, a rising in which many Presbyterians had fought and suffered for the republican cause, there had been a waning of both theological liberalism and republican sympathies within Presbyterian communities. Under the leadership of the orthodox Calvinist and staunch Tory, Henry Cooke, Calvinist evangelicals gained control of the Synod of Ulster during the mid 1820s, imposing strict tests of orthodoxy on all candidates for ordination. Cooke had the support of conservative landowners, including Lord Mountcashel and the Earl of Roden, who believed that Calvinist evangelicalism would encourage social and political quiescence.[21] The triumph of the evangelical Calvinists forced a secession of the Arians and theological liberals, under the leadership of Henry Montgomery, in 1830. Under evangelical leadership, the Synod of Ulster embarked on a vigorous programme of church extension, temperance work and home mission. In 1840 it united with the orthodox Calvinist Secession Church to form the Presbyterian Church in Ireland.[22] There was renewed Presbyterian interest in revivalism, inspired in part by James Seaton Reid's account of the Six-Mile-Water Revival which appeared in 1834 in the first volume of his *History of the Presbyterian Church in Ireland*.[23] In 1853, the Presbyterian Church founded the Assembly College in Belfast. Modelled largely on the conservative envangelical Princeton University in the United States, the Assembly College contributed to the growing interest in religious movements outside Ireland, including the new measures of American revivalism.[24] By the mid 1850s, Presbyterian clergymen were looking to American revivalism as a means of restoring a communal identity that was being threatened by rapid industrialisation, urbanisation and changing patterns of agriculture.

This evangelical Calvinism and interest in revivalism was in large part a response by Ulster Presbyterians to the new strength and confidence of the Roman Catholic Church. During the second quarter of the nineteenth century, the Catholic Emancipation and Repeal campaigns under the leadership of Daniel O'Connell had contributed to an identification of Catholicism and Irish nationalism. The years after the famine, moreover, brought to the Irish Catholic Church an improved ecclesiastical discipline, an increased number of priests and nuns relative to the Catholic population, increased use of aids to devotion (rosaries, missals, pictures, statues) new church building, and new forms of mission, in what Emmet Larkin has characterised as a 'devotional revolution'.[25] This strengthening of Catholic organisation and confidence was associated with the leadership of Cardinal Paul Cullen, who became archbishop of Dublin in 1852 and exuded an air of Catholic triumphalism.[26] It also reflected the emergence after the famine of a substantial class of Catholic 30–100 acre farmers, and a new missionary fervour and doctrinal confidence of the Church as a whole during the pontificate of Pius IX. The Catholic community became increasingly assertive, refusing to tolerate the remaining symbols of Protestant ascendancy. In the summer of 1857, Belfast suffered serious sectarian rioting, as Catholics, now representing a third of the city's population, responded with violence to Protestant 12th of July marches and open-air evangelical preaching.[27] Presbyterians had reason to fear becoming a marginalised minority in a predominantly Catholic and nationalist Ireland – unless they could renew their historic ties with their covenanting past and with the larger transatlantic Protestant world.

III

The Ulster revival of 1859 began in the Connor district of county Antrim.[28] This district had been cultivated since the mid 1850s by local evangelical Presbyterian clergymen who had regularly visited homes, distributed tracts, organised local prayer meetings and Sunday schools and employed a direct, conversionist style of preaching. There had been heightened evangelical activity among the farmers and linen weavers in the area from as early as September 1857, including the spread of prayer meetings, and there had been unusual excitement at the spring communion of 1858. During 1858 and the first months of 1859, lay converts from Connor began circulating through the surrounding countryside, giving emotional testimony of their conversions and encouraging the formation of prayer meetings in homes and schoolhouses. The movement broke out into revivalist enthusiasm in mid-March 1859. A vast crowd of perhaps 3,000 gathered for the spring communion occasion in the First Presbyterian church in Ahoghill, where the minister, David Adams, was an enthusiastic supporter of his Church's call for revival. Following the address of a recent convert at the Monday thanksgiving service following the communion, the excited crowd had to be cleared from the church. The meeting, however, continued outside in the rain, where amid impassioned scenes many were physically 'struck down' in the process of being converted.[29]

Reports of the events at Ahoghill were spread to neighbouring districts by lay converts, while evangelical ministers encouraged local enthusiasm. Prayer meetings multiplied and there were outbreaks of religious enthusiasm at spring communions and Sunday services. During April and May, revivalist fervour spread rapidly through the Presbyterian communities of Antrim, and then fanned out across much of rural Ulster during the early summer. Observers compared its spread to that of an epidemic disease, with people speaking of individuals 'catching' the revival as they might a contagion.[30] It tended to affect entire communities, gaining numerous converts in neighbourhoods already bound by kinship associations and sympathetic attachment.[31] The movement, however, did not affect all districts equally, and some communities remained totally unaffected by the revival. The revival tended to have its greatest impact in areas of Presbyterian settlement, and was therefore strongest in Antrim and Down, and weakest in the south and west of the province.[32]

The movement reached Coleraine, Belfast and Derry in early June. In the towns, the revival became more interdenominational, receiving active support from Methodists, Baptists, Congregationalists and Church of Ireland Evangelicals. Evangelical ministers of different Protestant denominations co-operated in organising open-air revival meetings and regular union prayer meetings, which served to weaken barriers and blur theological distinctions. The urban revival meetings frequently became large-scale events, bringing together thousands, including the curious and revellers, as well as the anxious and pious. In Coleraine on 7 June, perhaps 7,000 gathered for an open-air revival meeting, which was followed by days and nights of prayer gatherings in private homes which claimed 150 converts. A mass revival meeting in Belfast's Botanical Gardens on 29 June – chaired by the Moderator of the General Assembly of the Presbyterian Church – attracted an estimated 35,000, including 15,000 who travelled into the city on special trains from Antrim, Derry and Armagh. A second mass meeting in Belfast, held in the Botanical Gardens on 17 August, had an estimated attendance of 20,000. An All-Ireland Union Prayer meeting was held in the religious centre of Armagh on 21 September. Again special trains brought people in from the surrounding districts, with an estimated 20,000 attending, who were organised into eight separate congregations in the open field. The large urban mass meetings also represented a departure from the communal aspects of the early stages of the revival in Antrim. The emphasis began to shift from the preservation of traditional Presbyterian communities to the salvation of individuals through direct, conversionist preaching and 'new measures'.

During the summer, the movement attracted celebrated preachers to Ulster, including the 'gentleman' lay preacher, Brownlow North, the professional revivalist, H. Grattan Guinness of Dublin, and the American Methodist lay preachers, Walter C. and Phoebe Palmer.[33] In mid-June, clerical supporters of the revival issued a call to ministers in Britain to come and assist with preaching and with instruction of the new converts. The ministers in Belfast, it was said, were being overwhelmed by the numbers of converts, in the same way that doctors had been overwhelmed by the numbers of stricken during the cholera epidemic.[34] In response to the call, scores of clergy travelled across from Scotland and England to preach and assist at prayer meetings. The revival also attracted hundreds of lay visitors – anxious to view the revival scenes – from Scotland, England, the United States and the European Continent. During the summer of 1859, it could indeed be claimed that Ulster had come under the gaze, if not of 'universal Christendom', then certainly of the transatlantic evangelical world. 'Now, I tell you', proclaimed Dr Edgar at the Belfast meeting of 17 August, 'you are pledged; we are before the world, and we must show to the world that our actions are equal to our words – that this is not a mere evanescent movement'.[35]

IV

For many Presbyterians, the main work of the revival was to renew their sense of identity as a covenanted community, a peculiar people set apart by God, who would be preserved against the social dislocations of industrialisation and urbanisation, and who need not fear the growing strength of the Catholic Church or of Catholic nationalism. From the beginning, the Ulster revival of 1859 had a strong communal dimension, expressed in particular through local prayer meetings. In the towns, as has been noted, different Protestant churches co-operated in organising united prayer meetings, which often met nightly through the summer in one of the larger churches. But a more striking feature of the revival was the multiplication of informal prayer meetings that were conducted in private homes, barns or local schoolhouses. These were usually organised and led by lay men and women, and involved wide participation by the community as a whole. With the coming of the revival to Connor, the Presbyterian minister there reported that over 100 separate prayer meetings were being held regularly in the parish, all of them conducted by lay members.[36] These prayer meetings brought together converts and inquirers from the lower and middle social orders (though few from the ranks of the gentry or professional classes). They enabled women and children to express themselves, even to assume leadership roles in the communal religious life – in some cases in prayer meetings organised along the lines of sex and age, but more often in mixed meetings alongside adult males. The meetings provided forums for extemporaneous prayers and addresses by lay converts, which could be liberating for communities which had known only worship dominated by the minister and the lengthy sermon. Indeed, the clergy were not always welcomed at local prayer meetings, where their presence tended to dampen the new-found lay confidence. Local prayer meetings could call forth impressive displays of eloquence from labourers and farmers, who were otherwise unaccustomed to public speaking. 'For the first time in the history of Ulster Presbyterianism', noted one Presbyterian historian, 'laymen became prominent as preachers'.[37] New converts often began preaching publicly within a few days of their conversion, filled with an overwhelming need to communicate their new-found peace and assurance to others. Some clergy expressed concern over these illiterate lay preachers, often possessing little knowledge of Scripture or the Westminster Confession, who swarmed over the countryside addressing meetings. Others, however, were impressed by the way in which the revival drew out the latent capacities of the common people:

> The most fervent and energetic prayers were offered up; persons who had never prayed before seemed urged on by some unseen power or influence, and poured forth the most eloquent and fervent petitions, without any apparent difficulty, or the least hesitation in expressing themselves.[38]

The prayer meetings became expressions of communal conversion and renewal, as local communities subordinated their differences to the idea of the renewed covenant. Pressure was placed on the unconverted to come forward, confess their sins openly, and reconcile themselves with God and the community of the godly. Samuel J. Moore, Presbyterian minister in Ballymena and a leading figure in the revival, observed of the prayer meetings that 'any person whom they consider to be one of themselves, "a brother" or "a sister", as they say, they will receive with open arms'. 'I have seen', he continued, 'Christian mothers embracing their lately converted sons, sisters their brothers, companions their old associates in sin, now in Christ, with the deepest intensity'.[39] The prayer meetings brought a highly emotional worship – including personal testimonies from converts, the singing of hymns and gospel songs, and swaying or jerking movements among participants – which was far removed from the subdued forms of worship prevailing in most Presbyterian meeting houses. William Magill, Presbyterian minister of rural Dundrod, left the following description of reconciliation and renewal in a prayer meeting in his parish:

> The multitude heaves to and fro like a ship in a storm and like drunken men in the streets the people stagger and fall with a shout or a deep sigh. Tears are shed, and groans, as if from dying men, are heard. Prayer and praise, tears and smiles, mingle together. Husbands and wives are locked in each other's arms, weeping and praying together; while those who came to scoff stand still, and in 'fear and trembling' contemplate the strange thing that is going on before

their eyes. The dead are rising from their graves, as if at the sound of the archangel's trumpet, for the lord is quickening those who were dead in trespasses and sins. As the people separated, they formed into groups, and marched to their respective homes, some singing, some praying, some mourning, and some rejoicing. One or two had to remain all night.

Such features, Magill insisted, were exhibited at every prayer meeting in his district, 'with little variety'.[40]

The confessions from new converts who for years had abused spouses and children, fought with neighbours, gambled and stolen, were often heart-rending events, accompanied by trembling and unleashing pent-up tears. Confessions and repentance in crowded prayer meetings recalled the Presbyterian ideal of corporate discipline, of confession before the kirk-session of elders and penitence before the congregation, which until the later eighteenth century had played a central role in Presbyterian communal piety and identity, but which by the 1850s was largely neglected by the Church.[41] The prayer meetings also resembled the semi-annual rituals of the Presbyterian communion occasions, in which community members confessed openly the secret sins that might bring divine displeasure on the whole community, and repented the wrongs committed against family and neighbours.

Under revival influences, communities endeavoured to express their new found spiritual identity through moral reforms – the closing of public houses, the enforcement of strict Sabbatarianism, the silencing of profane songs, the suppression of cock-fighting and gambling, the elimination of crime. Converts were expected to conduct daily family worship, and to fulfill their obligations as children, parents or spouses. The able-bodied receiving poor relief were to become self-supporting. Children were also to be converted – and the enthusiasm expressed over the revival movements that swept through schools in Coleraine and Armagh, for example, reflected in part the desire to perpetuate religiously-based communities by winning the young, who were being increasingly drawn away from the home and locality by the new forces of industrialisation, urbanisation, agricultural change and geographical mobility.[42]

Some believed that the downpouring of the Spirit would eliminate the sectarian divisions of the past and usher in a spirit of brotherhood between Protestant and Catholic. They hoped the revival would bring an end to the Orange lodges – which many evangelical Presbyterians viewed as centres of sin, encouraging heavy drinking, brawling and sectarian hatred. The leading Presbyterian supporter of the revival, Professor William Gibson, was confident that the revival had delivered 'a fatal blow' to the order and its 'baneful influence'.[43] The 12th of July passed very quietly in 1859, with Orangemen in many districts joining in prayer meetings. In Newtownards, reported an evangelical school teacher, 'the 12th of July, the anniversary of Satan as well as of the Orangemen, came and went, and left no trace behind. "Not a drum was heard", not an arch was erected, not a shot was fired. The prayer-meetings took place as usual – were thronged as usual'.[44] In Monaghan, Orange lodges celebrated the 12th of July with prayer meetings instead of marches, while the Presbyterian minister, John Blakely, reported that never in his long career had he witnessed 'such a state of kindly feeling towards Roman Catholics on the part of the Protestant population'.[45] A 'red-hot' Orangeman of county Monaghan, known for provoking and threatening Catholics, insisted after his conversion that 'now he loved his Roman Catholic neighbours, and would not willingly offend any one of them'.[46]

While some Protestants had expected the revival to result in large-scale Catholic 'conversions', the results of proselytising efforts proved meagre and relatively few were converted from Catholicism. Those who were, appear to have come largely from the margins of the Catholic community. An elderly widow, for example, had been raised a Presbyterian but converted to Catholicism when she married a Catholic. Perhaps feeling isolated and unwanted among her Catholic relations, she took advantage of the revival to return to her previous communion. A Catholic woman from county Derry had married a Presbyterian who subsequently became a drunkard; she may have hoped that her conversion would have a positive effect on her husband. A number of converts were adolescents, such as a servant boy in Carrickfergus, converted in the home of his Presbyterian employer, who later claimed that he was beaten and doused with holy water by his mother at the instigation of the local priest.[47] These were, however, hardly the large numbers of converts that might have been expected from a downpouring of the Holy Spirit. Protestants soon ceased to look for extensive Catholic conversions, especially as Catholics in many districts closed ranks against the revival.[48] There was never much effort invested in proselytising; the revival from the beginning was primarily concerned with the life and faith of Protestant communities.

The most notable and controversial feature of the Ulster Revival of 1859 was the widespread prevalence of the 'physical manifestations', which included a variety of phenonema – prostrations, convulsions, cries, uncontrollable weeping or trembling, temporary blindness or deafness, trances, dreams and visions. The manifestations appeared with the beginning of the revival in Connor and Ahoghill, and continued throughout the course of the movement. While supporters of the revival argued that only a minority of the converts – perhaps only one in ten – were struck down in a physical manner, large numbers were clearly affected. Some were struck down in prayer meetings and open-air services, and meetings were frequently interrupted by cries and prostrations. After one open-air meeting in county Antrim, an observer noted that 'the lawn was literally strewed like a battlefield with those that were stricken down in this mysterious manner'.[49] The prostrations, moreover, were not confined to religious meetings and people were struck down on roadsides, in fields, at workplaces or in homes. In many cases, the prostrated became unconscious for hours, and might afterwards take to their beds for several days, surrounded by family and concerned neighbours. Prostrations appeared almost exclusively among the lower social orders, though among the poor they affected men and women, young and old, and rural and urban dwellers.[50] Young unmarried females seem to have been especially susceptible, perhaps, as Peter Gibbon has argued, as a result of their vulnerable situation and diminished prospects of marriage at a time of high immigration of young men.[51]

Most prostrations probably resulted from extreme emotion – terror at the prospect of eternal punishment and profound relief at being released from the wages of sin through grace.[52] The fears were frequently aroused by the direct conversionist preaching style adopted by many evangelicals, which was designed to impale individuals with a burning sense of sin until they embraced salvation through grace; indeed, some preachers evidently measured their success by the number of prostrations they could bring on in a sermon.[53] The emotional response to the revival message could be intensified in overcrowded and overheated prayer meetings, in which a few incidents of fainting, uncontrollable weeping or anguished cries often elicited similar behaviour from others until a large portion of the crowd was affected. In many cases, those who had experienced physical manifestations felt compelled to bring others to have similar experiences. Prostrations could become a badge of identity, a sign that a person had been touched by the Spirit and was a part of the community of the converted. 'I have seen', observed a Church of Ireland minister, '[affected] females rush forward to kiss each other. They express the greatest delight when their friends are visited in the same way, and frequently pray for them that they may have an attack'.[54]

Many converts also began claiming visions and charismatic gifts. A Church of Ireland observer asserted that 'almost every girl now "struck" in Belfast has "visions", and would be greatly disappointed if she had not'.[55] Sometimes the visions came in the midst of prayer meetings or church services, as in Derry when a man during a church service saw a vision of hell opening up beneath him and felt a force drawing him down – forcing him to stagger out of the church.[56] J. Whitsitt, minister of Drum in county Monaghan, claimed that during a prayer-meeting in his church 'a dark cloud formed on the ceiling, and, in the course of a few minutes, a number of forms burst out. One in particular was of human appearance, and . . . descended to a pew, in which a young woman was rejoicing. The appearance lasted for three minutes, or more, produced no terror, but joy, especially among the converts'. 'All present did not see it', Whitsitt admitted, 'Perhaps 300 saw it, and can testify to its reality'.[57] Those going into trances frequently claimed to be transported to heaven or to hell, to wrestle with the devil, to embrace Christ, to meet dead relations, or to foresee the eternal fates of their neighbours.[58] Some Protestant women believed themselves to be visited by apparitions of the Virgin, prompting a leading Presbyterian to observe that 'if the Protestant Church comes to trust in visions, it will soon find itself far outstripped by the Church of

Rome'.[59] Claims to charismatic gifts included healing and prophecy. In Comber, county Down, there were reports of healing, with people recovering their sight or the use of their limbs.[60] In Belfast, women claimed to have marks on their bodies left by the Spirit – representing mystic words or symbols – which validated their claims to prophetic power.[61]

Prostrations, visions and charismatic gifts were not unusual in revivals, and had certainly been prominent during the Cambuslang revival in Scotland in 1742 and during the First and Second Great Awakenings in America. There was indeed biblical warrant for expecting a revival to be accompanied by the gifts of the Spirit. Charismatic powers – visions, prophecy, healing – enhanced the sense of the imminence of the Spirit, enabling Christians to recover the awe and wonder in their religion. Many were impressed by the fact that the Ulster prostrations were occurring within the most advanced industrial state in the world, amid the claims of Victorian science to explain the world rationally – and yet for believers science seemed incapable to explain the phenomenon. Ulster could thus be viewed as a field of mystery; two visiting Scottish ministers were struck by what they described as the 'peculiar atmosphere' in Ulster, in which the air was 'charged with some spiritual electricity' filling them with a 'new and strange power'.[62] The manifestations seemed to restore Christianity as a living, spontaneous faith in the modern world – not a set of doctrines defined as orthodox by the letter of Scripture or the Westminster Confession, but a faith that transcended logic and forced itself on the scientific world, a faith to be experienced in fear and trembling.[63] The widespread belief in the charismatic claims among Presbyterians may have been a reaction against the rigid orthodox Calvinism imposed on the Presbyterian Church by Henry Cooke and his supporters. The visions and charismatic claims may have also resulted from the new-found freedom of the laity in prayer meetings to express their religious beliefs and aspirations, without fear of censure from the theologically educated ministers.

One effect of the physical and charismatic manifestations was to elevate further the individualistic aspects of the revival at the expense of the communal, a process that began with the mass revival meetings in the larger towns and cities. As those involved in the revival became increasingly absorbed in the subjective experiences and extraordinary spiritual powers of individuals touched by the Spirit, the concern for the corporate renewal of traditional communities waned. The Spirit was increasingly seen as acting upon individuals rather than communities; conversion became more a private than a corporate experience. The 'physical manifestations' attracted considerable attention from the press, both in Ulster and in Britain, and a steady stream of visitors – clergy, scientists, sceptics, religious journalists – travelled to the revival scenes to study the phenomena at first hand. Individuals who had been struck down or who claimed charismatic gifts were often repeatedly visited by the curious and encouraged to describe their prostrations or visions, sometimes receiving payment for their efforts. In September 1859, a Scottish Presbyterian periodical expressed concern about the stream of British religious tourists following the now well-trodden route from Belfast to Ballymena and Coleraine:

> In each town or village they procure a list of the converts there, and make the round of them, regarding them with a curiosity such as might be evinced at the sight of some singular phenomenon – Tom Thumb, for example, or the Siamese Twins. Having exhausted their last list, they return to report what they have seen and heard to their expectant friends at home.[64]

Such attention was no doubt attractive for some converts, especially among the poorer classes, and the crowds of visitors encouraged fraudulent claims and extravagant behaviour.[65]

Ulster Protestant leaders were divided in their responses to the 'physical manifestations'. For sympathisers of the revival, the manifestations represented the work of the Holy Spirit acting upon sinful humanity. While there were some incidents of fraud or self-delusion, the vast majority of those struck down had been genuinely affected by a heart-felt release from the burden of their sins. Further, whatever the educated classes might think of them, the manifestations made a powerful impact on the lower social orders, who had often proven immune to traditional evangelical methods.[66] Others, however, expressed serious concerns about the physical manifestations. In a paper presented at the Conference of the Evangelical Alliance in Belfast on 22 September 1859, James McCosh, Professor of Moral Philosophy at the Belfast Assembly College, maintained that the prostrations were a normal physical response to extreme emotion, and that it was not surprising they should occur among people suddenly released by grace from the prospect of hell. However, he continued, if individuals repeated the prostration experience (as many did) amid the enthusiasm of the revival meetings, the emotional strain could result in nervous disease, even hysteria – and this might account for the disturbing reports of trances and visions.[67] For Edward Stopford, the Church of Ireland Archdeacon of Meath, the prostrations represented an epidemic of mass hysteria, that struck particularly among young working-class girls in the textile mills of Belfast. Susceptible young women, he maintained, were often weakened by poor diet and craved sympathetic attention. They were emotionally exploited by ambitious revivalist preachers and encouraged by misguided sympathisers to make false claims of visions and spiritual gifts.[68] For another Church of Ireland observer, the prostrations were simply expressions of blind terror, resulting from delusions inspired by Satan.[69]

In Britain, the Churches and the press took a keen interest in the Ulster revival. British Christians were divided over the meaning of the extraordinary events occurring among the usually sober and hard-headed Ulster Protestants. Liberal nonconformists and Anglicans, on the whole dismissed the revival as an outburst of religious enthusiasm, reminiscent of the charismatic excesses of the movement associated with Edward Irving which flourished briefly during the 1830s.[70] British evangelicals, on the other hand, tended to view the Ulster revival as a genuine work of the Holy Spirit, part of a larger movement that had swept through the United States, and they prayed and prepared for the revival to reach Britain.[71] The Ulster revival had probably its greatest influence on the conservative evangelical Free Church of Scotland, which had forged close links with the Presbyterian Church in Ireland at the Disruption of 1843. The Scottish Free Church had its own strong revivalist traditions, and now took an intense interest in the revivals in both America and Ulster. During July 1859, many Free Church clergymen travelled to Ulster to assist with the revival, returning to Scotland with reports of the dramatic meetings and conversions. Ulster lay converts travelled to Scotland to address meetings and testify to the work of the Spirit. On 10 August, representatives of the Presbyterian Church in Ireland attended a special meeting of the Commission of the Free Church General Assembly devoted to the Ulster revival.[72] In the same month the revival made its appearance in Glasgow and the West of Scotland, in Aberdeenshire, and in fishing villages along the east coast of Scotland. The revival in Scotland continued for over two years and affected tens of thousands. It was characterised by emotional prayer meetings, interdenominational co-operation and prostrations, although the Scottish Presbyterian clergy were quick to bring the movement under their control in order to avoid the charismatic excesses of the Ulster revival. The Scottish revival breathed new life into the Free Church and strengthened the historic connections of Irish and Scottish evangelical Presbyterianism.[73] During the summer of 1859, the revival also spread into England and Wales, becoming a general British movement and ushering in what has been described as the 'revival decade' of 1860–70, which brought dramatic increases in membership in existing churches and laid the foundation for new mission initiatives, including the development of the Salvation Army and the Moody and Sankey British campaign of 1873–75.[74]

In Ulster, the revival came rather suddenly to an end in the autumn of 1859 – just as it was making its impact felt in Britain. The Presbyterian districts in the province had been largely 'burned-over' in the heated excitement of the summer, with most individuals open to the revival influences having been converted. Interdenominational co-operation, moreover, had begun to break down, as churches and denominations competed for the membership of the revival converts. Presbyterians, for example, accused other denominations – especially Methodists and Baptists – of taking advantage of the revival excitement to attract members away from the Presbyterian Church.[75] Perhaps more important, the excesses of the physical manifestations and charismatic claims had convinced Church leaders, especially in the Presbyterian Church, of the need to dampen enthusiasms and reassert clerical control. At its annual meeting in July 1860, several months after the end of the revival in Ulster, the General Assembly of the Presbyterian Church in Ireland issued a pastoral letter, which 'lamented' the many cases of 'self-deception' and fraud during the revival, called for greater clerical control over the lay persons allowed to lead prayer meetings, and summoned elders and congregations to support and strengthen the authority of the ordained ministers.[76] There were concerns of 'doctrinal errors' emerging from the teachings of lay preachers and popular gospel songs.[77] The revival could no longer be allowed to move in its own directions; rather, the clergy needed to direct the spiritual and emotional forces into proper ecclesiastical channels. As the spontaneity was brought under control, the movement lost most of its power and influence.

V

The Ulster revival of 1859 had resulted in thousands of converts and had increased church membership significantly. During 1859, the Presbyterian Church in Ireland had gained 10,696 communicants. Other Protestant denominations also experienced increases. The Wesleyan Methodists, for example, grew from 19,406 members in 1858 to 22,860 in 1860, and the Primitive Methodists from 9,158 in 1858 to 15,341 in 1860.[78] The numbers of students preparing for the Presbyterian ministry at the Assembly College, Belfast, nearly doubled in three years, from 64 in 1858 to 104 in 1860 and 125 in 1861.[79] Through the prayer meetings and hymn singing, the revival had introduced a more emotional style of worship to the Ulster churches, and especially the Presbyterian Church.[80]

The revival had given Ulster Presbyterians a renewed confidence – a sense that they formed the centre of the transatlantic revival and received the admiration of the evangelical world. At the General Assembly of 1860, the report on the revival struck a note almost of Protestant triumphalism. 'God', the report asserted, 'has exceeded our expectations':

> The spiritual and moral effects have been such as to attract universal attention. They have excited the interest and inquiry of far distant nations. Strangers have come from England, Scotland and America, and many nations of the Continent of Europe, to look upon the work of the Lord. They have seen it with wonder and admiration, and thanksgiving.

The Presbyterians of Ulster need no longer perceive themselves as a threatened minority in a predominantly Catholic Ireland. The revival had renewed the covenant between God and the Ulster Presbyterians, and given them a place of leadership in the transatlantic Protestant world. Through the revival, Ulster Presbyterians could now set their own universalist claims against those of the Roman Catholic Church:

The consequence is that Ulster has become an object of contemplation to the whole religious world. Our own Church especially has been compared as 'a city set on a hill that cannot be hid'. Like Judea of old, it has been looked upon as a light shining in the midst of a dark world. Our country is regarded as though it were assuming again its ancient title of an 'Island of Saints'. This is a position of high responsibility. It well becomes us to tremble for the Ark of God, which is committed to our care.[81]

While it strengthened the ties of the Ulster Presbyterian Church with the larger transatlantic Protestant world, however, the revival had also weakened traditional Presbyterian communal identities. Increasingly, the Presbyterian identity became based, not on the largely self-contained communities of pre-industrial Ulster, but rather on a larger Protestant evangelical culture extending to the trans-atlantic world. The revival diminished concern for Calvinist orthodoxy or for covenanted communities – fostering instead a warm personal religion, with a simple gospel message emphasising the moment of 'deciding for Jesus'.[82] It strengthened the tendencies, already evident before the revival, for Presbyterians to concern themselves with the new measures of American revivalism, or the evangelical mission culture developing in urban centres in Britain. Many of the Presbyterians affected by the events of 1859 drifted out of the Presbyterian Church and found their way into other evangelical denominations with livelier forms of worship, more conversionist theologies or greater emphasis on assurance of salvation. The revival brought the growth of a diverse evangelical mission culture in Ulster, including the expansion of the Plymouth Brethren and the YMCA. During the 1860s and 1870s, new interdenominational evangelical societies began to exercise influence – the Salvation Army, the Irish Evangelization Society, the Faith Mission, and the Irish Christian and Missionary Workers Union. Mission halls appeared in many towns; freelance professional evangelists became increasingly a part of Ulster religious life.[83] The experience of interdenominational co-operation during the revival had diminished for many the importance of denominational differences and theological distinctions. Protestant worship, especially Presbyterian worship, appealed increasingly to the emotions, with more singing of hymns and congregational responses, and less emphasis on the lengthy sermon. Rather than restore the ideal of the covenanted community, under the leadership of an educated and ordained Presbyterian clergy, the revival had instead contributed to the spread of a personal and subjective faith, deeply concerned with personal salvation and open to charismatic influences. The revival had served to weaken the Presbyterian tradition of an intellectual and liberal clergy, exercising a moral control over their congregations.[84] The attempts of the Presbyterian clergy to reassert their former authority in the aftermath of the revival had not on the whole proved successful. After 1860, if a minister took an unpopular position, members of the congregation were likely to leave his church for another – as was the case in the churches of many Liberal Presbyterian ministers during the Home Rule crisis.[85] Religion in Ulster became increasingly voluntary in nature, a matter of personal choice; the revival was, as the historian Peter Brooke has noted, 'another substantial step towards religion becoming a subjective personal commitment rather than the organising principle of a unified community'.[86] Moving away from the communal traditions of rural Ireland, Ulster Protestantism increasingly reflected the mood of liberal mid-Victorian Britain, with its emphasis on laissez faire industrial capitalism, religious pluralism, self-help and individual autonomy. It also resembled in many respects the United States, with its denominationalism and voluntaryism. As a result of the revival, noted the Presbyterian historian, W. T. Latimer, in 1893, 'our worship is becoming more emotional, and our theology either Broad Church or 'Evangelical'. A majority of our younger ministers incline to Broad Church views, while most of our people are evangelical'.[87] Through the revival, Ulster Presbyterians shared increasingly in the ethos of British nonconformity and American denominationalism, perceiving themselves as part of a British, or Anglo-American liberal evangelical Protestantism.

In drawing Ulster Presbyterians into this British evangelical nonconformist culture, the revival of 1859 contributed to the growth of Ulster Protestant Unionism. At the beginning of the revival, Presbyterian leaders such as William Gibson had expressed hopes for an Irish awakening, one that would bring large-scale conversions and transform society throughout the island. The downpouring of the Holy Spirit would affect the whole of the Irish people. However, while there had been some revival activity among Protestants in the southwest and around Dublin, the revival had been mainly confined to Ulster – emphasising its separateness from the rest of Ireland. Further, there had been relatively few converts among Irish Catholics. Evidently, the Holy Spirit had passed the Catholics over during 'the Year of Grace'; at any rate, it became clear after 1859 that there would be no major Protestant inroads into the confident and assertive Irish Catholic nation. Many Protestants no doubt shared the opinion of the layman who in 1859 assured his minister that the Roman Catholics could not be converted: 'between you and me, I don't believe God would have anything to do with them'.[88] With the growing influence of an evangelical mission culture among the Protestant laity, such views many well have become more prevalent – spreading the perception that Roman Catholics were among the reprobate. Catholics could thus be seen as something other, from whom Protestants had nothing to learn, with whom they had nothing to share. After 1860, Ulster Presbyterians increasingly subsumed their traditional communal identity into a larger mass identity based on an emotional evangelical mission culture and voluntary religion.[89] The majority of Presbyterians also became increasingly committed to maintaining the union with Britain, perceiving themselves more a part of religiously pluralistic Britain than of Ireland, with its traditional religious communal identities. The language of covenant was preserved as a badge of identity, but in the aftermath of the revival of 1859 such language came to represent the Protestant and Unionist population of Ulster, rather than the Presbyterian communities of the Six-Mile-Water revival and the communion occasions.

Notes to Chapter 7

1. D. G. Boyce, *Nineteenth-Century Ireland: The Search for Stability* (Dublin, 1990), 133.
2. W. Gibson, *The Year of Grace: A History of the Ulster Revival of 1859* (Edinburgh, 1860), p. 372.
3. R. F. Holmes, *Our Irish Presbyterian Heritage* (Belfast, 1985), 115–25; P. Gibbon, *The Origins of Ulster Unionism* (Manchester, 1975), 44–66; P. Brooke, *Ulster Presbyterianism: The Historical Perspective* (Dublin, 1987), 190–97.
4. M. Hill, 'Ulster Awakened: The '59 Revival Reconsidered', *Journal of Ecclesiastical History* 41 (July 1990), 443–62.
5. M. J. Westerkamp, *Triumph of the Laity: Scots-Irish Piety and the Great Awakening* (New York, 1988); L. E. Schmidt, *Holy Fairs: Scottish Communions and American Revivals in the Early Modern Period* (Princeton, 1990); N. Landsman, 'Revivalism and Nativism in the Middle Colonies: The Great Awakening and the Scots Community in East New Jersey', *American Quarterly* **34**; 2 (Summer 1982), 149–64.
6. Brooke, *Ulster Presbyterianism*, 193–94.
7. D. W. Miller, *Queen's Rebels: Ulster Loyalism in Historical Perspective* (Dublin, 1978), 7–24.
8. Gibson, *The Year of Grace, op. cit.,* 5.
9. Westerkamp, *Triumph of the Laity*, 31–34.
10. *Ibid.,* 135.
11. *Ibid.,* 136–64; Schmidt, *Holy Fairs*, 11–68.
12. Schmidt, *Holy Fairs*, 192–206; J. F. Fishburn, 'Pennsylvania "Awakenings", Sacramental Seasons and Ministry', in D. B. Clendenin and W. D. Buschat (eds) *Scholarship, Sacraments and Service* (New York, 1990), 86.
13. Carwardine, *Transatlantic Revivalism*, 3–28.
14. W. W. Sweet, *Revivalism in America: Its Origin, Growth and Decline* (New York, 1944), 112–39.
15. J. Kent, *Holding the Fort: Studies in Victorian Revivalism* (London, 1978), 71–2.
16. Kent, *Holding the Fort, op. cit.,* 71.
17. Carwardine, *Transatlantic Revivalism, op. cit.,* 159–69; J. E. Orr, *The Second Evangelical Awakening in Britain* (London, 1949), 13–37.
18. Gibson, *The Year of Grace*, 14.
19. J. T. Carson, *God's River in Spate* (Belfast, 1958), 12.
20. *Ibid.,* 12–13.
21. R. F. Holmes, *Henry Cooke* (Belfast, 1981), 44, 52.
22. R. F. Holmes, *Henry Cooke* (Belfast, 1981), 139.
23. Holmes, *Our Irish Presbyterian Heritage*, 121–22.
24. Brooke, *Ulster Presbyterianism*, 195.
25. E. Larkin, 'The Devotional Revolution in Ireland, 1850–1875', *American Historical Review*, **77**; 3 (June 1972), 502–23.
26. D. Bowen, *Paul Cardinal Cullen* (Dublin, 1983), 293.
27. Holmes, *Henry Cooke*, 190; Miller, *Queen's Rebels*, 67–71.
28. Supporters would later claim that the revival in Connor began in September 1857, at the same time as the beginning of the American revival – thus showing the two revivals to emerge from the same downpouring of the Spirit.
29. D. McMeekin, *Memories of '59, or the Revival Movement* (Hull, 1908), 15–17.
30. 'Christian Revivals', *Westminster Review*, n.s., 16 (January 1860), 198.
31. 'Revivals', *North British Review*, 33 (November 1860), 496.
32. Hill, 'Ulster Awakened', 449.
33. Orr, *The Second Evangelical Awakening*, 232.
34. *The Witness* (Edinburgh), 18 June 1859.
35. Weir, *The Ulster Awakening*, 154.
36. Weir, *The Ulster Awakening*, 15–17.
37. W. T. Latimer, *A History of the Irish Presbyterians*, 2nd edn. (Belfast, 1902), 492; Gibbon, *The Origins of Ulster Unionism*, 48.

38. W. Steuart Trench, *Realities of Irish Life*, 5th edn. (London, 1870), 332.
39. S. J. Moore, *The History and Prominent Characteristics of the Present Revival in Ballymena* (Belfast, 1859), 11.
40. Cited in Gibson, *The Year of Grace*, 132.
41. Brooke, *Ulster Presbyterianism*, 191.
42. Hill, 'Ulster Awakened', 458–9; Gibbon, *Year of Grace*, 68–70, 268–70.
43. Gibson, *The Year of Grace*, 155.
44. Gibson, *The Year of Grace*, 184.
45. Weir, *The Ulster Awakening*, 201–2.
46. Gibson, *The Year of Grace*, 305.
47. Gibson, *The Year of Grace*, 313–35.
48. See, for example, the report of Catholic hostility from William Craig, Presbyterian minister in Dromara, cited in Weir, *The Ulster Awakening*, 207.
49. Trench, *Realities of Irish Life*, 338.
50. J. C. L. Carson, *Three Letters on the Revival in Ireland*, 8–9; W. M. Wilkinson, *The Revival in its Physical, Psychical and Religious Aspects* (London, 1860), 80–81.
51. Gibbon, *The Origins of Ulster Unionism*, 58–62.
52. Trench, *Realities of Irish Life*, 332.
53. E. A. Stopford, *The Work and the Counterwork; or, the Religious Revival in Belfast* (Dublin, 1859), 39–42.
54. G. Salmon, *The Evidences of the Work of the Holy Spirit* (Dublin, 1859), 47.
55. Stopford, *The Work and the Counterwork;* 50.
56. Weir, *The Ulster Awakening*, 134.
57. Wilkinson, *The Revival in its Physical, Psychical, and Religious Aspects*, 112.
58. Stopford, *The Work and the Counterwork*, 85; Anon., *Revivalism: Is it of God or the Devil?* (Belfast, 1859), 8.
59. J. McCosh, *The Ulster Revival and its Physiological Accidents* (Belfast, 1859), 12–13; Wilkinson, *The Revival in its Physical, Psychical and Religious Aspects*, 13.
60. Gibson, *The Year of Grace*, 172.
61. Gibson, *The Year of Grace*, 141–3; McMeekin, *Memories of '59*, 83.
62. D. MacColl, *Among the Masses; or Work in the Wynds* (London, 1867), 251–2.
63. Wilkinson, *The Revival in Its Physical, Psychical, and Religious Aspects*, 89–90.
64. *United Presbyterian Magazine*, n.s., vol. III (September 1859), 400.
65. 'Revivals', *North British Review*, 33 (November 1860), 503.
66. *The Witness* (Edinburgh), 13 August 1859; 'Revivals', *North British Review*, 33 (Nov., 1860), 512.
67. McCosh, *The Ulster Revival and its Physiological Accidents*, 10–14.
68. Stopford, *The Work and the Counterwork*, 45–57, 75–76.
69. E. Hincks, *God's Word and Satan's Counter-works, as Now Carried Out in the North of Ireland* (Belfast, 1859), 7–8.
70. Eg., B. Scott, *The Revival in Ulster: Its Moral and Social Results* (London, 1859), 8–9; P. W. Perfitt, *The History, Character, and Consequences of Revivalism in Ireland; An Appeal to the Common Sense of Englishmen* (London, 1859); 'George Gilfillan of Dundee on the Irish Revival', *The Witness* (Edinburgh), 22 June 1859.
71. J. E. Orr, *The Second Evangelical Awakening in Britain*, 78–171.
72. *The Witness* (Edinburgh), 13 August 1859.
73. J. E. Orr, *The Second Evangelical Awakening in Britain*, 58–77; *Proceedings and Debates of the Free Church of Scotland* (1862), 175–87.
74. G. Kitson Clark, *The Making of Victorian England* (London, 1962), 188–89; Orr, *The Second Evangelical Awakening*, 262–67.
75. *The Autobiography of Thomas Witherow*, eds., G. Mawhinney and E. Dunlop, (Draperstown, 1990), 95.
76. *Minutes of the Proceedings of the General Assembly of the Presbyterian Church in Ireland*, vol. 2 (1851–60), 892–3, 899–900.
77. McMeekin, *Memories of '59*, 56.

78. Gibson, *The Year of Grace*, 404; Hill, 'Ulster Awakened', 455. Hill mistakenly gives the Presbyterian Church in Ireland as the Church of Ireland statistics.
79. Orr, *The Second Evangelical Awakening in Britain*, 200.
80. Holmes, *Our Irish Presbyterian Heritage*, 124–5.
81. *Minutes of the Proceedings of the General Assembly of the Presbyterian Church in Ireland*, vol. II (1851–1860), 866.
82. Brooke, *Ulster Presbyterianism*, 193–4.
83. Latimer, *A History of Irish Presbyterians*, 494–7.
84. 'Whereas before 1830 (the Presbyterian minister) might be understood as a bearer of cosmopolitanism, learning and *Logos* in the rural community, after 1860 the minister is unequivocally a messenger from *doxa*'. Gibbon, *The Origins of Ulster Unionism*, 64.
85. Anderson, *Story of the Presbyterian Church in Ireland*, 98.
86. Brooke, *Ulster Presbyterianism*, 193–4.
87. Latimer, *History of the Irish Presbyterians*, 495.
88. D. W. Miller, 'Presbyterianism and "Modernization" in Ulster', *Past and Present*, no. 80 (August 1978), 88.
89. Brooke, *Ulster Presbyterianism* 193–4.

8. THE EMPIRE WRITES BACK

Declan Kiberd

In 1983 the Trinidadian dramatist Mustafa Matura rewrote John
Millington Synge's most famous play under the revised title *The Playboy
of the West Indies*. He altered the main characters' names, so that Christy
became Ken, Pegeen was reborn as Peggy, Mahon was shortened to Mac,
and Shawn Keogh was turned to Stanley: and, naturally, he substituted
the Trinidadian for the Hiberno-English dialect. The final moments cap-
ture the flavour of the text:

> MAC (untying KEN): An we go have a good time telling people bout de
> blood thirsty village a Mayaro, an de fools dat live here. Come boy.
> KEN: Boy, I en no boy, but I go come wit you like Robinson Crusoe an he
> Friday an you go cook me food an buy me rum, because a could beat you in
> any fight from now. Go on you. (Pushes MAC).
> MAC: Do push me man.
> KEN: Go, a yell yer. (Pushes him).
> (MAC walks out).
> MAC: Well look at me crosses, me mind gone again.
> (MAC goes).
> KEN: A said greeting wen a come in an a say greetings wen a go out, because
> a tank all yer, all a yer, fer turning me into a real saga boy an Bad John.
> From now on I go romance an fight wit de best an all a meet, till wat de
> almond tree didn't do, de good Lord go do, an in he good time. (KEN goes
> out).
> MIKEY (picking up tables): After all dat, yer mean all we left wit is peace,
> peace, ter drink. Le we fire one, girl.
> (PEGGY goes to get bottle, glass. STANLEY goes to her at bar).
> STANLEY: Am. As soon as a run home an change, de Post Mistress could
> marry me. Wha yer say?
> (PEGGY turns her back on him).
> PEGGY: Oh Lord, oh Lord, oh Lord. A lose im, a lose im, a lose de only play-
> boy a de West Indies. (Goes into room).

What was remarkable was how little Matura added to Synge's masterpiece, a lot less than Aime Cesaire had to add to his rewritten version of
The Tempest. After successful productions in Oxford and London,
Matura's work was recorded by BBC television and this version was seen
widely in Ireland.

Ever afterwards, Irish versions of Synge's *Playboy* were transformed, becoming astoundingly violent, raw and dirty. By the mid-nineteen-eighties the peasant girls in the Druid production of Galway seemed more like harridans with horrendous muscles and missing teeth than like the fresh-faced colleens so beloved of the National Theatre at the Abbey in Dublin. In the words of one rather caustic critic, they seemed to have stepped straight down from a Girl-Meets-Tractor poster from the Soviet nineteen-thirties. The Druid production as a whole was very physical, intentionally barbarous: it emphasised the violence of Synge's world at least as much as the poetry. It was like no version seen in Ireland before, except perhaps the opening production mounted under Synge's watchful guidance in 1907. Then the bloody bandage on Old Mahon's head and the threatening movements of the actors onstage had inflamed an audience to riot. Ever since that outbreak, producers and actors had settled for a tamer option: to play up the 'hearts a wonder' poetry; to encourage defin-itive 'national' actors like Cyril Cusack and Siobhán MacKenna to lilt the beautiful lines; and to present onstage a community which epitomised Eamon de Valera's Ireland of athletic youths and comely maidens at a crossroads dance. Prisoner of a state subsidy, the National Theatre in Dublin converted a revolutionary play into a revivalist pastoral, in much the same manner that Irish critics had erased the subversive potentials of their own people's texts, or in the manner of a government minister ban-ning republicans from the airwaves.

Against this backdrop, the bafflement of many critics was understand-able: for the clear implication of the new versions, at the Gaiety theatre as well as the Druid, was that violence, though always regrettable, might in some ways be redemptive. By studying the available notes on Synge's intentions for his first performance and by incorporating their own expe-rience of growing up in the impoverished west of Ireland, members of the Druid Company had come up with a Fanonite production. The Abbey Theatre in Dublin – museum-custodian of this and other masterpieces – had undergone a vitalising challenge from peripheral Galway; and a fur-ther impulse from Trinidad helped to restore to Synge's work the open-ness it once, briefly, had.

The society depicted in *The Playboy of the Western World* is a colony in the throes of a land war, as the last phase of the campaign against feu-dalism in Ireland is enacted. Pegeen Mike refers with excitement as well as fear to the thousand militia then crossing county Mayo, scene of so many evictions which have left thousands of vagrants in the streets. Synge did not suppress the ugliness of colonialism – 'the loosed khaki cut-throats', 'the broken harvest', or the rigged juries 'selling judgements of the English law' are all mentioned – but this is mere backdrop. Synge was less interested in the colonial present than in the postcolonial future. Assuming the inevitability of Home Rule once socialist ideas had spread in England, he tried instead to see so profoundly into the Mayoites' cul-ture that the shape of their future might become discernible.

So he took the violence of the colonisers as read: his deeper interest was in how the colonised cope with the violence in themselves, their situation and their daily life. There is no obvious outlet in the world of the play for these instincts. The Mayoites offer no allegiance to the hated English law, which might allow them to channel their violence into socially-sanctioned punishments like the hanging of a murderer. The allegiance to the Catholic church, which by its sacrifice of the Mass helps to appease the human taste for violence, is also very weak. Father Reilly is so peripheral a figure to these fundamentally pagan people that Synge does not allow him to appear on the stage at all: only Shawn Keogh speaks of the priest without irony. Yet the villagers are saturated in violence and its attendant imagery. Sarah Tansey is willing to travel miles to set eyes on the man who bit the yellow lady's nostril by the northern shore. Such a people desperately need a hero who can bring their instincts to violence into a single clear focus: a hero, moreover, whom they can then convert into a scapegoat, onto whom may be visited any troublesomely violent tendencies that are still unfulfilled. This figure must come from outside the settled community, for otherwise he might exact a terrible revenge through the intervention of angry relations. So, Christy Mahon comes from 'a windy corner of high distant hills'. This permits the community the luxury of believing that with him the cycle of incremental violence will come to a final halt. Hence the importance of reading into Christy all the ills and frustrations that flesh is heir to. As his father so vaguely, yet so magnificently, says: 'Isn't it by the like of you that the sins of the world are committed?' This would also account for Christy's radical blankness as a personality on his arrival: he is the seductive male version of those gorgeous but empty female models into whose faces men can read their most vivid fantasies. Except that in this case the role of sex-object is played by the male lead.

A person thus sacrificed harmlessly drains off the evil in a village and, in the very act of being disposed of, becomes endowed with the glamour of a holy healer who has the power to bind the community back together. So, in *The Playboy*, the very hand that dealt the seeming death-blow to the father is watched acutely, even worshipped, by the village girls; and when he conceals it behind his back, Christy is asked 'Is your right hand too sacred for to use at all?' They bring him food, half-aware that they are fattening him for the scapegoat's slaughter.

In his study *Violence and the Sacred*, René Girard defines the sacred as 'all those forces whose dominance over man increases or seems to increase in proportion to man's efforts to master them. Tempests, forest fires, plagues . . . and human violence'. The presence of a murder among a people may, in folk belief, bring about any of these disasters as a manifestation of sacred wrath. In the play, Christy is asked 'Would you be bringing plagues and pestilences, and the cholera morbus and the old hen?' In the ritual crisis which ensues, violence becomes the great leveller and everyone the twin of his or her antagonist: so Synge shows how the old grow like the young, men like women, and so on. If all antagonists are secret doubles, one figure can be arbitrarily selected as scapegoat to become the double of all, the sole remaining object of hatred and revenge. In *The Playboy* Christy does indeed serve as the apparent opposite but unexpected double of Widow Quin (both are lonely murderers), of the settled Pegeen (both are frustrated children of autocratic fathers), of old Mahon (both are expelled from polite society). Thus instituted as a universal scapegoat, he offers the hope that with his expulsion will go all memories of past violence. This human desire to deny the very violence which marks human society is captured in Michael James's injunction to the scrappers in his shebeen:

> Go to the foreshore if it's fighting you want, the way the rising tide will wash all trace from the memory of man.

Girard climaxes his book with the claim that ritual sacrifices which pretend to appease forces external to men and women are actually designed to feed the unadmitted taste for violence in many persons. And why? 'Because men cannot confront the naked truth of their own violence without abandoning themselves to it entirely' – a point astutely made by one of the original actors who warned Synge during rehearsals that so much bad temper and aggression onstage could easily spill over into the pit. There could be few better illustrations of Girard's contention than the riots which greeted *The Playboy*, a drama which questions the conceit that society is held together by consent and contract rather than by a force which can never admit itself as such. This is the central intimation of the psychoanalytic process and of Greek tragedy: that there is always a hidden truth which a person cannot afford to see, for if it were told, it would illuminate but also shatter its subject. People, entire communities even, elaborate myths which help them to avoid such painful disclosures, which are kept at the level of paradoxical embodiment rather than analytical expression. The instincts which impose a colonial culture are no less violent – by very definition, they must be more violent than – the instincts which they oppose and override. To make this painful identification of barbarism and civilisation, it takes a hero like Christy or, indeed, Synge (for, as Shaw said, the real Playboy was Synge and his libel on Ireland was the truth about the world). Synge's particular offence in the Irish context was to have exploded the most beloved of all middle-class myths (the notion of 'the social contract'), before the new Irish bourgeoisie had had time to come fully into being as a social formation. What Girard observes of free, non-colonised societies would have been even more notable of pre-revolutionary Ireland: 'they have never had a very clear idea of this violence, and it is possible that the survival of all human societies in the past was dependent on this lack of understanding'.

In other words, socially-sanctioned violence is seldom called by that name at all, so masked is it by official decorum and virtue. The word is usually reserved for unsanctioned, oppositional forms, which are never as 'mindless' as they are subsequently made to seem. Insurrectionary violence is usually motivated by the desire to tear the mask of respectability from the face of the ruling class and to reveal the essential barbarism of its underlying consensus. This was, indeed, Antonin Artaud's definition of the Theatre of Cruelty:

> . . . it causes the mask to fall, reveals the lie, the slackness, baseness, and hypocrisy of our world . . . and in revealing to collectivities of men their dark power, their hidden force, it invites them to take, in the face of destiny, a superior and heroic attitude they would never have assumed without it.

Far from being crazy, such violence is often deeply analytical, since it discriminates the latent from the manifest content of a society. Moreover, its agent, however emotionally charged at the moment of committing the act, has the effect of compelling all those in its vicinity to reconsider and redefine their values. Not all, of course, will do so. Under this provocation, the mercantile mind of a Michael James will still try to cover all violent effects rather than subject them to conscious critique.

Clearly, there were many such minds in Synge's audience on the night of the riots. 'It is as if we had looked into a mirror for the first time and found ourselves hideous', wrote a columnist for *The Irish Times:* 'we fear to face the thing. We scream'. The monstrous spectacle of a deformed colonial life may have defeated the very sympathies which it could have aroused among nationalists in the audience. The frustration of knowing that they were more nauseated than sympathetic may have led many spectators to insure themselves against ensuing guilt by converting the play, through vilification and hearsay, into a genuine 'monster'. The physical assaults on the actors would be of a piece with this, since their effect would be to enhance the deformation and monstrosity of the players. Synge's play, and by extension Synge himself, thus became – like Christy – a scapegoat for the violence visited upon one another by the colonised. Not long after Synge had served this function and died an early death, Patrick Pearse, repenting of his earlier attacks on play and playwright wrote of him as an authentic martyr and contrasted that martyrdom with the facile careerism of a colonialist:

> Ireland, in our day as in the past, has excommunicated some of those who have served her best, and has canonised some of those who have served her worst. . . . When a man like Synge, a man in whose sad heart there glowed a true love of Ireland, one of the two or three men who have in our time made Ireland considerable in the eyes of the world, uses strange symbols which we do not understand, we cry out that he has blasphemed and we proceed to crucify him. When a sleek lawyer, rising step by step through the most ignoble of all professions, attains to a Lord Chancellorship or an Attorney Generalship, we confer upon him the freedom of our cities. This is really a very terrible symptom in contemporary Ireland.

By 1913 Pearse had endowed Synge with the saintliness of his own putative sacrifice for the work of art called Ireland. This moment had been
adumbrated at the end of Synge's play: for not long after the scapegoat
Christy serves his function of uniting previously quarrelsome men so that
they can enjoy 'peace for our drinks', he is invested with the insignia of a
lost redeemer by the very woman who evicted him: 'O my grief, I've lost
him surely. I've lost the only Playboy of the Western World'. But the
play, on the night of the disturbances, was not heard properly to that
concluding line: so it may be useful to seek out other reasons for the
riots.

The stock explanation is that nationalists rejected a work which
appeared to satirise a drunken, amoral peasantry at a time when all patri-
otic dramatists of the National Theatre were expected to celebrate a
sturdy people ready for the responsibilities of self-government. It is also
said that pious Roman Catholics resented the insulting use of sacred
phrases in lines like 'With the help of God, I killed him surely, and may
the Holy Immaculate Mother intercede for his soul'. There is some validity in these arguments, but not much, given that other plays by Synge,
even more extreme in these respects, were presented without disorder.
The situation was, of course, rich in ironies, the most obvious being that
the protesters shouted 'We Irish are not a violent people' and then sprang
at the actors to prove their point – confirming Synge's conviction that
some were.

One says *some*, for little credence should be given to the cliché of the
fighting Irish, a notion strangely popular among Anglo-American peoples who send entire armadas and armies thousands of miles to defend
rocks in the south Atlantic or deserts in the Middle East. The Irish have
a reputation for violence (due perhaps to the overcrowded conditions in
which their emigrants lived in British and American cities) but also a
shrewd distaste for it. Though their island has been occupied, in whole or
in part, by a foreign power for over 800 years, they have never put a
disciplined nation-wide army of resistance into the field. In the same
period, the English have fought literally dozens of wars, and yet there are
still millions of English people able to convince themselves that the Irish
are bellicose. The major discrepancy in the attitudes to violence of both
peoples can be illustrated by the events which followed the Easter Rising:
for the story of 1916 is not so much the story of the insurrection as of the
executions. To the British authorities, the handful of rebel leaders were
mere traitors, not greatly different from the dozens of soldiers in the
trenches of Europe who deserted or defected every week. Their fate was
that of the traitor and, as such, would have merited scarcely a paragraph
on an inside page of a newspaper. However, the Irish people, passive and
peaceable by nature, had no stomach for these reprisals and so they were
appalled by the protracted orgy of official violence in Dublin. The key to
the rise of Sinn Féin in subsequent years lies not in an Irish addiction to
violence, so much as in a principled recoil from it. Sinn Féin prospered in

the elections of 1918 on the basis of its anti-conscription policy, which was later embodied in the principled neutrality of the independent Irish state. In so far as Sinn Féin became implicated in bloody deeds over the years, its reputation suffered significant reversals. Only the British could have come up with forces like the Black-and-Tans and B-Specials to copper-fasten support for Irish rebels. As George Bernard Shaw wearily observed 'the notion that Ireland is the only country in the world not worth shedding a drop of blood for is not a Protestant one, and certainly not countenanced by English practice'.

Though some Irish people have professed to admire 'mythic' violence, they have more often than not shied away as individuals from the thing itself: and Yeats was, in this respect, a representative instance. In early plays, he celebrated the redemptive violence of Cuchulain, the Irish hero who defended his people against attack and whose exploits made blood-letting seem glamorous. Patrick Pearse had adopted Cuchulain as the role-model for his pupils at the school, St. Enda's, along with the warrior's motto: 'I care not if I live but a day and a night, so long as my deeds live after me'. One former student would later write that 'at St. Enda's, Cuchulain was an important, if invisible, member of the staff'. What this meant in practice could be instructive: one young lad who won a poetry competition in the school was astonished, when he went up before the boys and their parents on prize-day, to be presented not with a Bible nor indeed a book of poems but a new rifle. Pearse was making explicit for the boys – many of whom would emulate Cuchulain's last sacrifice in the Post Office in 1916 – the intimate connection in the mind of the Irish nationalist élite between poetry and violence. And no sooner did the rebels make themselves martyrs to British firing-squads and to Yeatsian texts than the national poet began to have second thoughts about the 'terrible beauty' then born. The anxiety of 'Easter 1916' derives from Yeats' attempt to separate his admiration for the ancient hero from his clear distaste for the spectacle of his dead imitators in the contemporary city. Years later, in 'Ancestral Houses', Yeats would finally concede that he wanted the poetry but not the violence:

> O what if levelled lawns and gravelled ways
> Where slippered contemplation finds his ease
> And childhood a delight for every sense
> But take out greatness with our violence?

Yeats was too forthright to deny that those images of eternal civility, the Big Houses of the Anglo-Irish, were built by 'some violent, bitter man', and so must be taken as documents in the history of a barbarism suffered by the extirpated Irish, who hewed the wood and drew the water that made those images complete. Yet he could not help but feel, also, that the urge to destroy might also be a creative urge: the argument of his poem 'Meru' is that it takes equally intrepid souls to build a civilisation up and to break it down. So, to the end of his days, Yeats was quite capable of using the word 'violence' in honorific ways, for its evocation of youthful vitality in the face of an enervated middle class and for its therapeutic effect:

> Even the wisest man grows tense
> With some sort of violence,
> Before he can accomplish fate,
> Do his work, or choose his mate.

Violence to some past self, in his system, became the necessary precondition for the remaking of a new one: yet when that violence ceased to be rhetorical or psychic and became real, Yeats was filled with scruple.

Synge's extraordinary influence on the middle period of Yeats' poetry was attributable to his insistence that violence and poetry went hand in hand. There was, most strikingly, his declaration in the Preface to his own *Collected Poems*, which he submitted for editing and publication to Yeats, that 'before verse can become human again it must learn to be brutal'. That sentence voiced his revolt against the artificial poetic diction which had so emasculated English poetry in the later nineteenth century. He believed that 'the strong things of life are needed in poetry, also, to show that what is exalted or tender is not made by feeble blood'. The weakness of Swinburne and Rossetti lay in their cultivation of a tenderness that was cloying rather than tough, while the problem with realists like Ibsen and Zola could be found in their naturalist depiction of sordid urban conditions unmitigated by any sense of beauty. In the life and language of western Ireland, however, Synge found a world that managed to be both tough and tender. A visit to the Aran Islands liberated the frustrated artist in Synge, who thanked Yeats for sending him with the remark that 'style comes from the shock of new material' (Hemingway, another lyricist of violence, once said 'what amateurs call a style is usually only the unavoidable awkwardness of first trying to make something that has not before been made'.) Accepting the romantic symbol of the poem as a tender flower, Synge added that there was no flower which had not strong roots among the clay and worms. A major investigation is conducted in *The Playboy* of the relationship between the flower and the crude life at its roots, between style and shock, which is to say between poetry and violence. In a private letter to an admirer, written soon after the riots, Synge remarked that 'the wildness and vices of the Irish peasantry are due, like their extraordinary good points, to the *richness* of their nature, a thing that is priceless beyond words'. So if the violence and the poetry sprang from a common source, it would have been impossible to separate them without a diminution of both.

In the opening act of *The Playboy*, Synge describes a people who only rise to intensity of feeling when they are recounting deeds of violence. Folk who once sat spellbound at the stories about Cuchulain now regale one another with tales of a more tedious sadism: of Daneen

Sullivan who 'knocked the eye from a peeler' and 'the mad Mulrannies were driven from California and they lost in their wits'. Tales of the bodily flawlessness of Cuchulain have been replaced by notations of the deformities of Red Linahan 'has a squint in his eye' and 'Patcheen is lame in the heel': but the ancient impulse is still there, however diminished. When Christy arrives at the shebeen, 'slight, tired and frightened', he must seem to the audience a carbon-copy of Shawn Keogh (the actor who first played the part was only five feet three inches in height and was used to playing the fool in Abbey comedies); but the village girls yearn for a hero and so a hero he must be. Christy himself makes no claims: the villagers simply imagine the lineaments of a hero and proceed to read those qualities into him. They do not wish to hear immediately of Christy's terrible deed, preferring to speculate about it (larceny, robbery, indecent assault, shooting a landlord, shooting a bailiff, are all excitedly suggested). They spin out their fantasies to such lengths that an impatient Pegeen feels obliged to force a confession out of Christy by a straightforward denial of his deed: 'You're only saying it. You did nothing at all. A soft lad the like of you wouldn't slit the windpipe of a screeching sow'. This is a wonderfully sibilant alliteration to poeticise an essentially agricultural image.

Christy's terse confession spurs rather than dispels further speculation, this time about the weapon: did he use a gun or hilted knife, or did he hang his father by rope?

> ... the way Jimmy Farrell hanged his dog from the license and had it screeching and wriggling three hours at the butt of the string and himself swearing it was a dead dog and the peelers swearing it had life.

So obsessively are poetry and violence interwoven in the mental fabric of the Mayoites that the women seem incapable of describing poetry except in terms of violence, and unable to imagine violence except as a kind of poetry. To the comparatively reticent Christy of Act One Pegeen exclaims:

> If you weren't destroyed travelling, you'd have as much talk and streeleen, I'm thinking, as Owen Roe O'Sullivan or the poets of Dingle Bay.

– and she mentions the eighteenth-century Gaelic poet Eoghan Rua Ó Súilleabháin specifically, because his hot temper led to a tavern brawl and death from injuries received:

> ... I've heard all times it's the poets are your like, fine fiery fellows with great rages when their temper's roused.

Later still, Pegeen returns to the equation of poetry and violence when she tells Christy that he is a grand fellow 'with such poet's talking and such bravery of heart'. The two notions are likewise coupled in her rejection of Shawn Keogh as 'a middling kind of scarecrow with no savagery or fine words at all'.

At the end Christy has tamed his resurrected (and delighted) da with the twin boast that he is 'master of all fights' and will 'go romancing through a romping lifetime'. Like his creator, he still equates brutality and romance. It is left to Pegeen to dismantle the equation in the name of the Mayo villagers, if only because as accessories to another attempted murder, they might incur the wrath of the law – an English law, of course, in which they do not believe. They have professed to be exponents of rebellion, but are now terrified at the prospect of a visit from the police. There is no horror at the barbarity of Christy's second murder-attempt: rather, it is a case of peasant cunning overwhelming peasant respect for energy. Pegeen goes through her own Yeatsian struggle to disentangle images of savagery from high rhetorical words:

> I'll say a strange man's a marvel, with his mighty talk; but what's a squabble in your back yard, and the blow of a loy, have taught me that there's a great gap between a gallous story and a dirty deed.

These lines are Synge's exposure of the ambiguity in Irish attitudes to violence. Knowing that the 'fighting Irish' are only an Anglo-American fabrication, he taunts his people with a more radical diagnosis: that they can only endure the *idea* of violence when the deed is committed elsewhere or in the past, but are actually nauseated by the fact of carnage in their own backyard. If barbarism and culture are linked, then it is the poetry rather than the brutality which finally impresses them most. They will sing ballads of the Thompson gun or the armoured car, but in order to remain 'a grand story', these should be told about a place which exists only in fiction, or at least a hundred miles away on the far side of a patrolled border.

Over eight decades after the death of Synge, that ambiguity persists, as schoolchildren are taught by their history-books to revere the memory of Michael Collins, who had British civil servants assassinated in their beds before their wives and children, but to revile the current terrorists of the Irish Republican Army, who try to continue that policy. They are caught between the First World in which they think they live – a clean, well-ordered place – and the Third World narrative which long ago made that fragile security possible but which now threatens to interrupt it all over again. Young educated products of a system which offers few posts commensurate with their qualifications, many of them have predictably concluded that the Druid Company's version of *The Playboy* makes good sense: and so they read it, in the way in which they read Joyce's *Dubliners*, as a taunt to the effect that the besetting vice of the Irish may not have been pugnacity but paralysis. Pegeen's separation of gallous stories and dirty deeds is excessive: the 'great gap' which she proclaims between them is the death-knell for any society, where *IS* and *OUGHT* no longer usefully touch and interrogate one another. The space opened at the end by her between poetry and violence is, if anything, even more sinister than her earlier, absolutist identification of both. So, at the close, Mayo suffers the extreme colonial torpor described by Shaw: the facts seem more brutal than ever, the dreams even more unreal. Instead of closing with one another in a dancing dialectic, they move farther apart, leaving society unredeemed and apparently unredeemable. A revolution occurs, but it is happening offstage.

'Deeds are masculine, words feminine', says a proverb, as if to ratify Pegeen's separation: but *The Playboy* tells a more complex truth about how these categories interpenetrate one another. Its men commit most of the verbal violence onstage and are actually less aggressive in action, whereas the women, schooled to repress their instincts, are consumed by unappeased pugnacious impulses. There is violence in Pegeen, as in many persons, and it has not been assuaged by the gallous story: this becomes clear when she lights a sod of turf to cripple her former lover. This brutal act, pronounced beyond belief by many of the play's first critics, is entirely in keeping with her character as revealed from the start of the play. Emphasising this scene, the Druid production underscored Synge's brilliant insight: that those who made rhetorical denials of their own violence invariably end up committing even more. In that sense, at least, the rioters finished the play for Synge with a demonstration of its central point. In all likelihood, its members thrilled to the poeticised accounts of a distant violence in the opening acts, only to be nauseated by the deglamourised onstage repetition in the flesh: their revolt against the second murder may have arisen from a sudden onset of shame at how easily they had themselves accepted the first 'killing'. They may have been angered at the implication about their own self-deception, at a time when so many nationalists were nerving themselves for the coming battle with England. Like future Abbey producers, indeed like the Mayo villagers themselves, they repressed the violence in the text and subordinated it to the poetry, only to find the energies which they denied unleashed in the pit.

Small wonder, then, that the Druid production struck such a chord among the young in an Ireland still suffering the effects of post-colonial torpor. This was an Ireland racked by bombings and agonising over whether the appropriate response was to remove the pictures of Michael Collins from schoolroom walls and to demolish the statue of Cuchulain in the General Post Office. The fear was that, in losing these images, Ireland would lose a part of itself: for it, too, was trapped in the dilemma of Pegeen Mike, whose aggression turned out to be an inextricable part of her vitality. To reject the 'dirty deed' of Christy, she must also deny that element within herself, and yet, in following the dictates of polite society, something good has been lost.

Synge's sympathies may have become clearer at this point. Though formally a pacifist in the 1890s – when he resigned from Maud Gonne's

Irlande Libre because of its proposal to bomb English cities – he appears in the following decade to have changed. Exposure to the raw realities of peasant life in the congested districts may account for that. He saw Yeats and Lady Gregory glorify the violence of the Cuchulain tales, while they conveniently ignored the same brutality in the lives of the people who still told these stories.

Synge was more forthright in *The Aran Islands:*

> Although these people are kindly towards each other and to their children, they have no feeling for the suffering of animals, and little sympathy for pain when the person who feels it is not in danger. I have sometimes seen a girl writhing and howling with a toothache while her mother sat at the other side of the fireplace pointing at her and laughing at her as if amused by the sight.

He realised that along with the gentle beauty of western life ran a streak of high brutality to man and beast. His challenge was to transcend merely scandalised, conventional responses and to engage with that violence in all its authenticity at the level of the imagination. The widespread tolerance for petty violence to animals was a legacy of the Land Wars of the 1870s and 1880s, during which the maiming of a landlord's cattle or indeed the shooting of a landlord might be referred to with pride.

As his health deteriorated in his thirties, Synge may have been visited by a genuine envy of the man of violence, or, more precisely, of that man's *capacity* for violence, doubly fascinating to a sick person. Synge was amused to think that the great deeds of a Cuchulain were typically applauded by men too timid to think of emulating them. In the Irish Ireland movement of his time, there were basically two schools of writing: one devoted to the heroic legends of Cuchulain and other ancient heroes, the other to a vision of the western peasant as a secular saint and Gaelic mystic. By recreating *some* of the traits of the ancient hero in a puny peasant playboy, Synge offered his own caustic comment on the similarities and dissimilarities between the Irish past and present. His was a challenge to both schools, to concede, if they would, the savagery as well as the glamour at the heart of their cultural enterprise.

If Synge's art were simply an analysis of the *relation* between barbarism and culture in Ireland, it would merit our respect: but it gains an added depth by serving also as an *example* of that relation. All culture is parasitic: what lives, feeds off what died, and feeds without scruple. Synge's was in truth a carrion vision, but he was always critically aware of its costs: and this is what distingishes him ultimately from a writer like Lady Gregory. She once filled a notebook in a Galway workhouse with a rich collection of tales from the derelicts who lodged there, and, as she left, she remarked on the strange discrepancy between the poverty of the tellers and the splendour of their tales. She was beguiled and moved by the contrast, as are many people who note that the black man, in losing so many battles, was compensated by all the best songs: but she left her analysis in that unresolved state, too pleased with the paradox, perhaps, to explore it further.

Synge was quite different. In his writings, he worried constantly about the gap between a beautiful culture and the poverty that can underlie it. In *The Aran Islands*, for instance, he notes how every piece of furniture, every chair, every table, has a personality of its own, lovingly imparted to it by its maker, albeit at immense cost in terms of time, trouble, pain – so great a cost, indeed, that the maker often seems to have been robbed of his identity in the very making, as his self passed into his production. The critic Mary King has astutely observed that the islanders are depicted by Synge as persons obsessed with the price of everything. This is because they are people who can scarcely afford an individuality. In *Riders to the Sea*, a drowned man is identified not only by his bruised and broken body, which even his mother would be 'hard put' to recognise, but by a dropped stitch in his stocking, a mere object. The few traces of personality shown by his mother, her self-absorption in grief, are massive liabilities, almost criminal acts of self-indulgence, within the subsistence economy of the islands. Her final speeches of compassion, spoken as 'an old woman' on behalf of all mothers left living in the world, represent a triumph over that selfishness, a return to folkloristic impersonality. Synge records all this with a terrified and terrifying accuracy, because he knows that, however spare and beautiful such a culture may seem to the outsider, its costs in human terms are just too high. Like Joyce's Stephen Daedalus, he senses that a few scattered phrases of Elizabethan English, or a few quaintly-turned versions of Irish idiom, are hardly a sufficient compensation for the loss of the Irish language.

So he checks his own tendency to be charmed by the well-wrought stool or the beautifully-hewn table. Turning his back on William Morris and the folk radicalism of his youth, he reminds himself of a harder socialist school, and honestly concedes that all these beautiful effects are bound up with a social condition near to penury. He knows that that condition cannot last and so it has, therefore, the added charm of an exquisite, dying thing: and he does not finally oppose the change. He is sufficiently self-aware to admit that his very presence on the islands is a portent of that change. Though beguiled by much of the backwardness, he is an agent of that change, bringing the first alarm-clock to the islands (with the attendant notion of clock-time, efficiency and measurement) as well as his camera (itself creating a new narcissism among the islanders, which he observed with some disgust, since the camera was a curiosity employed by him to win the confidence and respect of the people). Seeing his photographs of them, the islanders tell Synge that they are seeing themselves for the first time.

Synge knows that he is only an interloper on Aran, a tourist, one of the first, and, perhaps one day, one of the most famous among many: and that the more successful is his book called *The Aran Islands*, the more extreme will be the consequent disruptions of tradition by the day-trippers who will come in his wake. Indeed he has – though he never quite says this – a vested interest in those disruptions, because after they have had their effect, his book will be even more evocative than ever. He himself will feed off the death of the old Gaelic culture, as do all coroners and morticians. The covert desire of his book, to *make the present past*, is something that Synge shares with all his major creations, whether Maurya looking forward to the relative serenity of the long nights after Samhain, or Deirdre imagining how the story of her current exploits will be told forever. *That* is the only actual control which these women achieve over their lives. Otherwise, Deirdre is at the mercy of events, and Old Maurya is unable to bless a departing son because 'something choked the words in my mouth'. Both are doomed to repeat lines already known by heart, so that the striking beauty of their language is in direct contrast with its ineffectuality. The so-called exoticism of Synge's language is related to the remoteness of his characters from the 'big world' with its standardised versions of English. The greater that displacement, the more untamed the life and the more colourful its deviations from the linguistic norm. But the dislocation which makes these people colourful is also that which leaves them powerless.

The mortal charm of Synge's dialect is the beauty that inheres in all precarious or dying things. It is traceable to the Gaelic *substratum*, those elements of syntax and imagery carried over from the native tradition by a people who continue to think in Irish even as they speak in English. George Moore's joke – that Synge discovered that if you translated Irish word-for-word into English, the result was poetry – turns out to be a true enough account. Even the 'jawbreakers' – words like 'bedizened' or 'potentate' – are in the tradition of hedge-schoolmasters nervously advertising their new mastery of English polysyllabic effects to impress the parents of their putative pupils, in the absence of a more formal diploma. The tradition was at least as old as Goldsmith's village schoolmaster:

> While words of learned length and rumbling sound
> Amazed the gazing rustics ranged around;
> And still they gazed and still their wonder grew,
> That one small head could carry all he knew.

The potency of Synge's idiom derived in great part from the reported death of Irish; and the deader (or, at least, the more doomed) that language, the more vital the semantic energies that passed into Hiberno-English and the more magnificent that language seemed.

Hiberno-English, like Christy Mahon, owes its force to the apparent murder of its parent: and *The Playboy of the Western World* may thus be read as a critical reflection upon its own linguistic parasitism. The bleak joke, of course, is that standard English was itself rather jaded by cliché-mongers when Synge began to write. In Deleuzian terms, Synge saw that a deterritorialised Irish might yet deterritorialise that English, leading to a bilingual weave more vital than either of the standard languages between which it stood. Yeats's crusades for a formal recognition of that dialect have been already discussed: against a 'school-master's ideal of correctness', which led to such clichés as 'flagrant violations' and 'shining examples', he pitted the dialect of country people, which was 'an imitation of nothing English'. The accusation against Synge's peasants came, he said, from those whose minds were full of sentimental Kickhamesque novels written to an English literary formula.

This demand for an official recognition of Hiberno-English went unan-swered. Nationalist leaders could celebrate standard Irish as a counter-vailing discourse to standard English, but they could not entertain the suggestion that the people, in their rapid shift from Irish to English in the nineteenth century, had themselves created a new language, which Synge was magnifying in its carrier Christy. Most nationalist commentators pre-ferred to treat Synge as an unapologetic ascendancy parasite, stocking up his tourist's notebook with self-serving studies in a dying culture. D. P. Moran dubbed the dialect a 'hopeless half-way house', neither good Irish nor good English, but a sort of bastard lingo which grew in the no-man's land between two authentic cultures. More recently, Seamus Deane has added an Adornian inflection to that analysis, describing Synge as one who creamed off the Gaelic culture in the few remaining areas where his class had failed to exterminate it, but where he could not appropriate its energies on the eve of their distinction.

Such an analysis ignores Synge's critical awareness of the points which might be made against his own cultural project; and it slights the skill with which he infuses that awareness into his writings in the ways just described. Far from being a secret snob, Synge was a radical who grew up in a colonised society, impressed by its cultural richness but even more horrified by its costs. The contention that the rioters against *The Playboy* were outraged by his ascendancy attitudes to peasant religion or rural psychology is a *retrospective* fabrication by nationalists who pretended that their objection was to snobbism. In 1907, it was the radical ideology in the play, as well as the accompanying violence, which upset the nation-alists including the pre-revolutionary Pearse. Seamus Deane's critique of Synge, though not penned as such, is probably the most eloquent defence yet written of the *Playboy* rioters; and the strength of its arguments should remind us that those who disrupted the performance were no ran-dom collection of hotheads, but some of the most sensitive and intelligent thinkers of the time, risking arrest and imprisonment for the stand which they took. Nevertheless, Deane's reading of the play is mistaken, because it is based on revivalist productions and on a scholarly tradition which claimed Synge as one of Anglo-Ireland's crowning glories. (The major exponent of this interpretative tradition was T. R. Henn, who liked to portray Synge as a martyr to the Irish mob, perhaps because this assuaged his own guilt about ascendancy mistreatment of the natives).

Synge was, by his own say-so, a radical, whom he defined as 'someone who wanted to change things root and branch'. He was a student of such texts as Marx's *Das Kapital* and *Communist Manifesto*, the works of William Morris, *L'Anarchie, Problems of Poverty, Principes du Socialisme* and *Basic Socialism*. He went to Paris in 1896 with the intention of immersing himself in the socialist movement: 'he wants to do good', lamented his mother, 'and for that possibility he is giving up everything'. This was no passing youthful fancy: for in the last days of his life, at the Elpis Nursing Home in Dublin, he repeatedly sought to engage the nurses on the topic of feminism. The protestors may have known exactly what they were doing. They were middle-class nationalists who did not want a revolution: and so, with exquisite logic according to their own lights, they stopped his play as it moved into its liberationist third act. This process must now be explained.

When Christy leads his father out towards the end of that act, 'like a gallant captain with his heathen slave', the pair constitute the image of a revolutionary community, while the villagers lapse into revivalism. In such a world-turned-upside-down, the old take their cue from the young (rather than the other way round). As Frantz Fanon reported from the Algeria of *A Dying Colonialism* in the 1950s, the native father counselled obedience, but the son, in rejecting obedience, did not reject the father: 'What he would try to do on the contrary would be to convert the family. The militant would replace the son and undertake to indoctrinate the father'. So the stage directions emphasise Old Mahon's delight at this new assertiveness in his offspring. 'At no time do we find a really painful clash', adds Fanon: 'The father stood back before the new world and followed in his son's footsteps'.

Such a moment also leads to a masculinisation of women and a corresponding feminisation of men. In Algeria, Fanon noted how women declared their independence of fathers and husbands, often appearing more manly than their partners. As families disintegrated into their separate elements under the new stress, the meaning of a national revival emerged: 'each member of the family has gained in individuality what it had lost in belonging to a world of more or less confused values'. These reversals constitute that political and sexual unconscious, systematically explored in the Irish writings of Wilde and Shaw, Joyce and Yeats: but it was Synge, more than any other, who dramatised that moment when 'the person is born, assumes his autonomy, and becomes the creator of his own values'. He seems to have believed that such reversals had always been possible to artists: for example, in suggesting to Molly Allgood that they write a play together, he proposed that he write the female parts and she the male. A revolution, however, would open such possibilities to all, on the anarchist principle that every man and woman could be an artist.

In *The Playboy* the women take the initiative in wooing; they enjoy the experience of trying on the hero's mud-spattered boots; and, generally, they disport themselves with a sort of locker-room bravado. The foremost among them, Pegeen, 'would knock the heads of any two men in this place': while the men of the village do seem to score more modestly on an available virility-test. The women complain that the Widow Quin's 'sneaky' murder of her husband won 'small glory with the boys itself', as if the boys are a lot more easily cowed than the girls. Moreover, the sexual chemistry of the play vindicates Freud's contention that manly women are attracted, and attractive, to womanly men. The phrase 'female woman' is used by Old Mahon as if to indicate a pained, sexist awareness that there is another kind: the kind attracted by his son. It was the female women who, of course, made of Christy a 'laughing joke', but what mesmerises *all* of the women is his femininity. Pegeen praises his small aristocratic feet (as if he is a fetishised sex-object of her starved imagination); the village women enjoy his nuances of delicate phrasing ('It's a grand story . . . He tells it lovely'); and the Widow Quin has fantasies of putting him into a woman's dress by way of securing his liberation from persecution.

Perhaps the most telling moment is that when the village women burst in upon the risen Christy of Act Two, only to find him preening himself in a mirror: 'Didn't I know rightly I was handsome, though it was the devil's own mirror we had beyond, that would twist a squint across an angel's brow?' It was the cracked looking-class of a servant, in fact: but now he knows the heady delights of a Caliban seeing his own face in a flawless mirror. The ensuing scene is Synge's mischievous repudiation of that sexist tradition, which encouraged male artists to paint nude females, into whose hands they put mirrors. Such paintings, though composed by some men for the delectation of others, purported to be high-minded commentaries on female narcissism: and, accordingly, the woman was rendered holding the mirror up to her face, or her breast, and the painting duly entitled 'Vanity'. In a boldly feminist reversal, Synge has an embarrassed Christy unwittingly mock the stereotype by hiding the mirror behind his back and holding it up against his bottom, to the vast amusement of village women who comment: 'Them that kills their fathers is a vain lot surely'.

There was ample sanction for such reversals in the utopian plays of Wilde and Shaw, but Synge added a Gaelic resonance entirely absent from their writings, and based on his knowledge of poetry in the Irish language from the seventeenth and eighteenth centuries. There, in works like *Cúirt an Mheáin Oíche* (The Midnight Court) by Brian Merriman, the writers had denounced the new anglicisation of sexuality in rural Ireland. Merriman was especially scandalised by the high-heeled shoes, the artificial cosmetics (*Púdar*) and the clothing (*húda*) which characterised the new fashions, and his use of the accompanying anglicised slang-words in the poem signalised his deep contempt. Though revivalist critics preferred to read all this as a nationalist critique of English culture by a defender of Gaelic values, there is much more than that at stake. What is under attack in such texts is the reification of the female body to the point where it becomes a fetish of the male, puritan imagination, the real curse of Cromwell. Merriman's poem contains many other elements which would have been congenial to Synge: it is based on the idea of a court of love ruled by women; these complain of enforced marriages to spent old dotards, very much as Nora Burke complains in *The Shadow of the Glen;* they are frank rather than genteel in asserting their sexual urges, and the male poet is mocked, as Synge was on Aran, for being over 30 years of age and still unmarried.

An even more explicit critique of the anglicisation of sexuality in eighteenth-century rural Ireland may be found in 'Bodaigh na hEorna' (The Churls of the Barley) by Art Mac Cubhthaigh. Here the poet denounces the vulgar fashions worn by the females of a south Ulster Family, which has circumvented the Penal Laws against Roman Catholics by making a small fortune from distilling:

> Níl aon chailleach bhuí, chrón a lásaibh ag stró
>   Dá gcruinneoidh dornán saibhris,
> Nach mbeadh síoda agus sról agus sciorta ar a tóin,
>   Agus putóg nó dhó ina héadan.
>
> Is tócuil an tseoid níon bhodaigh sa ród
>   Is cha ghlacann sí cóiriú Gaelach,
> Mur mbeadn hata uirthi ar dóigh, is crios air den ór,
>   Is cleite ag treabhadh na gaoithe.

> There is no tan-yellow hag struggling in her laces
>   Who, if she gathers a fistful of money,
> Doesn't start wearing silk and satin and a skirt on her bottom,
>   And a ringlet or two down her forehead.
>
> The daughter of a churl is a proud jewel on the road
>   And she does not wear Gaelic fashions,
> But a hat in new style, with a golden braid,
>   And a feather ploughing the wind.

Mac Cubhtaigh's viciousness only emerges fully in the following stanza:

> Na sneadha 'na ndornaibh casta 'na coip
>   A putóg 's í ag dortadh dréise,
> Is amach óna srón teacht theas na Féil Eoin
>   Go bhfaicfí an míol mór 's é ag aoibheall.

> The nits come out in twisted fistfuls in her company,
>   As her ringlets pour out grease,
> And out from her nose on the feast of St. John
>   The great monster snot comes gadding.

Prose texts from the same period such as *Parlaimint na mBan* (The Parliament of Women, 1703) were even more elaborate in their critiques of a male chauvinism which had relegated women from public life to the domestic periphery. One year after Daniel Defoe's *Good Advice to the Ladies* (1702) the male author of the *Parlaimint*, Dónal Ó Colmáin, complained that the female sex had lost much of its power through lack of education and through the accompanying fetishisation of the woman's body. Doubtless, in Gaelic Ireland as elsewhere, there were those for whom imbecility in females represented a great enhancement of their charms, but Ó Colmáin captured the authentic anger of those who would not brook such marginalisation:

> Do chítear daoibh go léir go mbíd a gcomhairlí agus a gcomh-thionóil ag na fearaibh go laethúil ag déanamh a ngnótha agus ag tabhairt aire do gach ní bhaineas riu féin, i gcás, an uair bhíd siad ag trácht orainne, gurb amhlaidh bhímid mar chaitheamh aimsire, mar chomparáid, nó mar stoc magaidh aca de ló agus d'oíche. Agus fós, ní admhaíd siad gur daoine sinn ar aon chor ar bith, ach gur créatúirí sinn do cruthaíodh in aghaidh nádúir, agus nach bhfuil ionainn ach *malum necessarium*, 'drochní is riachtanas do bheith ann'.

> It is evident to you all that the menfolk had their meetings and conferences on a daily basis, doing their business and taking care of all that pertained to themselves – so that, whenever they mentioned us, we were simply a pastime, a comparison, or a source of mockery to them by day and night. And even still, they will not admit that we are human at all, save only that we are creatures created against the forces of nature, and that we are nothing but a *malum necessarium*, a bad thing which is necessary.

Of course, as a male writer Ó Colmáin was speaking on women's behalf, just as a male poet Merriman voiced the female protest against false gentility in the *Cúirt:* two facts which, in themselves, indicate just how far Gaelic women had fallen from earlier times. For it was well known that the ancient Irish laws were remarkably liberal in their attitude to women. A woman could divorce a sterile, impotent, or homosexual husband, could marry a priest, could give honourable birth to a child outside of wedlock. Merriman's poem was not the foreign-inspired debauch complained of by some puritans of the national revival, but a dynamic plea for a return to more radical traditions: according to one historian, however, 'the natural development of these liberal customs was cut off by the imposition of English law on Ireland in the seventeenth century'.

Synge was well aware of the loss of these liberal traditions, but he delighted in pointing to those areas, such as the Aran Islands, still largely unaffected by the changes. The women of Inishmaan were, he noted, 'before conventionality' in their frank, easy manners, which left them untainted by the false Victorian gentility of the women in Dublin, Cork or Galway. Instead, they 'share some of the liberal features that are thought peculiar to the women of Paris and New York'. The latter, he added in a footnote, 'have freed themselves by a desperate personal effort from the moral bondage of lady-like persons'. He was doubtless recalling the New Woman whom he had known on the Left Bank of Paris in the 1890s, women who earned their own livings as dancers, writers, artists. At a time when the wild, passionate and masterful women of the ancient Celts were being rediscovered by scholars, Synge put the debate about rural womanhood back on the agenda in the persons of Nora Burke and Pegeen Mike. After all, *The Playboy* starts and ends with Pegeen's plight as a trapped rural woman in a landscape virtually bereft of enterprising men, most of whom have been lost to English jails or to the emigration ship. The girls are all agreed that theirs is a dull life, 'going up summer and winter (to the priest) with nothing worthwhile to confess at all'. Mayo is a community of timid apple-lickers, people who if tempted in the Garden of Eden, would have licked rather than bitten the apple.

Into this mediocre zone comes Christy, to all intents a landless, propertyless Shawn Keogh, but to all purposes a pure invention of Pegeen Mike. He starts out as and strictly is a nonentity, until he discovers in himself an unexpected gift for mimicry. Noticing the propensity of the Mayo villagers to narrate deeds with reference to the points of the compass, he retells his own deed in these derived terms: 'he gave a drive with the scythe, and I gave a leap to the east. Then I turned my back to the north, and I hit a blow on the ridge of his skull, laid him stretched out to the knob of his gullet'. In Act One, it is Pegeen and the villagers who speak poetically, telling Christy who he is: and in Act Two, he is saluted as a poet merely for returning to the community, lovingly distorted, a magnified version of its own language.

It is one thing to parody the speech-patterns of interlocutors: it is quite another to appropriate the images, ideas and intensities of an entire literary tradition, as Christy does in wooing Pegeen. The dozens of borrowed lines deployed from *Love Songs of Connacht* may testify to Synge's versatility as a new kind of writer, but, within the play itself they also expose Christy's initial hollowness as a person, especially when declaring his love in phrases looted blatantly from the songs of the folk. Most of these borrowings occur in Act Two and the earlier part of Act Three, when Christy's desire has abandoned the language of reality for a fictitious and flowery dialect. Not everyone, of course, would find such behaviour contemptible: there is a sense in which Christy becomes a kind of nationalist hero in these moments by creating a tradition for himself out of nothing but folk culture, thereby restoring to people an image of themselves. This was, as has been shown, one of Yeats' highest aspirations, never fulfilled in his own person, but envied in the achievement of Hyde.

For Synge's own purposes, Christy *has* to be an empty man at the outset, so that he will carry no baggage from his degrading past into the revolutionary future. He rejects a false image of self (in the broken mirror) and chooses instead *to be*, creating instant, improvised traditions of himself out of the shreds of popular culture. Denied identity and freedom by his father's misrule, he is the living evidence of the nullity to which oppression may reduce a person or a community. Yet that very nullity is also the source of his charm, for it offers the Mayo villagers an empty space into which they can read their fondest dreams, but at a safe distance. In the first two acts, Christy is the locus of village desire, carrying himself like a revivalist leader on a resistible rise to absolute power. That power is, of course, bogus, since it is a function of the community's mediocrity and since it prevents either the leader or the members of that community from constructing themselves from within. But it is the gift of all desperately oppressed peoples: witness the Irish search for a messianic hero through the nineteenth century, from O'Connell to Parnell a catalogue of revivalist icons made and then broken. As saviour and scapegoat; as poet and tramp, Christy is their logical embodiment at the level of artistic imagination. For, after the famines and emigrations of the 1840s, 'Ireland' had almost ceased to exist in the old Gaelic way: what was left – the remaining voices confirmed this – was a terrifyingly open space, in places and in persons.

It is this very emptiness in his personality and in his contexts which has allowed generations of critics to read so many different meanings into the character of Christy, whether Parnell, Cuchulain, Christ, Oedipus or artist. In doing this, critics simply repeated the actions of the Mayo villagers, using Christy as a mirror in which to read and explore themselves. Indeed, the recorded responses to the play are, undeniably, extensions and imitations of its innermost theme. The villagers onstage discover that the radically transformed society which they had 'read into' Christy is not what they wanted at all: and so they go back to their farce of revivalism, of fireside tales told about past heroes. Similarly, Synge's audience decided that they could not brook such innovation and versatility in a text, and so they attacked it on those very points of its strength, Synge's knowledge of Gaelic Ireland. Excessive rhetorical claims had been made for Synge by Yeats and others (he was 'the chap who writes likes Sophocles, Shakespeare, etc.'), which helps to explain some of the vehemence of the reaction against his work. This recapitulates the progress of Christy who makes no stylised claims for himself – other than the parricide, which he genuinely believed himself to have committed. The case for his own heroism is not made by him, but for him.

Chief among the claimants is Pegeen, whose invention Christy really is, her *animus* returned after centuries of anglicisation to the level of female consciousness. Her lament in the play's final lines is less for the physical man just gone offstage than for lost possibilities of her own womanhood. Christy has liberated an unsuspected femininity in her ('to think it's me talking sweetly, and I the fright of seven townlands for my biting tongue') mainly because he was so at ease with the female qualities in himself: and the woman in him took an undisguised pleasure in the man in her. Pegeen, being more of a traditionalist, could not fully reciprocate in this androgynous fashion. Though prizing his femininity, she oppressed her man by compelling him to live up to an extreme of hypermasculinity. He did this to an extent by winning all before him at the sports, thereby establishing that men who consciously recognise their *anima* are less effeminate than the Shawn Keoghs who are unconsciously enthralled by the repressed female element: but this was not sufficient for Pegeen. Like Lady Macbeth, she wanted her partner to exemplify a manliness which she could not fully confront or contain, so much was there of it in herself. Doubtless the woman in him, having established her right to exist, connived in all this by demanding the usual proofs that, despite the contra-sexual admission, the partner is still reassuringly male.

Christy, revealed as having *not* killed his father, fails her test. It is a mark of her conventionality that such a test, at this late stage, should still seem necessary. No sooner does he attempt another killing on the spot than she denies the very violence she had courted. When she drives him out at the end, it is as if her *animus* has been repressed back into the unconscious and demonised accordingly. The revolution occurs, but off-stage and in the black-out. She, for her part, surrenders to gentility, kills off her *animus*, and opts to become a 'proper' country girl of the kind lampooned by the Gaelic poets. As such, she will be a fitting mate for the 'puny weed' Shawn Keogh. He restores the old patriarchy in the village by *telling* Pegeen to burn Christy's leg: and she submits, doing something which, in all probability, Shawn would be afraid to do himself. This is no contradiction, however, since the weakness of the ineffectual male has traditionally masked itself behind a pose of patriarchy, issuing orders and striking postures but achieving little for itself. Repressing a female dimension which it would require courage to confront, such men are enslaved to the *anima* and enfeebled accordingly. Repressing a male dimension which she briefly flirted with, Pegeen becomes once again enslaved to her *animus*, which explains her reversion to the harsh, sharp-tongued exterior which she presented in the shebeen before the onset of Christy. Compared with Shawn's dithering, this may give her actions the appearance of decision and despatch, but in any comparison with Christy she emerges as a coward who could not live up to the image of freedom for which they both had reached. She lets Christy go at the end, not really because he is weak, but because he has grown too strong for her. From now on, her *animus* denied, she will continue to obey Shawn Keogh.

The radical implications of the manly woman of Gaelic tradition were deflected by the Mayo villagers, even as the sensuous images drawn from the love-songs of Connacht were denounced as titillating by some puritans of the Gaelic League. It was ironic to recall, in this context, that the League's own president had edited the book from which Synge looted some of the most disturbing lines. Synge shrewdly remarked, however, that a writer could get away with things in Irish which would not be tolerated in English: a point depressingly confirmed in the 1940s when the independent state banned an English-language version of *The Midnight*

Court, though the far more ribald version remained available. Revivalism was proving rigidly selective of that which was worthy to be revived and translated into popular versions. Sexuality, it seemed, was not to be de-anglicised. The conclusion of Synge's play proved bitterly prophetic of the sexual politics of the new state, which would deny the manly woman epitomised by Constance Markievicz and Maud Gonne, opting instead for de Valera's maidens at the rural crossroads, themselves a pastoral figment of the late-Victorian imagination. And thus a people who, in the nineteenth century, had thought in Irish while speaking English, came in the twentieth to 'think English' even while they were speaking Irish.

The spark that lit the *Playboy* riots is well-known, memorialised in the famous telegram sent by Lady Gregory to Yeats in Scotland: 'Come home at once. Audience broke up in disorder at use of the word "shift"'. These controversial lines represented a modest, if mocking reworking by Synge of a scene in the national epic. In the play, Christy tells the Widow Quin 'it's Pegeen I'm seeking only, and what would I care if you brought me a drift of chosen females standing in their shifts itself maybe, from this place to the eastern world'. In Lady Gregory's *Cuchulain of Muirthemne* the hero regularly returns from combat filled with a *battle-rage*, which leads the men of Ulster to forbid his entry to the city of Emhain Macha. They fear that his perturbation might destroy peace and damage city buildings, and so they conduct earnest discussions of the ways in which his ardour might be cooled. This is finally achieved by sending 30 women, stark naked, across the plain of Macha in serried ranks: and when the hero sees them, he blushes to his roots, casts down his eyes, and with that (say the manuscripts) 'his *battle-rage* left him'. In his original version, Synge had a 'drift of naked females' but was clearly advised by Yeats that the more puritanical members of the Abbey audience could not tolerate such candour. (With commendable innocence, Yeats appears not to have realised what Hugh Hefner would later so profitably prove: that a scantily-clad woman can be even more inflammatory than a naked woman to the puritan male mind). The word 'shift' had been used without offence in Hyde's *Love Songs of Connacht* (in Irish, of course, as *léine*): but when Synge politely pointed this out in a newspaper interview, the point was left unexplored in the ensuing controversy.

It is hard, at the same time, not to feel some sympathy for the riotous audiences in the play's first week. Most were nationalist males who frequented the theatre for political reasons, since the Abbey was the one national institution of occupied Ireland. Few men anywhere in the Europe of 1907 could have coped with Synge's subversive gender-benders, least of all a group committed to the social construction of precisely the kind of Cuchulanoid heroism which the playwright was so mischievously debunking. Irishmen had been told that when they protested their voices rose to an unflattering female screech: and so they were offloading the vestigial femininity of the Celtic male onto icons like Cathleen ní Houlihan or Mother Ireland. These were the men who accused Synge of 'betraying the forces of virile nationalism' to a movement of decadence. They were hardening themselves into hypermasculinity, in preparation for an uprising, rather than adopting the more complex strategy of cele-brating their own androgyny. That Synge preferred the latter option is clear from the tripartite structure of his play, which corresponds very neatly with Fanon's dialectic of decolonisation, from occupation, through nationalism, to liberation.

In Act One, Christy finds a false image of himself in the cracked mir-ror of his father's cruel home, the very image of Irish self-disgust under colonial misrule. In Act Two, he then discovers an over-flattering image of himself in the perfect mirror of Pegeen's shebeen, the very acme of Irish pride under the conditions of a self-glorifying revival. But national-ism, as Fanon warned, is not liberation, since it still persists in defining itself in categories imposed by the coloniser. A revolution couched in such terms is taken away from a people even as they perform it: it is only by breaking out of the binaries, through to a third point of transcendence, that freedom can be won. Only in Act Three can Christy forget about the good opinion of others, throw that mirror away and construct himself out of his own desire (as opposed to allowing himself become the locus for the desire of others). Only then does he lose the marks of a provincial who is doomed to define himself through the distorting mirror of a pub-lic opinion shaped in some faraway centre of authority.

The Mayoites, on the other hand, never achieve a rudimentary self-awareness, but abjectly defer to a set of laws which they privately despise. Like hopeless provincials, they have no sense of their own presence. Christy's by-play with the mirror in the second act may be narcissistic, but it does serve to *frame* his face, raising it from a commonplace thing to the realms of self-reflexive art. The very *representation* of that face bestows on it an interest it would otherwise have lacked, the growth of consciousness in various characters being indicated in the repeated phrase of recognition 'Is it me?' This is what Jacques Lacan has called 'the transformation which takes place in the subject when he assumes an image' . . . like those Aran islanders who, contemplating Synge's photographs saw themselves as if for the first time. (Likewise, in *The Well of the Saints*, Martin and Mary Doul set everyone talking about 'the way they looked in the face', recalling the pleasures and perils of living at the intensity of the artist). The perfect mir-ror in *The Playboy* points forward to that moment when Christy will form a conception of himself, rather than existing as a conception of others. This is the first act in any revolutionary agenda, a moment reminiscent of that recounted by Carlos Fuentes, when an insurgent Mexican peasantry breaks into the great houses of landowners to be stunned at the sight of their entire bodies in the vast mirrors.

Until this point, Christy has been repeatedly described as one who is afraid of his own shadow, that shadow which is emblematic of his hidden potential, the dark, repressed aspects of himself: but he proceeds from that fear to active self-reflection in the mirror in the second act. This is, as yet, a somewhat superficial activity, an adolescent contemplation of ego rather than of self, but it nonetheless provides the means from which the self may finally be inferred. It is the psychological version, within the individual, of that rather revivalist form of nationalism which is self-conscious but not self-aware. Knowledge of the self rather than mere ego would be the personal version of liberation: and even as nationalism is a phase which a community must pass through *en route* to liberation, so the ego is an essential precondition for the revelation of self. If whole peoples can mistake nationalism for liberation, so there are egos which demand to be identified totally with the self, such as the inflated ego of Christy in Act Two. Equally, there are others which identify solely with the shadow side, persistently asserting their unworthiness, the self-loathing Christy of Act One. Integration can finally be achieved only by those who admit both positive and negative sides as authentic elements.

Those, like Christy, who start with the shadow-side, are more likely to reach this terminus than those who blissfully bask, without reflection, in the ego-image of the perfect mirror. Worshippers of ego, lacking the critical capacity, become prisoners of their own impulses, whereas those who reflect on ego attain objective insights into their dark side and that of others. They learn, as Christy does, that the shadow of which they are initially afraid, is the mirror of an opposite within; the Yeatsian *antiself;* a set of elements all the more powerful for having been repressed. The ego is the mirror of the superficial person. Christy as a mirror-self in the first half of the play was like all mirrors lacking any image of *himself*, with the consequence that when an image showed in his mirror, it was the image of another's desire. By degrees, however, he moves from that passive state to one of active self-reflection, and so his behaviour is progressively less impulse-ridden and more deliberated: by the end, indeed, he can proclaim himself master of those forces which have been mastering him.

In Act One, Christy speaks prose; a prose which befits the frightened boy he is. In the next act, he perfects a factitious lingo, too flowery and exotic to be true: 'It's her like is fitted to be handling merchandise in the heavens above'. This is derided as 'poetry talk' by the Widow Quin, who sees in it a falsely idealised account of 'a girl you'd see itching and scratching and she with a stale stink of poteen on her from selling in the shop'. Such poetry talk is the interesting equivalent of the black-is-beautiful poetry of Negritude, cultivated among the writers of Martinique in the 1940s. Fanon and Cesaire were later to conclude that such exotic nativism was no final solution: and, in like manner, at the close of Act Three, Christy repudiates his former lyricism for an altogether more terse and telling language. He turns to the woman who had so recently loved him, but who now lights the sod to burn his leg, and on this occasion he offers no flowery speeches: 'That's your kind, is it?' After Yeatsian eloquence; Yeatsian terseness. After revivalist baroque; Joyce's style of scrupulous meanness, his dignified assertion of a people's right to be colourless. After nationalism; liberation.

Synge is arguably the most gifted Irish exponent of the three phases of artistic decolonisation described by Fanon. He effortlessly assimilated the culture of the occupying English and then proceeded to immerse himself in the native culture. Fanon's warning about the pitfalls of national consciousness is worth repeating at this point:

> The native intellectual who comes back to his people by way of cultural achievements behaves in fact like a foreigner. Sometimes, he has no hesitation is using a dialect in order to show his will to be as near as possible to the people. . . . The culture that the intellectual leans towards is often no more than a stock of particularisms. He wishes to attach himself to the people; but instead he only catches hold of their outer garments.

This, or something very like it, has long been the nationalist description of Synge, to be found most recently in the account by Seamus Deane: but it is, of course, a description of the Christy of the second act. Unlike that Christy, however, Synge does catch hold of a great deal more than the outer garments of a folk culture: and he never behaves like a foreigner. In the history of Irish writing, he was exoticism's first and foremost critic, exposing the ways in which a torrent of talk may be poor compensation for a failure to act. Denounced as a stage-Irish exaggeration, *The Playboy* actually offers a sharp critique of the verbal exaggeration associated with the stereotype. The play's counterposing of fine words and failed action makes it a caustic study of the fatal Irish gift of the gab. It was a measure of Synge's own artistic maturity that he could satirise his own great gift even as he exploited it most fully. In *The Playboy* his art reached such a pitch of sophistication that it could even raise doubts about the medium through which those doubts were expressed.

The only stage-Irish scenes enacted on the night of the riots were performed by the protestors in the pit. Synge himself claimed in an essay that the Abbey Theatre had 'contrived by its care and taste to put an end to the reaction against the careless Irish humour of which everyone has had too much'. That sentence broke out of the Anglo-Irish antithesis by shrewdly implying a criticism of both the colonialist stereotype and the nationalist reaction to it. In his own art, Synge wonderfully fused what was best in English and Gaelic tradition, often doing this within a single work, as in the short satire against the women who hated *The Playboy*:

Lord, confound this surly sister,
Blight her brow with blotch and blister;
Cramp her larynx, lung and liver,
In her guts a galling give her.
Let her live to earn her dinners
In a jail with seedy sinners.
Lord, this judgement quickly bring,
And I'm your servant, J. M. Synge.

The poem is in octosyllabic couplets, which Swift said were most suited to pungent, alliterative satire: but the notion of raising blisters on the brow of one who has spurned the writer's art is taken from Gaelic bards, who resorted to alliteration in such performances. So blended, the two traditions amount to something more than the sum of their parts, constituting – like the bilingual weave of Hiberno-English – a third term. Synge's *Playboy*, a product of similar blending, was a sort of blueprint for a new species of Irish artist. In his hands, the meaning of Gaelic tradition changed from something museumised to something modifiable; endlessly open. He sensed that the revivalists' worship of the past was based on their questionable desire to colonise and control it: but his deepest desire was to demonstrate the continuing power of the radical Gaelic past to disrupt the revivalist present. In the play, after all, Christy not only fails to kill his father but decides in the end that he doesn't even want to: it is enough to know that the old man is now happily tractable to his son's future designs. This play is the Fanonite 'seething pot', into which Synge cast the shards of threatened Irish traditions, out of which the learning of the future might emerge.

9. IRELAND'S ISLANDS IN THE CARIBBEAN: POETRY FROM MONTSERRAT AND ST. CAESARE

E. A. Markham

I've spent three years in the North of Ireland, as writer-in-residence at the University of Ulster, and enjoyed it immensely. About ten years ago a friend of mine, the American novelist William Wiser, also spent three years here, as writer-in-residence, this time at Queens. And he, too, recalls those years warmly, and his novel informed by the time spent here, *The Circle Tour*, though mischievously accurate about certain academics and poets was, in fact, a labour of love. Bill Wiser's ancestry is Irish, mine Montserratian and – as you will probably have forgotten, Montserrat was for some years an outpost of Ireland in the Caribbean. It's possible that the poem I've written, in response to my three years sojourn in Ulster – the poem that will constitute the second half of this lecture – strikes a different note from Bill Wiser's novel but – informed by the complex Ireland–Montserratian relationship going back 350 years and more – I might claim extenuating circumstance. More of this later.

I did warn the organizers that this would not be a conventional lecture. I couldn't address the original, suggested title: 'Post-colonial forces at play in West Indian Literature' – as we haven't, in my opinion, achieved post-colonial statehood – in all but a formal sense, and in some cases not at all. It's like talking, in Europe and America about post-feminism, when we haven't had feminism. But I *will* try to say something about the Irish Cultural connection.

I wanted to respond, not as an academic but as a writer, someone who feels more comfortable trying to understand his environment, his circumstances, through the media of poems, stories, plays, jokes. Another thing which makes me want to contribute to the debate about cultural matters concerning the Caribbean and the West Indies is to correct a little the distortion in these matters of those who see Caribbean and West Indian as synonymous, and Anglophone, thus doing violence to the geographical sprawl, from Cuba through Belize, taking in Martinique and Curacao in the north-west, to Barbados in the far east, to the Guyanas – all three of them – on the southern part of the Continent. That construct would, of course, be mainly Spanish-speaking, with some English and French, patois, Dutch, etc. Three years ago I edited a book of Caribbean and Caribbean-heritage poetry, a book called *Hinterland*, concentrating on Anglophone poets. I wouldn't, I think, feel able to do this today. This is just a recognition that we must put Anglophone concerns into a larger context when talking about our region.

So, it's obvious that Irish culture – a major literary culture and one in your language – would influence us in our part of the Caribbean. The influences of Joyce, Yeats and Synge have long been detected in the work of Derek Walcott, the Caribbean's finest Anglophone poet; indeed – with apologies to St. John Perse of Guadeloupe, and Aime Cesaire of Martinique, and Nicolas Guillen of Cuba and Edward Kamau Brathwaite of Barbados – Caribbean's finest poet.

But we note that Walcott was influenced, also, by W. H. Auden and Dylan Thomas, by those nearer home like Neruda and St. John Perse himself – as well as . . . Marvell, John Donne, Mandelstam . . . and by his own peers: Lowell, Cesaire, Brodsky, etc. Not something to apologize for, according to Walcott, and I agree with him. Walcott says in a much-quoted passage:

> Young poets should have no individuality. They should be total apprentices, if they want to be masters. (Or mistresses, we might add. But Walcott continues) If you get a chance to paint a knuckle on a painting by Leonardo then you say 'Thank God!' and you just paint a knuckle as well as you can.

And the newest generation of Anglophone Caribbean poets are not immune. Fred D'Aguiar acknowledges Yeats (again) in his *Mama Dot Warns Against an Easter Rising* (a poem about flying a kite on Good Friday and suffering the consequences – the consequences being a splinter in the heel of your bare foot.) So, new poets like D'Aguiar and David Dabydeen – both of Guyana and England – have self-consciously used Irish models as their leaping-off points. Dabydeen takes on Heaney (as well as some English northerners) in his *Coolie Odyssey*, a poem which starts:

> Now that peasantry is in vogue,
> Poetry bubbles from peat bogs,
> People strain for the old folk's fatal gobs
> Coughed up in grates North or North East
> 'Tween bouts o' living dialect,
> It should be time to hymn your own wreck,
> Your house the source of ancient song:

One to Heaney, I think.

In the theatre Mustapha Matura of Trinidad has given us *A Playboy of the West Indies*, a creolized version of Synge's still controversial masterpiece. Howard Fergus of Montserrat celebrates an uprising of black Montserratians, against the local Irish Catholics, in his *Heroes of St. Patrick's Day* poem: no one but a Montserratian, I suspect, would risk that sort of irony!

But of course this sort of thing isn't what really engages us about the influence of Ireland on our culture, our literature. It's the special position

of Ireland's relationship to the English language that has fascinated us in
our part of the Caribbean, and Walcott articulates what every Caribbean
Anglophone writer has felt in this area, when he says:

> I've always felt some kind of intimacy with the Irish poets because one real-
> ized that they were also colonials with the same kind of problems that existed
> in the Caribbean. They were the niggers of Britain. Now, with all that, to have
> those outstanding achievements of genius whether by Joyce or Beckett or
> Yeats, illustrated that one could come out of a depressed, depraved, oppressed
> situation and be defiant and creative at the same time. . . .

Walcott, of course, apologizes, for calling the Irish 'niggers'. But this is, in
a way, a continuation of the Stephen Daedalus train of thought when he
reflects – to jog your memory!

> The language we are speaking is his before it is mine. How different are the
> words *home, ale, master* on his lips and mine! I cannot speak or write these
> words without unrest of spirit. His language, so familiar and so foreign, will
> always be for me an acquired speech. I have not made or accepted its words.
> My voice holds them at bay. My soul frets in the shadow of his language.

When, in Kenya, the novelist Ngugi reflected on these questions, he
came up, finally, with the solution of abandoning English for the use of
his native Gikuyu, a decision which terrified the government. We, in the
Caribbean, were either more cautious or more fortunate. We have fun in
using all the different strains of discourse that we find, to forge a language
which is English, at one level announcing its West Indianness not so much
in its syntax and vocabulary but in its stresses and in the weighting of its
imagery. At the other end of the continuum, we have nation-language,
which in itself can be comprehensible to outsiders, or it can be used in an
attempt to exclude. The French and Dutch in the region have similar linguistic arrangements. (I'm not going to talk about literature and its role
in cultural nationalism – we are not yet, as I said, seriously engaged in
that task, in the Caribbean as a whole.)

Of course the position of Ireland created difficulties as well as opportunities for us in the Caribbean. Certain second-handed notions of
Ireland and Irishness couldn't fail to percolate through to us living then
in a book-worshipping but largely non-reading society, a hear-say society,
avid for rumour, pleased to hear the worst of others, pleased to find fel-
low-victims in potential victimizers. So, the endlessly recycled, mainly
pejorative notions of Ireland and Irishness, whether generated by a
Charles Kingsley's 1860 letter to his wife bemourning the fact that the
Irish were not black, for in that case their animal characteristics wouldn't
cause him so much pain – whether that, or, Matthew Arnold, in a series
of lectures advocating the establishment of a Chair of Celtic Studies at
Oxford, stressing the sentimentality of the Celt as the chief characteristic, a child-like, feminine quality (and he was no early feminist) as
opposed to the mature, masculine Anglo-Saxon – whether that or even a

culled reference from Tennyson's *In Memoriam* to 'the blood hysterics of the Celts' – such things couldn't help but inform us.

It wasn't lost on us that though they were the ones who effectively colonized Montserrat, Irish Catholics were so legally circumscribed – not being able to vote, etc., in the local Assembly – that it took them over 150 years, even, to be allowed to act as jurors! In reality, it wasn't until Wellington and his section of the Tory Party bowed to the demands of Catholic Emancipation, in 1831, that their constitutional rights were respected in Montserrat. The effects of the alleged Popish Plot, of 1678, was felt even in Montserrat, where Catholic priests had to disguise themselves as fishermen to carry out their duties. (To this day, when I come across a fisherman in an Irish play, I suspect him to be something else!)

So, for every Walcott influenced by Yeats there was an M. G. de Lisser of Jamaica who, in his 1929 novel, *The White Witch of Rosehall*, felt able to portray an Irish plantation owner, Annie Palmer, practising the Voodoo she has learnt in Haiti. The good thing about this is that it suggested that the Irish could be creolized. The unfortunate thing – the proportion of stage-Irish stereotype, needn't be elaborated upon.

Of course in Art no one knows quite what are good and what are bad influences. All of Nigeria celebrates the achievement of Joyce Cary. And, of course, at his best Cary is a fine novelist, but that's not why Nigeria is grateful for *Mister Johnson* – there Cary is not at his best. As Chinua Achebe explained to Lewis Nkosi in a 1962 interview, his own first novel *Things Fall Apart* was provoked by Cary's novel, which seemed to him to depict, and I quote, 'a most superficial picture . . . not only of the country, but even of the Nigerian Character'. And so he thought, quote, 'perhaps someone ought to try and look at this from the inside'.

But to the positive aspects. Ireland's proximity to England and complex relationship to English makes it easier for us, from outlying areas of Englishness, or Britishness, or English-languageness, to adopt and adapt its literary models without the political self-consciousness that would arise if those models were English – or perhaps, even, American. Ireland's lack of political and economic empire makes it easier for those of us who are Anglophone to accept its models and concepts as not being detrimental to us. So Mustapha Matura's play, already mentioned, could give shape to his Trinidadian drama, and pay tribute to John Synge *at the same time*, without having to make the self-conscious political point; without having to disavow the original – as he would have felt constrained to do if his model had been English. This probably hints at an immaturity in West Indian letters, but there it is. Mustapha doesn't have to be angry (in this instance) because his model is Synge.

If that sounds still grudging and negative, think of Derek Walcott's homage to Irishness in *Omeros*, his great epic, recently-published, 325 pages of poem – a Homeric – or Joycian enterprise, though the style of execution – *terza rima* – comes from Dante, and its main setting is St. Lucia. Yet among the most tender portraits in the poem is Maud Plunkett from County Wicklow. Maud is married to Dennis who is English, pig-breeding in retirement. Maud fills her days with gardening, sewing and – quote – 'marking the routes of passing liners'. She elicits from Walcott a language of polite accusation wonderfully appropriate to someone marooned in paradise. Here they are in the Evening –

> Maud with a needle, embroidering a silhouette
> from Bond's *Ornithology*, their quiet mirrored
> in an antique frame.

Again:

> The morning Maud died he sat in the bay window,
> watching the angel-hair blow gently from her face.
> That wax rose pillowed there, was his crown and wonder,
>
> a breeze lifting the curtains like her bridal lace.
> Seashells. Seychelles. The empire of cancer spread
> across the wrinkled sheets, etc.

At a reading of the poem Walcott very carefully explained away his tenderness for Major Plunkett. He was spiritually native, Walcott said. In honouring the couple he was honouring his own parents (though Walcott's own mother appears, poignantly, in the poem). Or as Paula Burnett, the critic and anthologist said of this couple: 'Walcott is presenting a complement to the group of black characters whose story is central to the work – a sort of fitting together of the divided halves of the world, an epic and ethical undertaking'. The point is it would have been harder, if the white-skinned Maud had not been Irish, for the Caribbean poet to treat her so lovingly, so poignantly, and put her at the heart of his book; and not feel the need of a disclaimer, even in conversation. Ireland, in fact, is saving us from the charge of racism.

My own personal engagement with all this, this Irishness, the culture emanating from Ireland, derives from the fact that I was, as I said, born in Montserrat, the tiny Caribbean outpost, colonized by the Irish in, we think, 1632. I expect you know the history better than I. There were Irish settlers on the neighbouring island of St. Kitts. There were also French settlers on St. Kitts, and the island was formally divided between England and France. St. Kitts is a small island. This is the 17th century. Events in far-off Europe make it difficult for three foreign nationalities to cohabit in a small space.

The Irish are thought to be unreliable. Soon, Irish Catholic dissidents (or suspects) find their way to Montserrat, about a hundred miles away. This is not a voyage of discovery. This is a haven, selected by the British, with the dual purpose of easing the problem in St. Kitts and having *some* presence in Montserrat in case the French from neighbouring Guadeloupe decide to claim it. They were always doing that sort of thing to outlying islands. So, we have the dissidents – suspects from St. Kitts, 1632. There was another inflow, we think, this time down from Virginia, the following year. And, of course, a few of Cromwell's political prisoners found their way there, after the business in Ireland in 1649–50.

Montserrat is uninhabited at the time – just as it was said to be uninhabited in 1493, when an Italian desperado – whose name I believe was Cristobal Colon – on his second voyage, passed by and, without landing, named it Santa Maria de Monserrate, after the Monastery of that name 30 miles north-west of Barcelona, in Spain. We know, from remains, that the Caribs had been there. Their absence on both occasions, 140 years apart, is one of the myths informing contemporary Montserratian literature – and there *is* a growing Montserratian literature.

But there is no doubt about the Irishness of Montserrat, then and now.

In my own family, the story is that a great, great, whatever, uncle worked on a farm of a couple of Irish sisters, as overseer. He was, apparently, not paid, and when the sisters decided to sell up and return to Ireland, they gave him part of the estate (and the shop which they ran) in lieu of payment. (I suppose, in a less racially-conscious time, he would have married into the family). The shop was called Trescellian House (Tresciollian = three leaf, in Gaelic, Trefoil) – even though my friends in Ireland insist that the name is Cornish. (Indeed, to this day, a Shamrock adorns the Government House in Plymouth).

But back to Trescellian House. It survives to this day, a general store, in Parliament St., Plymouth, Montserrat; and is owned by a first cousin of mine, Bertrand Osborne – Osborne being the name of the second Governor of the island – after Brisket and before Stapleton (names that populate my own fiction.)

In our own time, in the wake of the latest natural disaster, Hurricane Hugo, it seemed natural to me as a writer, to image a descendant of one of the early settlers, marooned back in Europe, sending condolences to the old island. I call him Kevin. Here is his response to the recent hurricane:

Kevin's Message to Montserrat

I'm in between certainties: here they call me
A man with an Irish accent. I'm the legend
Who set foot on your Emerald Isle in the 1630s,
Did a bit of this and that, built Trescellian House
(Damaged, I know, but still standing) and courted
My first wife under the Evergreen tree in Plymouth.
The Church I built among Temples of the Christians: how is it?

I suspect the Committee naming your hurricanes
To be bureaucrats unschooled in our history. Hugo
Seems an odd policeman, a pre-Enlightenment pirate

Of the wrong tribe. Ah, you're not interested in this.
(Distribute your Aid; give thanks to the Red Cross).
Here in Fun City, I wait by my car, clamped
By a rascal among the sex-labs to discredit me.

My thoughts, fellow-gamblers, are with you
From indigo, lime-grove to cashing in the chips. As you know
I have an interest in a bank on the island, off-shore
(No cumbersome buildings like Churches to tempt God).
From North, East, Cork Hill, Kinsale, we must pool
Our assets. I'm coming soon to celebrate with the little
Hamilton girl. Tell she I love she.

It is this special relationship which makes those of us from
Montserrat feel able to tell Irish jokes (for they are, indeed, our jokes)
without their carrying the connotation of similar jokes told by the
English.

Of course the culture that Ireland brought wasn't just literary.
(Indeed, no settler of any sort, brought a literary culture to the
Caribbean; that came later. But they brought other things – French
cuisine to our Francophone neighbour, Guadeloupe, for instance!)
The Montserrat national dish, *Goatwater*, is said to be based on a
Connemara housewife's recipe for stew. Here is a recipe, authen-
ticated by my friend Howard Fergus, historian and at present
deputy Governor of the island – which is still a British colony.
Howard Fergus – we recall his *Heroes of St. PATRICK'S Day* – is
a poet and a sort of historical and social commentator. One of his
many books is called *MONTSERRAT: EMERALD ISLE OF THE
CARIBBEAN* – and that's what the island was called in the years when I
grew up there.

Now, for the Goatwater recipe.

Goatwater

2 quarters goat or sheep
4 onions, cut up
Herbs and chible (local name for thyme)
¾ cups cooking oil
3 ozs. fresh marjoram
4 cloves garlic, minced
1 tablespoon whole cloves, crushed
1 tablespoon mace
2 tablespoons catsup
1 hot green pepper, whole
Salt and pepper to taste etc.

The interesting things which are now beginning to inform a
Montserratian literature, which is more organically Irish than any in the

Caribbean, are the floating images, the buried memories which Montserratians, including myself, are now attempting to trap into stories, poems, plays. There is the fisherman of our youth, an Irishman, minus a hand, bitten off or damaged at sea, badly enough to be amputated. And he does complicated things with the stump, leaps on to a moving bus, an old-fashioned bus open at the back, and he secures himself with the stump against the wooden upright. When, as a child, at night, you refuse to go to sleep at the right time, your grandmother threatens you with the Irishman with one hand. This is not an Irish joke but an important part of your heritage. The Irish impact on this literature will be distinctive. Here is that image, reclaimed:

> All who had failed, failed here.
> St. Caesare, spread out, was a map of the world's
> battlefields, from ancient to modern to now.
> Last week's Irishman from the sea minus a hand: what made
> him so generous to fish with bait that had caressed
>   maybe foreign, cool & freckled women in lace
> but *sickness* for our grape-coloured Geraldine?

This is from a recent poem of mine called *Maurice V's Dido*, in which the mythic qualities of the island of St. Caesare – an invented island to twin Montserrat, but with a stronger French influence – are acknowledged.

It seems to me that these qualities, these perspectives – consciousness of an Irish presence at home – a population which, in some senses distanced itself from the English (though only in some senses) encouraged in the native population the feeling that outside forces, however irksome, were not necessarily monolithic, that it was possible to make alliances with those who were not necessarily on one's side, when those alliances were useful, in the full knowledge that they might shift. It's like our own Montserratian version of the African Spiderman image, which figures so prominently in Caribbean literature generally. This was an experience which doesn't lead to easy stereotypes (My Methodist preacher, for instance, had an Irish accent!). There was a sense that the Irish (even though we had experience of brutal Irish land and slave-owners) provided something of a wedge between the English and ourselves; and that made us, I think, more ambivalent in racial matters, than most of our neighbours in the Caribbean.

It's interesting to note that Linton Kwesi Johnson, the Jamaican reggae poet, recalls that one of the things which made him think he might have access to the English language as a writer, was hearing John Arlot's Somerset accent on the radio, his cricket commentaries: the fact that that diverged from the then stock BBC radio voice, and that Arlot was nevertheless an authority figure made Linton think that another non-English voice – his own – might have validity in poetry. In a sense, in Montserrat,

the Irish vicar performed that function for us. He, too, was an authority
figure. But his voice wasn't the one that came over the BBC.

And now for the poem, broadening that Irish influence.

Letter from Ulster

i

For Mimijune

I'm 300 years old;
the partner arrives and is shown into
the drawing-room where someone makes her comfortable.
She is, we think, 40 years early.
The boy sits in an upstairs room, his back
to the window, typewriter on the bed
two-finger tapping a scene from the house
next-door – a young girl folded in the arms
of a man, open curtains with promise
that travel from St. Caesare to Ladbroke Grove
might fulfil. Neither typist nor writer he turns
too late, the curtains are closed.
Downstairs, mother entertains an in-law 40 years early
with scenes from a life more real than this:
the drawing-room floor is freshly polished, smell
of wax like flowers from the garden toasting
in the sun. Wasps nests have been removed
from gable and gallery, lizards and other irritants
dealt with by someone unseen who nurses
a better version of this house. Look out
of the window – through glass panes, a bridal
present for the young mother never to shed
hint of girlishness in the crossing – glass panes,
first on this side of the island –
at grapes with a hint of salt, though the sea,
as you see – so calm today, how could we be sick? –
is distant. . . . Ah. But will you take
ginger beer or coconut juice with ice? Downstairs,
in this recent house imposed on other houses where occupants
vanish in mid-sentence leaving you unsure of tricks
being played – downstairs, brothers talk of an election
coming up, promises that must be made
to us here in England, to us in South Africa,
to us everywhere as price of the vote. (Old Professeur
Croissant used to say in class: if you must lie,
lie intelligently. If you must, sell yourself
dearly, a play on words too risky for parents born
before our time.) Excluded from the couple
behind their curtain and from the brothers' debate
– and from what else? I plead
unreadiness to meet a partner, years early.

ii

Dear X,

They call it confidence to offer
false starts to an intimate this late
in the game, but what if no better version comes? . . .
though this stand colludes, perhaps, with failure.
So, dear X, skip these lines of self-
regard, worn apologies
for omission, unreadiness, these practised
ways of shoring *Self*. To you, to others
who have turned up early, these games
irritate; they bore. Mock the time
with family growing into the real thing.
Stray postcards confirm your luck, you've escaped
the jokes – remember when Puller & Parkhouse
were in contention to open for England? –
that no one understands. That off our chests – Oh chest! –
safe to revert to the present with a letter
from Ulster. Scenes of local colour
won't do the trick – too much blood
under the lamp-posts, Joke. 300 years seems
a short time to manage a life cleansed
of its past yet love-propelled;
but my time-creditor comes like an Assistant
at the Bank and says. Enough: others,
who are not bright, manage it in the slot
allotted. Think of lives you have put
on hold by slowing things to this pace. Your drawing-
room partner, distanced now by – whom? – a Stand-in
daughter, has outlived the house, the fantasy.
Brothers, far from downstairs, answering to other
cares protect themselves from new 'South Africas'
(child & wife & self-abuses, biologies with your name
on. And they go out to vote). And what, pray,
of that early couple behind the curtain?
But I promised you relief from a letter
too stiff to compel reading between
the lines. A limp letter, then, and addressed
to someone, on another continent, not tempted
to read between our lines.

Dear Jim & Elisabeth

This is not the letter, I know. I'll write
at the weekend to thank you for Canada
(lovely present, unspoilt, where will I put it?)
for good times remembered, the walk through the ravine
that beautiful Sunday with Elisabeth (we're adults now,
no Atwood childhood fears. Remember Cats Eye?)
Thanks for the hospitality, the space . . .
But first, let me clear my mind a bit
as resolution ebbs on this Coleraine–Belfast train.
Cutting it fine, as always, I crash the guardsman's
van, pleased, no seconds today, to spare –
and I'm missing a package, a bag – left
in the taxi, snatched on the steps? the race
over foot-bridge, messy: students pouring the other way
helped when the straps broke: white bag
with books, green bag MADE IN CANADA, my change
of clothing, a white top, for Belfast,
after a bath – fresh for the late-night studio.

I'm in the Guard's van. Maybe he thinks:
they need longer to recover breath
than men in our parts, all that running and jumping
on television. He makes small allowances
for this puffing race and settles a little more
in his skin. Today, bag-snatched, I see no reason
to take better care of his feelings than he does.
I rise to the occasion (It's a coarse time
but we'll outwit it) and see hoardes cross the bridge,
motorcycle-helmeted, Moll-painted, struggling
to don white Westing House gear and I . . . check myself in time.

Dear Elisabeth & Jim

iii

A government-suited man behind a desk: to show
he's human or to ease the tension, makes a joke
(not about the Chinese lady at Dhu Varren
railway station, though that comes to mind) . . . Which of us
will act this man's throwaway line
and end up in the Papers? And here we are coming out
of the film of the book, telling friends over a pizza
how the cut-price Bogart got it wrong. Across the road
filmed, too, in drizzle your tail lights a cigarette in the doorway. See!
Better to talk about the railway clock in Portrush Havishamed
at 11.25 encouraging old bachelors
to rewrite their history as literature.
I've caught the bug. Let me read you
the menu of the Chinese restaurant
(Lower Main Street) as a poem . . .

    You're right, my love. The act
    degenerates, distraction/from a life
    we might have lived/points
    to an analyst

    behind this glimpse of happiness,
    behind this naked breast, voices
    of old men unscramble/made human
    by translation, their toothless lives no longer
    excluding from the feast of family feeling
    those not dressed for table:
    the rhubarb chorus (something to rhyme with table?
    to swat the buzzing chorus?)
    makes you pause and turn away/careful
    not to repel the naked breast/I say

    having lost the prize:
    I will add some years to mine

    till it comes around next time.

iv

Meanwhile enter Horace
our Interlude, pink
ribbon in his hair, pink
shoe-lace in his memory-
pocket for a daughter
ever pink and beautiful:
Derringer's the name
name o'th'game, our Shaman
restored to humour.
Wars & roaming have dis-
tempered, slack-minded
this lover of Peace, stiff-
limping to action.
He appears on cue
against the tide of Comanche Cheyenne Sioux
back to you (he can do
the Ali shuffle, too!):
now at his piano miming
the old tunes. *In The Mood*
& *If I Give My Heart to You* . . .
(10,000 at Salamis, more at Zama
negotiations between the generals having failed)
Will You Handle It With Care . . .?
He is not blind, he outwits
doctors and family, this Special
Envoy to Europa, bringing *shhh*
(from St. Caesare, off
your map, don't look now)
Bustcrumvrst Mvst
Peace in his language,
in this or that language:
Messenger Horace broken-
toothed on his diet of phrases
WIR HABEN (try this one)
UNS MIT NACHBARN ÜBER DIE
BENÜTZUNG DES GARTENS ARRANGIERT
no pillow-talk now to Merles
& Sadies of Coderington
to Cathy and Sharon of Ealing & Edmonton.
but public lament for
Hrothvitha Hrothvitha
stage-wife and daughter
petals in the slaughter
to divert you from comfort,
from solemnity. And so –
May you never lack for caress
May your lover be left-handed and relentless
May Sally paint your door in bright colours
May you be the pick of your brothers

and so on and so on *Hrothvitha*
Hrothvitha a name no one claims for
these Sisters and Mothers.
Brokentoothed fly–
opened Horace ends
with a memory that he sings
unaccompanied, his own melody, pink-
ribboned melody, his
something-hearted melody, his
broken-charted melody, his
broken-hearted melody . . .

v
Puck

Just a note, darling;
I've had to explain you
appropriate you (for Mimijune &
Julieblossom) to see how you'd run:
Ama Ata Aidoo,
tripple A.
b. Ghana, 1939, Playwright,
novelist, etc. Address Zimbabwe
(see essay by Innes,
Lyn of Canterbury.) So,
you were my near-choice
for the Chair
to prick these Oberons,
these Titanians (immune with collars
and constituencies cross-
border (swing high, swing low . . .)
with a virus of compassion
as they learn to betray your name
in a common accent:
Ama Ata Aidoo
Chairperson to this Conference
not allowed
(by a daughter of Ghana,
Sister of Zimbabwe)
to break up
on this rock of malespeak
solid through the ages.

Mimijune, Julieblossom.
In the wings. My favourite things.

vi

I wake up howling: murder
has become easy to the long-lived. I'm committing
it again. The pistol in the pants
slugs a consenting victim
in the crotch. I do not have Aids,
I say. But the victim dies. Everywhere
it gets easier to kill. (And the coward
says: let me turn away from the loved one
before we wake. Meanwhile the years
are being used up. Solutions elude us.
How long, O Lord, is this string spun
from vanity, how long
will the earth sustain it?

      Dear John & Joan,

      (lacking courage
      for today again on the television, an outrage
      occurs – the plumber, shop-assistant outguesses
      me in the quizz of what I call my subject.
      Pride must be recovered before approach
      to another with intent.
      Lacking courage
      like the blind man at Sheffield Railway Station
      charging down the stairs, scattering passengers;
      like getting on with a former life;
      like dying early, I turn
      to another, slack letter, my darling
      and mild abuse of Canada. In lieu of lovers'
      cards, the codes untracked in the post,
      I blame the time, I blame the place.)

      My mispronounciations of Agincourt were deliberate.
      I, too, live in Henry V. country only when abroad.
      Just a letter from Ulster to thank you for Canada,
      big country, clean accent, etc. . . . And about me?
      O, fun times in Ballymena, Ballymoney. Limavady.
      Riding the middle of the train one day (not the first
      carriage or the last, making it safe, like a New Yorker
      story shorn of beginning and end) the second smoker
      lights up, the third girl-farmer splotches mud on my seat:
      I like it, folks, the wild North, I'm not too late
      for the rush. Later, I'll play myself in Hollywood.
      But competition is stiff for the films. At audition
      near Portrush (the place where the train, programmed
      to leave late surprises you one day by being early)
      I rated one line, the privileged extra . . .
      The time is evening, the place Dhu Varren, the train

not running. A bus – looking like bus – pulls up
and rail-passengers get on. Except for the Chinese
lady hovering, holding out. 'There's no train today',
the conductor treads on my cue, with no result.
The language-student wants a playback. So pointing
to UNIVERSITY bus, idling, he announces: THIS IS
THE TRAIN. This, a week after events at Teinenmen
Square where nobody died. This 'train' an English
joke in Ireland?

Old men used to say: Stones grow.
Men at home grew grey on such evidence.
No one thought of land-erosion. But the same men say:
cut me and I bleed, auditioning for Shylock;
trapped here, I die. Ah, if they thought of land-erosion
they would find ways out of this, with the family intact.
I stand accused of lengthening moments
into string, as if they were in short supply
in the average life.

O yes, I meant to say, they sent me
a list of 24 poets, names and addresses,
colleagues at the HARBOURFRONT, for a week. Telephone
numbers, too. How open. How good. Canada.

Mimijune, Julieblossom,

The change of clothing, the white top
reclaimed at home in Portrush, my oversight,
made me see how rash to write too soon
a letter from Ulster, to write to you
in innocence. In-between, the white top,
stolen on the road from London to Sheffield,
is another letter. But what of you?

vii

(Portrush: Fragments From the Journal)

(a)
Land, I think, though only just.
Gales from Iceland whistle through the caravel.
The seas, enraged at this obstruction threaten,
relent and come again, green-backed with teeth
straining from the world of myth. Some say
these monsters will not be ridden; these are tales
of desperate men far from home. Next will come
the triumph of supping with the devil
without the long spoon; and that will grant your wish
of keeping good folk at home.

(b)

The the land shrank back in a terrible roar
As the greenbacked, white-teethed
Mass made for the shore
Spitting sea-pebbles with venom
Like a line of snipers compelling
You to yield. This zealot's canon
Blends you down, crouches you in mime
Of humans in drink, each desperado
– And we have all been there in time –
Fantasising a railway-station pub at Portrush.
And some say the King of Spain
Has now laid claim to Portrush.
But on to the real El Dorado round
The promontory, our university teeming,
Its band of natives browned
By no sun & like the bless'd of the old
World, well-proportioned, except for webbed
Feet and tendency to walk backwards in leave-taking. Gold
Is our currency, though rival discovery
Of men with breasts or bird & fish aspect
Still serves, if not national recovery
Or fixing the State plumbing
To head off ruin and the Tower. The *cassique*
In chains, must fear our Second Coming.

(c)

Too dangerous to say what you've found.
The sealed envelope (Why should this be found?)
Would explain all should we suffer mishap.
A new god of hail descends like an icecap
Sneezing; unkind to flesh and eyeglass. Wind & rain
(And faulty instruments) make it hard to retain
Our humour. Exploring's no longer the sum
Of delights promised when the journey was begun.
Wet with indignity, men think this train
Of misery that brought them here, the same
That through Law of Averages, if not prayer,
Must lug back to those early stations of hope. Fair's fair.
In time a train stops unscheduled at Portrush
Where the spirits have not been propitiated. Portrush
Is a rooftop vandal hurling down slate at your feet
Daring you to assume safe passage to Main St.
You get home bleeding, fire-water the graze
& much else; relent, and sit down to write the day's
Journal when the light blows out.
I'm sitting in the dark; there are Christians about.

                                                                E. A. Markham

Notes

i:

St. Caesare: Imaginary island off the coast of Montserrat in the Caribbean.

Puller & Parkhouse: In the late-50s, early 60s, England cricket selectors cast about for opening batsmen who could give solidity to the innings. Of the two in contention here, Puller had some success against West Indies in 1959.

iv:

Comanche Cheyenne Sioux: Horace is moving *against* the trend, pushing back the damage. From about AD 1600, when enough Europeans were established on the east coast of America with superior weapons, the Indians were driven westwards into the territory of westerly neighbours. The succession of great battles – between the Chippewa and the Sioux – at Mille Lacs in the 17th Century; at Elk River in the 18th and at Cross Lake in 1800, have become part of our myth. In the 19th century, the buffalo gone, the pressure westwards continuing, the defeated Sioux pushed the Cheyenne (and others) further west. The Cheyenne eventually drove the Comanche back towards Mexico.

Salamis and Zama: The naval battle at Salamis between the Greeks and the Persians (480 BC.Sept.) led to a notable Greek victory and heavy casualties. At Zama (Oct.–Nov. 202 BC) the Second Punic War ended with Scipio Africanus overcoming the Carthaginians under Hannibal. The entire Carthaginian army of 35,000 was killed or captured, though Hannibal escaped. His infantry was semi-trained and his elephants confused by Scipio's blast of trumpets and horns along the whole length of his line. Also, by 202, Hannibal had had 16 years of continuous high-command.

WIR HABEN . . . : We've come to an arrangement with the neighbours about the use of the garden.

Hrothvitha: 10th century Saxon nun who wrote plays – generally with a Christian subject – in the style of Terence.

vi:

Agincourt: The Canadian town with an English pronunciation.

Harbourfront: Toronto. Certainly, the most splendidly-organized poetry-reading event in the west. Presided over by Grey Gatenby.

vii:

'tendency to walk backwards in leave-taking': An observation first made by Dr. Richard Bradford of Portrush, in conversation.

Cassique: Local ruler in the Americas during the time of conquest, often roughly treated at the hands of the Colóns & the Raleighs . . .

Christian: (?)

10. IN SEARCH OF THE MOTHER TONGUE

Christopher Whyte

I

The questions agitating your minds as I prepare to speak are very probably 'Who is this Christopher Whyte?' and 'What does he have to say to
us?' In answer I can suggest that there are at least three Christopher
Whytes, and that each of them would speak to you with a different
voice.

Since the age of twenty-three I have earned my daily bread mainly by
lecturing at universities, for some nine years in Italy and more recently at
Edinburgh and Glasgow in Scotland. The voice of the lecturer would be
detached and apparently logical, with perhaps even an aspiration to be
scientific, the voice of one who knows, or is at least required by his function to pretend to know, and whose judgement is not swayed by personal
or emotional considerations. But an effect of years of lecturing is that one
grows very tired of that particular voice and of that masquerade. Silence
comes to seem a more and more attractive prospect or, if silence is not
possible, at least the right to say: 'I don't know. I don't have any answers.
And what makes you think that, in the last analysis, there are any
answers?'

Nearly two years ago I edited an anthology of eight Gaelic poets entitled, after the closing line of a poem by Meg Bateman, *An Aghaidh na
Siorraidheachd* or, in English, *In the Face of Eternity*.[1] Many people had
considered putting together a book of this kind, in part to balance the
authoritative anthology of an earlier generation's work published in
1976, *Nua-bhardachd Ghaidhlig* or *Modern Scottish Gaelic Poetry*.[2]
There was a feeling that the older book needed, if not to be superseded,
at least to be put in perspective. It was Meg who suggested the idea to me,
and when she had outlined the reasons why she had no wish to edit the
book herself (reasons I will not go into here) I went ahead on my own,
found a publisher and contacted the poets. I put a lot of work into the
introduction to that anthology, which had to present an accurate critical
assessment of each of the participants while also promoting them and the
book. It was a kind of manifesto for those writing Gaelic verse today and
who, despite their disparateness and in many cases ignorance of each
other's work, for the purposes of the introduction constituted some kind
of a group.

So the second possible voice would be that of the editor. But I feel I have done my job, at least for the moment, as promoter and spokesman for a younger generation of writers. It was made all the more difficult because I was a self-appointed spokesman, and a learner of the language. All the time I was conscious that, whatever path a Gaelic poet approaching forty is supposed or expected to have followed, mine had been very different. Under no circumstances could I claim to be representative.

Today I want to make things easy for myself. I want to shrug off the responsibility of being representative along with that of being objective or authoritative. I don't want anyone to feel they can check up on what I have to say, or to measure it against a standardised paradigm. To speak for others, or to speak for one's generation, is a dangerous and even thankless task, and one I am very happy to set aside in order to do something rather more exciting, if potentially even more arrogant.

I want to speak with the voice of the poet. I want to be resolutely personal and autobiographical. This does not mean I will tell the truth. After all, everyone knows that autobiography is merely a subtler form of fiction. The possible stories of one's own life are like successive glimpses of the place one lives in got from a low-flying aircraft, exhilarating moments of power and pattern which must inevitably culminate in a return to earth and the loss of any perspective whatsoever.

II

What are characteristics of the poet's voice? And in particular, of a poet speaking prose, and prose in a language different from that of his poetry? I see the poet as someone who is always elusive and relentlessly disruptive, never more uncomfortable than when he or she is confronted with some kind of communal assent or unanimity. Especially when speaking in public, what I expect of a poet is to voice the unacceptable, to say the things each of us thinks in private but dares not utter, even to those we hold most dear. When speaking effectively, a poet will transform an audience into a conglomeration of single individuals, embarrassed to catch each other's eye in case some secret acknowledgement of what is being said should escape them. Poetry in our society is still overwhelmingly a solitary activity, and it is endlessly reassuring that poets themselves are normally not there to assess our reactions. We need only share our solitude with words.

I want to trust that my own particular experience, in so far as it is personal and inimitable and seems to break the rules, encloses its own kind of truth, which has a value beyond that of any detached overview or summary I might concoct. If I do not directly answer the questions on the conference programme, I may unwittingly offer indirect answers. But it will be up to you to arrive at them, and I hope that for different listeners the answers will prove to be different. Indeed, I suspect the question I am really expected to address is 'why do you write in Gaelic?' And after prolonged thought, I am convinced it deserves the simplest of answers: 'Why not?' Would anyone dream of asking a poet writing in English why he chose this tongue? The choice of English is taken as axiomatic by those who subscribe to current linguistic and cultural power relations, but it is not axiomatic to me.

Perhaps I can be permitted an excursus at this point and say just how mysterious I find the world of the monoglot English speaker, or the world of anyone who commands just one language. In saying this I am deliberately turning the tables, because I so often come across people who find my attitude to language peculiar. I've been overwhelmingly fascinated by language for as long as I remember, and in particular by languages I do not quite, or am only just beginning to understand. It is as if, when listening to a language I am in the process of learning or whose meaning I have just the faintest glimmering of, I am much closer to the reality of language than when dealing in one that is habitual to me.

I have great difficulty in thinking of languages as discrete, separate compartments. Very often, when seeking out a word, it will come to me in a language other than the one I want, or a sequence of sounds will linger in my mind for some time before I am able to assign it to a language or a particular meaning. Therefore, at times it is hard for me to think of English and Gaelic as being separate from one another or in some way opposed, and to imagine that if Gaelic were to disappear English could remain unaffected or even benefit.

I am particularly fascinated by how the mind, in this case my mind, deals with language. Especially I remember one evening some eight years ago, when, after ten days in Zagreb during which I had listened to and spoken about as much Croatian as I could possibly cope with, I stopped off on the way back to Rome at the house of friends in Bologna and, after a late, hurried meal, clambered into bed. My night was filled with an up-rush of Croatian words and sentences, some of them genuine, many of them not, like a well working in reverse and emptying out all its contents in a great surge to the light of day. And the following morning everything was tidied away, absorbed, so that I was able to go back to speaking Italian without any difficulty or interference.

It seems to me that the monoglot is deluding himself if he imagines he lives in a watertight, hermetically sealed linguistic world. Words and concepts from other languages are constantly seeping in, whether it be 'glasnost', 'intifada' or 'chili con carne'. In fact, I would defy anyone who thinks he uses only one language to get through the course of a normal day without using some words whose provenance is entirely different.

Then again, language is like a potted plant we might keep in our front room. From one season to the next, it grows and alters its appearance, but at no point in time can we actually perceive this process in action. Each single speech act changes the language in ways that may only become perceptible in the arc of a lifetime, so that any illusion that language is self-consistent, any aspiration to fidelity or purity has to be abandoned.

Indeed, this is a major problem for someone like myself when writing in Gaelic. If I were to be faithful to some principle inherent in the language, to some content it carried with it and evoked, my poetry, and the language itself, would be completely dead. To write in any language is an act of tremendous *hubris*, of interference, of disrespect. And the disrespect is especially evident with socially underprivileged languages because these, much more than a language which is politically powerful, are circumscribed by and identified with a particular subject matter and place.

Languages develop through and are enriched by mistakes and misunderstandings. Faulty pronunciations can eventually separate off and constitute words and concepts of their own, which did not previously exist. Most fascinating of all are the words that never quite got spoken, the syntactical variants that never came into being because at that moment an old peasant woman involved in some rambling and reflective monologue was interrupted by a pot boiling over on the fire or someone knocking at the door, and the mistake she was about to make, the unprecedented turn of phrase she was about to use, was forgotten.

III

So far I have been trying to give you some idea of what language means to me, language seen as a whole, a single organism which cannot be itemised or compartmentalised into discrete units. I think the best way to experience this reality of language would be to travel from central Europe down in a slowly curving arc to the coast of the Black Sea, beginning in one of these places that has names in three languages – Ljubljana, Laibach, Lubiana – and traversing a linguistic continuum that gradually transforms Slovenian into Bulgarian, embracing Croatian, Serbian and Macedonian on its way, yet with transitions so multifarious and imperceptible that it would be impossible to halt in a particular village and say this is where one language stops and another begins. Against this background I can begin to speak of Gaelic and of the role it has played in my own life. In a poem from the sequence 'An sgoilear a' seailtainn air ais/*The scholar looks back*' I tried to describe the city I was brought up in:

Ach rugadh mi ann am baile cruadalach,
daoin a' chaill gach dochas air seachran ann
mar thannasgan tiamhaidh, glaist' am braighdeanas.

Bha 'm fulangas sgrìobht' air an aodainnean
le litrichean goirt, a b' urrainn eadhon
do leanabh a thuigsinn gu furasda.

Leugh mi an sin duilleag a' pheacaidh
ann an cainnt ùr, a dh'ionnsaich mi
bho fheannagan creideamh an duilgheadais,
is fhaclan-san cho fuathasach

sgreataidh 's gun do dhubhadh a-mach
cainnt eile, anns am bitheadh mo chorp

a' dèanamh suirghe ciùin rim anam.
(Chuireadh stad ar an còmhdhail).
Dh'fhàg na feannagan air mo làimh dheis

truaghan lomnochd crocht' ri crann,
a bha a cholann na leòn gu lèir
air nach b'urrainn dhomhsa beachdachadh

gun oillt, is a' tuiteam bho a cheann
droighinn a dh'fheum mi coiseachd orra.
Is thubhairt mi rium fhin: ma bhitheas tu

balbh, is dòcha nach mothaichear dhut.

But I was born in a cruel city,
men who had lost hope wandering it
like captive, melancholy shades.

Suffering was written on their faces
in bitter letters even a child
could easily understand.

I read there the page of sin,
in a new language taught to me
by the carrion-crows of the faith of sorrow,

its words so ugly and dissonant
another language was blotted out
in which my body had been used

to make love to my soul.
(An end was put to their discussion.)
At my right hand the crows placed

a naked wretch fixed to a tree,
his whole body one wound, so that
I couldn't look at it without

disgust. Thorns would fall
from his head: I had to walk on them.
And I said to myself 'If you keep
quiet, maybe they won't notice you'.[3]

Glasgow is today a transformed city, although many would argue that it is more the image of the city that has been transformed than the place itself. When I was born there in 1952 it was a very terrible place indeed, and had been so for at least three decades. I think there are political and historical reasons for this. Glasgow is a stepchild, or an orphan. Its parent died long before the city took its present form. Industrial Glasgow has never experienced or been a part of an independent, organically functioning Scotland. It has always been a vacuum where political power is concerned, even when it was the second city of the Empire. And this meant that the Industrial Revolution took a particularly savage form there.

Specific factors compounded my own unhappiness. I came from a lower-middle class family, upwardly mobile in a slow and shambling sort of way. This meant that I was cut off from many of the city's saving graces: its rich popular life, its energetic coarseness, the raciness, humour and humanity of its vernacular. Moreover, I was a member of an immigrant community. Of my grandparents, only my father's father was born in Scotland, and to him I owe my Scottish surname with its putative Gaelic antecedents. The other three were born in Ireland, one in Mayobridge, one in Killyclogher and one in Glenties. Because my mother gave the home its cultural stamp (and the same may have been true of my father's family), we never felt ourselves to be genuinely Scottish, and the shibboleths of Scottishness, such as haggis and Burns, kilts and other Highland paraphernalia were looked on with suspicion. A few years ago, my mother visited her only living sister in an old folk's home. My aunt was demented, but one of the last coherent things she said, in an undertone, was 'The people here are very *Scottish*, you know!' Both sisters were born and raised just outside Glasgow, but at the end of their lives 'Scottish' still meant different from us, alien and, in some peculiar way, untrustworthy.

Education was highly valued in our home, not least because both my parents were teachers. A semi-private education could be had relatively cheaply in Glasgow in those days, and I was sent to a Jesuit day school, named after the scion of a Mantuan noble family in Renaissance Italy, cut off in his saintly and ascetic prime. Here the paradoxes of my position became even stranger. Although priests were not a majority of the staff, a majority of the priests were from a place we Scots euphemistically call 'down south'. The prevailing ethos was English and, in political terms, Conservative with a capital C. Now the purpose of the school was quite clearly to enable an immigrant community to produce its own middle class as quickly as possible. But until recently Catholics in Scotland voted overwhelmingly for the Labour party, given explicit or perceived religious prejudices of both the Tory party and the Scottish Nationalists. It is a rarely remembered but interesting fact that in the 1920s and 1930s the highest authorities of the Church of Scotland appealed repeatedly to the Westminster government to stem the tide of Irish immigration to Scotland. Many of the immigrant community saw the Labour party as the only political option available to them. So in the process of educating these boys, the Jesuits effectively alienated them, cutting them off not just politically and socially but also culturally from their own background.

As a child and adolescent I suffered from something I will call, for want of a better term, cultural asphyxiation. The term has a precious ring to it, but the suffering was very real. Alasdair Gray has given this predicament its classic formulation in his first published novel, *Lanark:*

> 'Glasgow is a magnificent city', said McAlpin. 'Why do we hardly ever notice that?' 'Because nobody imagines living here', said Thaw. McAlpin lit a cigarette and said, 'If you want to explain that I'll certainly listen'.
> 'Then think of Florence, Paris, London, New York. Nobody visiting them for the first time is a stranger because he's already visited them in paintings, novels, history books and films. But if a city hasn't been used by an artist not even the inhabitants live there imaginatively'.[4]

At secondary school we studied the English language, English history and English literature. The process which led me to find things English actively distasteful, rather than being merely indifferent to them, may have started at school. This is how I wrote about the distaste, retrospectively, in a poem published last year:

> Cha robh an t-suim bu bhige ghabhadh
> agam an cultur mòrdhalach
> ar nàbaidhean, am briathran sliobt',
> am fionnarachd, is sèisd nan càsd,
> a' ghibht cho priseil a thug iad dhuinn
> an cànain aca ùisneachadh,
> leabhraichean am bàrd a leughadh,
> direach mar gum buineadh sinn
> don nàisean-san, is sealbh againn
> air an dòigh 's am buadhan mòr'.
> B'e seòrsa marbhadh-fhaireachdainn
> a bh'annsa a' bhreislich aithghearr sin
> a bheireadh dìochuimhne gheàrr
> dhan a' bhròn dho-fhaothachadh,
> gum bu thràillean ciosnaicht', maslaicht' sinn.
>
> Bha goilean mo cho-nàiseantach
> cho tachdt' le còmhradh fòirneartach
> nan srainnsearan 's nach fhaodadh diog
> den cànain fhèin a thighinn àsda.
>
> Ach bha mi eòlach mar bho thùs
> air meud ar n-eadar-dhealachaidh,
> mar sin cha deach mo mhealladh fhìn
> le brìodalachd ar n-uachdaran.
> Thuig mi gun do chàiricheadh
> orm dàn gun bhreug-rèiteachadh,
> gur dìon is deuchainn e maraon,
> mo bhreitheamh is mo threunlaoch e,
> gur ann ro chùirt an fhacail fhìor
> a sheasas mi air latha a' bhràth.

I wasn't the slightest bit impressed
by the glorious culture of
our neighbours, their polished words,
their coldness, their obsession with class,
the inestimable gift
they made to us of using their language
and reading their poets, just as if
we could be part of their nation,
their customs and their victories.
That dizzying dream was a sort of
anaesthetic that could help us
briefly forget the unrelieved
pain of knowing we were trapped,
humiliated, deprived of freedom.

The mouths of my own people were
stuffed so full of foreign words
that not a syllable
of their own tongue could get out.

But I knew from the start
how different we were,
our rulers' beguiling words
had no attraction for me.
I knew mine was a fate
that excluded compromise,
at once a trial and a shelter,
a champion and a judge,
that I'd appear on the last day
before the court of the true word.[5]

The overall effect was of a double exclusion. Uncertain of my own Scottishness, I found myself at the edge of a community which was denied valid cultural expression, and I suffered their colonisation as if at one remove. Whatever art was, whatever crucial functions it might perform, none of it concerned my own place and experience.

The Catholicism I was brought up in was profoundly Philistine. It gave no value to art or artistic endeavour. Art was even demonized. At home, television and reading were censored. My mother expressed her concern openly when my sister read Nietzsche or I read Baudelaire. Beethoven and Mozart were acceptable, Wagner and Mahler not. Writers from strongly Catholic and strongly Calvinist backgrounds in Scotland have this in common, that for both the urge to create is a source of tremendous guilt.

IV

In this terrifying world everything – school, home, church, available or sanctioned television, music and books – presented a horrible uniformity.

One of the Jesuits would visit our house on Friday nights and debate with my mother the relative status of women's and men's souls, or inform her that she was permitted to wear make-up only in order to retain the affections of her spouse. A teacher made it clear to us that the madness and suicide of Joyce's children were more or less direct consequences of his rejection of the church and of the dreadful things he wrote in his books.

But there was a crack in this edifice, a fissure light could get in through and which, if I succeeded in making it big enough, might even offer a possibility of escape. As with so many other things, it was probably my sister who sowed the first seeds when, on a family outing to Loch Lomond, she piped up from the back of a stiflingly hot car: 'Dad, don't you think that if Scottish people are so bad at expressing their feelings, it may be because they're speaking the wrong language? That they shouldn't be speaking English at all, but Gaelic?' The language was not taught at my school, and the only people I had come across who might speak it, and who certainly never did so in my hearing, were a neighbouring family of rigid Presbyterian observance whose son was never allowed out on the street to play on a Sunday. And yet the existence, somewhere in this environment, impalpable but tantalising, of another language mooted a possibility of redemption. If this world could be described, could be experienced in other words, maybe it could be made into a different world. I could reinvent it.

Of all descriptions of the discovery of Gaelic by Scottish writers, that of the novelist Tom MacDonald, alias Fionn MacColla, is the one I can identify most closely with. Merely by murmuring a few words in Gaelic in the young boy's presence, his father

> caused the whole of my personal predicament and that of my contemporaries to become devastatingly clear ... *it was so inevitable that it seemed I had always known it.* ...
>
> The Proper language (known at some time or other as English) was completely foreign to my soul and sensibility, having a cramping effect, an effect of making shallow and artificial. I loved by contrast our language (nowadays known as Scots or Lallans) in which I felt my soul and sensibility free to move about and express themselves – *almost* to the full. Therein lay the crux. I had been conscious of the Proper language *as more totally foreign to me than the mere speaking of Scots as my first and loved language would have explained.*
>
> That postulated therefore that there must be somewhere another language capable of naturally doing to the *full* what Scots did certainly, but apparently *not quite to the full.* In other words I realised that Scots pointed to and implied another language which was *ours* too, but within which we should be able as it were to bathe and disport our sensibilities and this time completely and comprehensively to the uttermost that was in us.

My own discovery had none of the inevitability which MacColla celebrates so eloquently. If anything, the existence of Gaelic was an incredible piece of luck I could never have banked upon.

We often made family outings to the Trossachs, a kind of Highlands in miniature made up of lochs and hills in an enchanting setting some 40 miles north of Glasgow. There I was confronted with my inability to speak the landscape. It was such a strange experience to stand at the concrete, waist-high viewfinder, to trace summits on the horizon all around, saying 'That is . . . that must be . . .' and then to have to stop, because I could not pronounce the Gaelic names. Already, given the displacement my forebears, both Scottish and Irish, had suffered, I was fascinated by what it must feel like to inhabit a region where one's family had been for generations back, to have a bond with the land on which one lived. But here was an alienation that went beyond my own predicament. There are few countries in Europe where the placenames are not just impervious, but unpronounceable to the inhabitants. Language change has made the Scots foreigners in a part of their own land, like American frontierspeople confronted with bewildering toponyms in Indian tongues, incomprehensible to them and destined to disappear.

Gaelic, then, would not just allow me to reinvent my own sad world, it would enable me to speak my landscape, to speak to it. But the path by which I acquired the language was an unusual one that again makes me unrepresentative (in a way I suspect all individuals are). From the Jesuits I escaped to Cambridge, academic success providing an impeccable alibi for putting as much distance as I could, at the earliest possible date (I was not yet eighteen), between family, church and myself. At Cambridge two weekly essays and attendance at supervisions were the price to be paid for being left alone, and one that caused me little difficulty. I made the right noises, yet was left strangely cold by this forced acculturation into English ways. Indeed, what I was able to read of Verlaine, Rimbaud and Baudelaire seemed much more relevant than Keats or Browning to the recent torments of a Catholic adolescence.

By the end of three years, I understood exactly which saint had presided over my translation to Cambridge. It is one of the oldest stratagems of colonial powers to weed out promising individuals among the subject races and assimilate them to its own cultural norms, while concealing from them as long as need be the fact that they will never really belong, but will always in some way be second class citizens. So there was no question of my proceeding along this path to lucrative employment in London. At the same time, Glasgow was still too much like a bad dream I had just wakened from for me to want to return. And so I set out for Italy, for a break that should have lasted two years and in fact lasted eleven.

From journal entries at the time it is quite clear that I knew exactly why I wanted to go abroad. I needed to escape from the English language, to relativise it so that it would be no more my first or native language than French or Italian or German. Scotland did not offer me this possibility, because nowhere there could I find an integral linguistic or cultural world that was not compromised by English infiltration. It would be impossible for me to neutralise the forced acculturation I had undergone there, while in Italy it could and did happen.

It is very hard to convey in words what the experience of acquiring another language is like. If I had to sum it up in a single word, I would say that it involves a kind of relaxation. The mind has to become like soft wax so that it can receive and retain the most fleeting aural impressions. At the same time, one has to be something of a chameleon, to possess qualities which would be associated with the astrological sign of Pisces, of soaking up emotional and intellectual atmospheres like a sponge. It is useful to have a sufficiently ephemeral sense of the self to be taken over, briefly but perilously, by the selves and preoccupations of others. During a period of nearly a year, when I taught at the University of Bari in southern Italy, I spoke almost exclusively Italian because I disliked the two or three English people I had been introduced to and had little desire to communicate with them or spend time with them. This was, I think, the period when I spoke Italian best and was furthest from English.

V

I began studying Gaelic while riding on the backs of extremely bumpy buses in Rome. It would have been impossible for me to make any headway with pronunciation without direct contact with native speakers, and this I got almost exclusively on a three-month stint as dishwasher in a hotel in Skye. Nearly 16 years have passed since that summer, and the hotel, run by three spinsters and with a distinguished and deserved reputation for excellent cuisine, has long since closed. Incipient baldness and nostalgia for student life made for grim evenings as I bent over the sink. But there were compensations. At midnight, in June, there was so much light outside that I could read a book while lying on the grass. Across the bay the ridge of the Cuillins was silhouetted against the setting sun, like gapped, clenched and serrated teeth into whose maw the planet plunged. After rain, the gabbroid slopes would gleam like dragonhide. Looking southwards on clear days, I could make out Soay and even the dim scarf of Canna laid across the waters. My imagination peopled it with daffodils and crossroad madonnas, for it is a Catholic island.

The eldest of the spinsters read to me in the evenings and had me repeat, flying into rages when I could not reproduce her own dark liquid consonants. Her voice had endless resonances, and her reading of poetry had the grandeur of a world famous opera singer performing a scene for dramatic soprano. I found it impossible to tell which richnessess were Gaelic and which her own. Her sister spoke a fascinating cocktail of Gaelic and Scottish English over the phone. When I came home in the small hours from some dance, my mentor would be waiting for me by the fireside, her asthma easing off, and would laugh with satisfaction as I recited the list of my partners. Many of them were up from Glasgow for the summer, and she would connect them to fathers and cousins, or to a grandfather remembered for an enormous fart made during the Sunday service.

I understood these connections and realised I was being made at home. I cannot accept it was mere imagining on my part to feel that, late and unexpected and however inadequate, she had found in me the pupil to whom certain things could be transmitted, things that did not stop at the Gaelic language (though she herself had a first class degree in Celtic). And I believe I absorbed them, even though I have still to find a means of expressing them. This is a period of my life I have not yet written about. I wrote some poems in English there, and planned a long poem about coming back to Scotland from Italy and becoming a Gaelic writer. Since for many years these two things struck me as impossible, as things I was never going to do, I could not see my way to writing the poem.

I first got to grips with Gaelic through translation, in both directions. One project was to put the whole of Sorley Maclean's *Dàin do Eimhir* into Italian, and this I did, even succeeding in publishing a small number of lyrics in an Italian literary magazine.[6] There is no better way of coming to grips with a poet's work, of dismantling and reassembling the very fabric of each lyric, than to translate it, and in the process I became aware of the very different weighting, energy and semantic value of superficially equivalent terms in the two languages.

Working in the other direction was a more daunting prospect, and I made my first attempt during a Christmas vacation, in a westward facing room high on the eighth floor of a nondescript block of flats in the outskirts of Rome. I put four lyrics by Greek poets into Gaelic: three by Constantine Cavafy, and one by Yannis Ritsos. I worked from Italian translations, published face to face with the Modern Greek originals, which I could check although I could not read them fluently. The process thus excluded English and indeed, for a long time some of my most characteristic mistakes in Gaelic were syntactical patterns taken over, not from English, but from Italian. The Ritsos poem is particularly beautiful and, I think, was a good epigraph for a new poetic career:

Ag èirigh gu cabhagach airson an doras fhosgladh,
leig i às a' bhascaid le iteachain an fhuaigheil,
gan sgaoileadh fon bhòrd, fo na cathraichean,
anns na h-oisnean bu mhi-choltaiche:
fear, eadar an dearg 's an t-òr-mheas, an gloine an lampa;
fear eile, còrcair, am bonn an sgàthain;
am fear sin òr-bhuidhe – co às a thàinig e?
Cha robh riamh iteachan òr-bhuidhe aice.
Dh'fheuch i a glùn a lùbadh, gus an tional fear seach fear,
gus a h-uile rud a sgioblachadh mun d' fhosgail i an doras,
ach dh'fhairtlich e oirre. Bhuail iad uair eile.
Stad i gun ghluasad, eu-comasach, a gàirdeanan ri taobhan.
Nuair a chuimhnich i an doras fhosgladh, cha robh aon duine ann.

Co-ionann, uime sin, ris a' bhàrdachd?
Co-ionann dìreach ris a' bhàrdachd?[7]

Here is an English translation of my own Gaelic:

Getting up quickly to open the door
she dropped the reels of thread from the sewing-basket,
scattering them under the table, under the chairs,
in the most unlikely corners:
one, between red and orange, into the light bulb;
another, purple, deep inside the mirror;
that golden one – where did it come from?
She had never possessed a reel of golden thread.
She tried to bend down to collect them one by one
and tidy it all up before opening the door,
but it was useless. They knocked again.
She stood unmoving, helpless, her hands at her sides.
When she remembered to open the door, there was nobody there.

Is that what poetry's like?
Is that precisely what poetry's like?

I remember rushing into the sitting room in our flat in Rome and insisting that the Italian friends who were visiting should listen to the Gaelic rhythms I had produced, even though they could understand nothing of them. I sent the translations off to Derick Thomson, editor of *Gairm*, without delay, because I felt that if I held on to them I would lose my nerve and never do anything with them. His reply arrived on a Saturday morning, and I kept the letter in the back pocket of my trousers until Sunday night because I was so nervous about opening it. When I did, it did not, as I feared, accuse me of desecrating a language not my own and warn me never to trouble him again. On the contrary, Derick pointed out a few grammatical errors, suggested some improvements, and offered to print the translations in the next number of the magazine.

I was hooked. I went on to translate Anna Achmatova, working from Carlo Riccio's fine Italian translation, and Tadeusz Rozewicz from Polish, using my own rough English versions. However, it was not until some four years later that I felt able to produce original work of my own in Gaelic. Again, Derick Thomson was involved. He had commissioned a critical article from me on a nineteenth-century poet, and when my draft was returned it was so full of mistakes (I had done very little work with Gaelic that autumn and winter) that I felt incensed, and determined to show him, and myself, that I was capable of better.

The poems themselves came on a deliciously warm and sunny Edinburgh Sunday, while I was at a quartet concert at the Danish Institute with an Italian friend. It felt most peculiar to be wandering around Edinburgh in one's shirt sleeves so early on in the year, as it was only April. As I listened to Nielsen's music, ideas began to group themselves in my head. Realising this was not one poem, but a sequence of poems, I made some notes on the edge of the programme, whether in Gaelic or English I do not now remember. We spent the rest of the afternoon wandering from park to park and dozing on the grass, as the ideas firmed themselves in my mind, and that very evening I sat down at my Amstrad to sketch out the poems. There had originally been six, but one interposed itself in a most unexpected way between the third and fourth, and an extra one at the end brought the total of the cycle to eight.

VI

So that is the story of how I came to be a Gaelic poet and, although I have sometimes felt very confident about the quality of what I write and the importance my poems have for a wider audience than myself, there are of course also times when doubt takes over and I feel that only other people will be able to tell me if what I do has any value, and perhaps not for quite some time to come. My talk may have seemed anecdotal, too personal and even naive, but don't be misled. I am aware of the political and cultural implications of what I have said, but it seemed more useful and more modest to give you the raw material and let you reach your own conclusions. I am sure you will be able to offer different and equally valuable interpretations on my own rather peculiar story.

Perhaps the best way to finish is with another poem, in a very traditional mode, a love poem to the Gaelic language, entitled 'Mànran', that is, 'Lovetalk'.

Thusa, mo chànain
(is tha mi gun fhios
am fear no boireannach thu),
dè an sgeul seo, ràbhanach is daor,
san deach mo ribeadh?
Dè an rathad cagarach is cam
ris am bean do shàil cho aotrom
's gur gann gu lean mi thu?
Dhearbh iad orm gu robh thu aosd'
ach chuir t' òige fo gheasaibh mi.
Fhuair mi plathadh de do loinn
nach diochuimhnich mi gu bràth:
cas as lùthmhoir' chuirt' ri talamh,
deagh-chruth cluaise, slios is glùin.
Foillsich dhomh do dhùthaich,
ceadaich dhomh do ghràsan,
ann ad fhàrdaich adhair is ciùil
air bruaich fharsaing m' inntinne.

You, my language
(and I don't know
if you are a man or a woman),
what's this dear and complicated story
you've mixed me up in?
What's this whispering, twisted road
your foot touches so lightly
I can scarcely follow you on it?
They told me you were old,
but your youth enchanted me.
I got a glimpse of your beauty
that I can never forget,
the supplest foot that ever touched earth,
fine-modelled ear and thigh and knee.
Open up your country,
concede your beauty to me,
in your home of air and music
on my mind's broad hillside.[8]

Edinburgh, March 1992.

Notes to Chapter 10

1. Christopher Whyte (ed.), *An Aghaidh na Siorraidheachd: Ochdnar Bhàrd Ghàidhligh/In the Face of Eternity: Eight Gaelic Poets* A bilingual anthology (Edinburgh 1991). The poets featured are Meg Bateman, Myles Campbell/Maoilios Caimbeul, Anne Frater, Fearghas MacFhionnlaigh, Aonghas MacNeacail, Catriona NicGumaraid/Catriona Montgomery, Màiri NicGumaraid/Mary Montgomery and Christopher Whyte.
2. Dómhnall MacAmhlaigh/Donald MacAulay (ed.), *Nuabhàrdachd Ghàidhlig/Modern Scottish Gaelic Poetry* (Edinburgh 1976). The poets featured are Somhairie MacGill-Eain/Sorley Maclean, Deòrsa Caimbeul Hay/George Campbell Hay, Ruaraidh MacThòmais/Derick Thomson, Dòmhnall MacAmhlaigh/Donald MacAulay and Iain Mac a' Ghobhainn/Iain Crichton Smith.
3. Christopher Whyte, *Uirsgeul/Myth,* Gaelic poems with English translations (Glasgow 1991), pp. 2–5.
4. Alasdair Gray, *Lanark: a life in 4 books* (London 1982: first published 1981), p. 243.
5. Christopher Whyte, 'Eachdraidh-Beatha/ Life Story' in *Cencrastus* 40 (Summer 1991), pp. 11–13.
6. Fionn MacColla, *Too Long in this Condition (Ro fhada mar so a tha mi)* (Thurso 1975), pp. 54–55.
7. Gaelic first published in *Gairm* 123 (Samhradh 1983), p. 259.
8. Christopher Whyte, *Uirsgeul/Myth,* pp. 62–63.

11. AN T-ANAM MOTHALA/THE FEELING SOUL

Nuala Ní Dhomhnaill

Unlike Christopher Whyte, I don't wear three different hats; I am not academic. As the fox said to the donkey in the West Kerry folktale, –'ní haon scoláire mise is ní háil liom a bheith'. The last time I was ever in an exam situation was when I was doing my driving test, and it was so nerve-racking that I swore a solemn oath that I would never willingly put myself in such a position again. I do have the discipline of about 20 years of writing poetry behind me, but as poetry is nothing if not the delineation of the human soul, and this delineation occurs through the medium of each particular poet's skin and nerve endings and the invisible antennae with which she picks energies out of the air, and from the ground, and transforms them into the humanly accessible form of sound patterns on a page, then I have no choice but to have to speak from the personal.

I suppose I could call myself a third generation cultural nationalist. My grandfather, a native Irish speaker from An Clochán/Cloghane, Co. Kerry, when that area was still a Gaeltacht, if not a founder member of the Gaelic League (he was a little too young) was right in there in the fray nearly a hundred years ago. A former inmate of the Irish College in Paris, and a spoiled priest, he was unable to return home and face parental ire for a number of years but went to live in Cork city, where he was caught up in the IRB, the Gaelic League, was a Timire Gaeilge, did Celtic Studies under de Hindeberg, and was part of the great heave-ho of the time. Seán O Faoláin in his autobiography 'Vive Moi' calls him the only real revolutionary amongst his teachers and credits him for turning John Whelan into Seán O Faoláin. Graindeá subsequently became a School Inspector and was so disgusted by what happened during the Civil War that he never breathed a word about his youthful activities to any of his four sons. He was a member of the Cork Irish Language Mafia. Although his wife had no Irish, he spoke only Irish to his children. This was common enough behaviour amongst his peers and totally disgusted my mother, a Gaeltacht girl from a later generation who married into this circle of rather spurious cultural elitists. The story is still told about one of his like-minded friends, whose wife, though of little Irish, had spent her life doing her best to learn it. On her deathbed she asked for the pisspot, 'An áras', only to have her grammar corrected by her irate husband, 'An

170

t-áras, a bhean, an t-áras'. Those were the last words they ever spoke to each other. I mention this to put some forms of cultural nationalism in their right perspective, built as they are on a legacy of terrorized children and silenced women. I think one of the main things we in Ireland can tell the world about cultural nationalism is that if it is not strongly and firmly laced with whatever other forms of liberal philosophy as are in vogue at the time (and in our day these would mean Feminism, Ecology and Gay Rights, to mention but a few) the idealism behind it can very easily veer towards an appalling form of self-righteous fascism. What with the bad taste that a certain type of 'Gaeilgeoir' behaviour has left in our mouths, it is very difficult to conceive that at the turn of the century the learning of Irish was part of a genuinely empowering and liberating movement for all Irish people, as it can become again, as increasingly it is seen as a civil right, and not a burden imposed from above.

Probably in partial reaction to the idealism of the generation that went before them, my father and most of his brothers studied medicine. He met my mother, also a doctor, and jobs in Ireland being, as usual, impossible they set off on 'an bád bán' the emigrant ship, to England, where I was born and given the mythomanic name Nuala in a house, 406 Leach Lane, St. Helens, Lancs. which bore the equally improbable name of 'Banba', the second of the three ancient mythological names for Ireland. I never found out what the locals made of the name, or what they thought it might mean, though for all the world it must have sounded like a class of deer, a female form of Walt Disney's 'Bambi', perhaps. We still spoke Irish in the house in England, and a relation of my mother's, Noreen Keevane, was even brought over as an Irish speaking nanny, from about the time I was two years old, so I know that I had at least a passive knowledge of Irish from a very early age. Indeed my next sister, Neasa, arrived from England aged four with only one phrase of English to her name: – 'Mammy's car', the Irish word for car 'gluaisteán' having been too much of a mouthful for her to manage. When, after eight years in England, my father applied for and got a job as a surgeon in Co. Tipperary, North Riding, he jumped for it. He was fed up of the sheer racism of England, of the constant jokes about his name Seamus = shame us (this was in the days before Seamus Heaney made the name fashionable). My mother didn't want to leave at all. She was perfectly happy in England, ensconced as senior partner in her own practice, and gloriously happy in the pursuit of her great natural talent, the detection, diagnosis and healing of serious disease. In Ireland, subsequently, she was debarred from her own profession because of the so-called Marriage Ban, and once, on a trip to Lourdes in her medical capacity with the diocesan pilgrimage, found when she applied for a passport, that she had to get her husband's permission to leave the country. This, to a woman who had hitherto always gone by her maiden name, in good Gaeltacht fashion (does anyone remember Peig Sayer's married name?) was the last straw. The midlands, she was convinced, were aptly named the Doldrums, the Horse Latitudes

of Ireland. And so we were this Irish speaking family in the Gaeltacht of
North Tipperary, and very much 'éanlaithe isteach', – blow-ins. It is not
the most socially satisfactory position to find yourself in, as a child. My
friends would call to our door, and when my father addressed them in
Irish, they would run for their lives. That was often the very last I saw of
them. Know your friends, indeed.

What really ruined me for Tipperary, though, and subsequently for
everywhere else in Ireland, was that before we came to live there, in the
period of uncertainty about whether to come back or not, I was fostered
out to my aunt's house in Corcha Dhuibhne, the Dingle Gaeltacht.
Cathair an Treantaigh, or Cahiratrant, the village in which she lived, was
a world apart. Though ostensibly everyone could speak English, I could
understand their Kerry English no more than they could understand my
Scouse accent. I remember being at the table once and being thirsty and
calling for 'milk, milk' in my Lancashire accent and nobody paying the
slightest attention to me. Then I used the Irish word for it 'bainne' and
low and behold, it appears before me. This thing works, I decided, and
never looked back. I remember another day I was walking up the village
and I met an old man, Jeacksaí O Shea, coming down. 'Ce leis tu?' he
asked 'who do you belong to?', which was the traditional way of asking
my name. I bristled, and pulling myself to my complete height of five-
years, declared 'Ní le héinne mé. Is liom féin mé féin'. (I don't belong to
anyone. I belong to myself.) How I know that story at all, is that it went
around the village like wildfire and is still said back to me, even after an
interval of 35 years, especially when I have done something which is considered a bit 'bold' or 'too independent'. What I experienced in Corcha
Dhuibhne then can only be described as an atavistic reaction. I felt a
great sense of relief, a sense of belonging, of being a link in a long familial chain, something which had definitely been missing on a Lancashire
coalfield. I used to sit on a ditch, with my cousin Betty, and have her name
out to me all the townlands we could see from our vantage point: 'Fán,
Cill Mhic a' Domhnaigh, Cathair Boilg, Baile an Chóta, Cill Uraidh,
Baile an Liaigh, Com a'Liaigh, Imileach Lach, Baile Treasna, Rath
Fhionáin' . . . and so on, a marvellous litany of sonorous phrases. This I
used to make her do again and again, until I knew them all by heart. She
used to look at me as if I had two heads. I did. One head, still caught up
in Lancashire English and the other, in Irish, growing daily in strength
and depth and resonance. This initial language experience of Corcha
Dhuibhne imbues everything I have ever written and is maybe best
expressed in an early poem which I wrote when I came back to live in
Corcha Dhuibhne after being abroad for seven years.

I will read it in English first, to give an idea of the meaning of the poem.
The rough translation, or crib, is by myself, and though I have no preten-
sions to it being a literary artifact, it may help people with little or no Irish
to understand the particular gestalt of sound and image which is the
original.

I mBAILE AN tSLÉIBHE

I mBaile an tSléibhe
tá Cathair Léith
is laistíos dó
tigh mhuintir Dhuinnshléibhe;
as san chuaigh an file Seán
'on Oileán
is uaidh sin tháinig an ghruaig rua
is bua na filíochta
anuas chugam
trí cheithre ghlún.

Ar thaobh an bhóthair
tá seidhleán
folaithe ag crainn fiúise,
is an feileastram
buí
ó dheireadh mhí Aibreáin
go lá an Mheithimh,
is sa chlós tá boladh
lus anainne nó camán meall
mar a thugtar air sa dúiche
timpeall,
i gCill Uru is i gCom an Liaigh
i mBaile an Chóta is i gCathair
Boilg.

Is lá
i gCathair Léith
do léim breac geal
ón abhainn
isteach sa bhuicéad
ar bhean
a chuaigh le ba
chun uisce ann,
an tráth
gur sheoil trí árthach
isteach sa chuan,
gur neadaigh an fiolar
i mbarr an chnoic
is go raibh laincisí sioda
faoi chaoire na Cathrach.

IN BAILE AN tSLÉIBHE

In Baile an tSléibhe
is Cathair Léith
and below it
the house of the Dunleavies;
from here the poet Sean
went into the Great Basket
and from here the red hair
and gift of poetry came down to me
through four generations.

Beside the road
there is a stream
covered over with fuchsias
and the wild flag
yellow
from the end of April
to mid-June,
and in the yard there is a scent
of pineapple mayweed or
camomile
as it is commonly known in the
surrounding countryside,
in Cill Uru and in Com an Liaig
In Ballinchouta and in
Cathairbuilg.

And one day
in Cathair Léith
a white trout leapt
out of the river
and into the bucket
of a woman
who had led her cows
to water there;
a time
when three ships came sailing
into the bay
the eagle was still nesting
on the top of the hill
and the sheep of Cathair
had spancels of silk.

This feeling of being 'istigh liom féin', – bien dans ma peau – the for me rare and wonderful state of not being out with myself, was something I always associated with Corcha Dhuibhne, and was not at all the situation with which I lived in Nenagh. My Granny came to live with us, and she being of the 'spare the rod and spoil the child' persuasion, and the effect of a few early mutual run-ins being that I quickly learned that my mother would always take her side against me, I kept my head down, my mouth mostly shut, and my nose firmly stuck in a book. I don't really remember which of the two languages, Irish or English, we spoke in the house. Come to think of it, we didn't seem to speak either of them. As far as I can make out, we seemed to converse mostly in proverbs. Now a proverb in Irish still has a psychic momentum which its equivalent in English has long since lost, and my granny would sit in the corner firing them to left and right like brickbats;

> 'ní féidir ceann críonna a chur ar cholainn óg'
> 'ní thagann ciall roimh aois' . . .

and to be sure, none of them were complimentary to us youngsters, who were according to her, spoiled solid and full of badness and uproarious high spirits or 'teaspy' . . . and of course, 'teaspach gan dúchas is deacair é a iompar'. The only way you could learn to survive this constant barrage of proverbs was to learn to back answer her, pronto, with one that meant the opposite. This made for developing considerable presence of mind and speed of repartee and very good Irish but it was not exactly inducive to what would now be called 'meaningful conversation'. One of her all time favourite sayings was 'Muileann muilte Dé go mall ach muileann siad mín mín', 'the mills of God grind slowly but grind exceedingly fine'. Maybe I was just terrified of her, or was a small child with more imagination than was good for me, but I used to entertain this particularly horrible Hieronymous Bosch-like vision of all the poor naked people being ground down between these huge 'bróite muileann' or quern-stones. I think that it was as a way of finally exorcising this vision that, years later, I wrote the poem for my daughter Melissa, 'Dán do Mhelissa'. In it I postulate an alternative Eden, or what would have been written maybe, if a woman had been the author of Genesis, because in that case I don't think our first parents would ever have been put out, punished maybe, but in different, more subtle ways perhaps, but not banished from the garden:

DÁN DO MHELISSA

Mo Pháistín Fionn ag rince i gcroí na duimhche,
ribín i do cheann is fáinní óir ar do mhéaranta
duitse nach bhfuil fós ach a cúig nó a sé do bhlianta
tíolacaim gach a bhfuil sa domhan mín mín.

An gearrcach éin ag léimt as tóin na nide
an feileastram ag péacadh sa díog,
an portán glas ag siúl fiarsceabhach go néata,
is leatsa iad le tabhairt faoi ndeara, a iníon.

Bheadh an damh ag súgradh leis an madra allta
an naíonán ag gleáchas leis an nathair nimhe,
luífeadh an leon síos leis an uan caorach
sa domhan úrnua a bhronnfainn ort mín mín.

Bheadh geataí an ghairdín ar leathadh go moch is go déanach,
ní bheadh claimhte lasrach á fhearadh ag Ceiribín,
níor ghá dhuit duilliúr fige mar naprún íochtair
sa domhain úrnua a bhronnfainn ort mín mín.

A iníon bhán, seo dearbhú ó do mháithrín
go mbeirim ar láimh duit an ghealach is an ghrian
is go seasfainn le mo chorp féin idir dhá bhró an mhuilinn
i muilte Dé chun nach meilfí tú mín mín.

POEM FOR MELISSA

My fair-haired child dancing in the dunes
hair be-ribboned, gold rings on your fingers
to you, yet only five or six years old,
I grant you all on this delicate earth.

The fledgling bird out of the nest
the iris seeding in the drain
the green crab walking neatly sideways:
they are yours to see, my daughter.

The ox would gambol with the wolf
the child would play with the serpent
the lion would lie down with the lamb
in the pasture world I would delicately grant.

The garden gates forever wide open
no flaming swords in hands of Cherubim
no need for a fig-leaf apron here
in the pristine world I would delicately give.

Oh white daughter here's your mother's word:
I will put in your hand the sun and the moon
I will stand my body between the millstones
in God's mills so you are not totally ground.

But this sense of threat did not come only from the 'seanfhocail'. There
was very much a sense in our house that you could say whatever you

liked, so long as you didn't write it. Somehow the very act of writing, for a woman, was a terrible taboo. I mean writing the truth, not letters home from America, or anything like that. This may have been a general Gaeltacht thing. A very good example is the famous storyteller from West Kerry, Peig Sayers, who was collected from for over nine years by the full time folk lore collector, Joe Daly. Peig had an enormous vocabulary – something like 30,000 words, all active, and she knows how to use them too. Bhí caint láidir aici – she was wont to call a spade a spade, and yet, when Joe would be about to write this down from her she used to turn and say, 'Ná scrígh é, a Joe, Ná scrígh é'. It was one thing to say something, but it was a different thing entirely to write it. This is what gives rise, in her book 'Peig' which she dictated to her son, An File, Mícheál O Guithín, to a terrible 'holy Joe' sanctimoniousness, which has been the bane of school children ever since, and was utterly unlike the Peig Sayers that everybody knew. In the beginning of that book she speaks about how her mother was very fond of her when she was a child because she had lost nine children previously in stillbirths or miscarriages, attributed to the malevolent influence of the fairies 'na púcaí' who lived in a large rath on their farm in Cill Mhic a'Domhnaigh. The mother prevailed on her husband to swop the lease of the farm for another one back in Baile Bhiocáire in the parish of Dunquin, where Peig was born, and lived, much to the delight of her mother who doted on her 'chun gur dhóigh leat gur as mo chúl a d'eirigh an ghealach is an ghrian', which Brian McMahon translates, rather disingenuously I think, as 'you'd swear twas from my pole that the sun and the moon rose', when anyone who knows an iota about Hiberno-English, not to mention anatomy or for that matter astronomy knows that that is not the particular part of the human anatomy that the heavenly bodies shine out of. This was all perfectly in line with my mother's very serious advice to me, never to put in writing anything that I would not stand up to in a Court of Law. Not much room for manoeuvre there, as you might imagine, and hardly the kind of thing that was going to turn me into a budding writer. The Irish American novelist, Mary Gordon, in a recent article entitled 'I can't stand your books' speaks about this particular form of silence, a kind of camouflage, that Irish Americans took upon themselves, and about how emotionally barren and debilitating it is, but I think that this is not a purely American phenomenon, but a habit of mind that crossed the Atlantic from this side. What ever you say, say nothing. I was feeling very pressurized once when I was living in West Kerry by these sanctions on speech, and I determined to break the conspiracy of silence, and speak out against this web of Chinese whispers that was gradually enveloping me, and just because I was paranoic didn't mean they weren't out to get me! So I undertook to write a poem, as a charm, an 'ortha' a magic circle of sound to protect me from the demons and it came out as – *CLAONINSINT*. (I give first a rough translation, or 'crib' by myself, and then the poem in Irish.)

Claoninsint. (Falsely) Reported Speech

Oh we know, they said,
where you spent the summer, they said,
down in Crosshaven, they said,
what you did everyday, they said,
you went down on the strand, they said.
You didn't go swimming, they said.
Why didn't you go swimming?
Because it was too cold, they said,
too cold for your bones, they said
your bones that have gone soft, they said,
soft with wanton excess and downright hard living and sex
that you couldn't cope with, they said.

Claoninsint

Tá's againn, a dúradar,
cár chaithis an samhradh, a dúradar,
thíos i mBun an Tábhairne, a dúradar,
cad a dheinis gach lá, a dúradar,
chuais ar an dtráigh, a dúradar,
nior chuais ag snámh, a dúradar.
Canathaobh nár chuais ag snámh?
mar bhí sé rófhuar, a dúradar,
rófhuar do do chnámha, a dúradar,
do do chnámha atá imithe gan mhaith, a dúradar
bodhar age sámhnas nó age teaspach gàn dúchas
gur deacair dhuit é a iompar, a dúradar.

This terrible sense of threat, the awesome terror of breaking a taboo, a societal and familial sanction that is implied in everyday life, if never actually mentioned (In Ireland nothing is said directly, but the whole society functions on the nod and the wink and the half-said word) is a very real barrier to women developing as writers. Women in Ireland live in a symbiotic relationship with the family, the extended family, and the society in general. We exist deeply embedded in a mesh of relationships, familial and otherwise. This can prevent more than writing. Edmund White, the American novelist, when he was over here last year for the International Writers Conference said that even in America, 'you can't come out as a homosexual in the town that your parents grew up in'. Well, given the smallness of Ireland, and the interrelatedness of everyone on this small island, it is a problem even to come out as a heterosexual, not to mind writing about it. The constraints on women to hold their tongue are such that it is a wonder that any of us end up capable of writing in either of the two official languages.

In a way, though, I have always been more free to be myself in Irish. You could get away with murder in it. This goes back to my experience of boarding school, where I wrote a daily diary, mostly as a survival exercise.

My problem was that I was just not good boarding material. I was, if anything, at 12, already almost a fully-fledged recluse, and the enforced proximity of about 100 other girls, not to mention 40 nuns, was more than my
nerves could take, even at the best of times. Not that I got much sympathy for my problems, if anything boarding school was considered just
what I needed, 'to cut the corners' off me, the general atmosphere
towards what was seen as malingering being, that the only cure for it was
'cic maith sa tóin' or a good kick up the arse. I kept my diary in Irish, in
code, because there was no sense of privacy in the boarding school, but
the one nun who could be counted on to snoop in one's private papers
had no Irish, while the one nun who had good enough Irish to be able to
read them was a born lady, and could be counted on never to stoop so
low. This diary, a gradual accumulation of shilling copies all sellotaped
together, was my lifeline during my five years in boarding school, yet
when it came to writing poetry, I wrote it in English, for though the 18th
century Munster poets were my great joy, and I learned off by heart
reams of 'meadracht an amhráin' that was not on our school course, yet
the writing of poetry in Irish was not quite something intellectually cred-
ible. The first few poems I ever wrote, published in the school mag. – ele-
gies for Martin Luther King and Bobby Kennedy and the likes – were all
in English. I realized myself that they weren't bad, they were all right, but
why oh why did they seem so derivative of Austen Clarke, who wasn't
even a poet that I particularly liked. Then one autumn afternoon in the
boarder's study, literally in mid-poem I suddenly realized what was going
on. Austen Clarke's main drive had been to bring the rhyming patterns
and devices of Irish into English, – the 'aicil' and 'uaim', the alliteration
and half-rhymes. And that is exactly what I had been doing in English,
unconsciously echoing the rhetorical and poetic devices of Irish. It
seemed to me like a very stupid thing to be doing. Why wasn't I doing it
in the first place in Irish, where it belonged? So literally in mid-poem I
switched from English to Irish, and the result was immeasurably better,
so much so that the poem involved, 'Sabhaircíní i Samhain', was included
in my first collection, 13 years later, if only as an example of juvenilia.
Like my initial use of Irish as a communication method at the table in
Cahiratrant when I was five, the penny had dropped. This thing worked.
I never looked back. Nevertheless, what I was producing was still verse,
rather than poetry.

It took a major emotional catastrophe before that came on the scene.
When I was nineteen something so awful happened to me, something so
utterly traumatic that I have spent the remainder of my life trying to
make sense of it, and still cannot. The biographical details do not matter,
suffice to say that I fell through the meshes of the patriarchal mindset
which underlies all of Western discourse. Physically I responded by losing three to four stone, and developing a severe and chronic year-long
depression. I dragged myself through my final year in college in an utterly
dazed state, well and truly 'out of it'. John Montague, who was a recent

addition to the teaching staff at UCC at the time remembers me as 'a spooky kid' and once described me as looking like that character in the Ancient Mariner:

> her lips were red, her looks were free,
> Her locks were yellow as gold;
> Her skin was as white as leprosy,
> the Nightmare Life-in-Death was she,
> Who thicks man's blood with cold.

Nine months afterwards, almost to the day, as if some kind of strange gestation had taken place, during a few days of very high warm wind, as if the external elements were whipping up an internal storm, I produced a series of poems subsequently called the 'Mór' poems, which were to appear in Innti 3, and of which Seán O Ríordáin was to say in the *Irish Times*, 'beidh trácht orthu seo feasta'. I didn't know at the time that these had to do with the ancient story of Mór Mumhan, one of the large cluster of Sovereignty Myths which are central to the whole of Irish Language literature. In fact the poems could be described as an epiphany, though I did not know it at the time. As far as I was concerned, they were built about the character Mór, a 'cailleach' or old hag that I knew about all my life from the stories or Dinnsheannchas that I had been hearing since I was a child. It is not a coincidence that the townland that my mother was born in is known as Baile Móir, Mór's Home (if it were 'mór' meaning big it would be pronounced locally 'muar' which it is not.) The ancient structure known as Tigh Mhóir, and mentioned in the Annals of the Four Masters; (ní raibh géim bó le clos ó Thigh Mhóir go Caiseal Mumhan) was in nearby Dunquin. In fact the whole parish of Dunquin rejoices under the name of 'búndún Mhóire' or Mór's Backside! I still feel that it is quite extraordinary that when I fell out of the so called 'real world' or the reality principle, the straws that I clutched at in my desperation, 'le greim an fhir bháite', were stories from the Dinnsheannchas that I didn't even know I knew.

Now the word Dinnsheanchas was translated in Lane's Dictionary at the turn of the century, as the 'naming of high or holy places' and more recently in O Dónaill's dictionary as, quite boldly, topography, so much has the last bastion of Irish fallen to the egregious vice of the kind of all-consuming empiricism which states that if it moves, measure it and if you can't measure it, it doesn't exist. Dinnsheanchas, in my opinion, is the result of our emotio-imaginative involvement with the physical features and landscape of this island in which we live. In the oral tradition for many millenia, and in the written tradition for over 1,500 years we have been involved with this landscape, projecting outwards onto it our interior landscape, the 'paysage intérieur' which is the landscape of our souls. This has resulted in an enormous repertoire of stories about it, not just in the written dinnsheanchas, but the sort of thing a farmer taking a break from bagging potatoes in a field will tell you if you ask him what is that field called, or why is this road called such and such a thing. This is a living and vital knowledge and true for the whole length and breadth of the island, wherever there are people who have been in the place a long time. What you have is a covenantal relationship with the landscape. I take this rather biblical term from the work of Rosemary Radford Reuther who in her book 'Sexism and Godtalk' quotes from Vine Deloria's book about the native theological traditions of North America 'God is Red'; – 'the Indian lives on, not as an isolated individual, but in the collective soul of the tribe. The ancestors survive, not in a distant heaven unrelated to everyday life, but within the Earth in communion with present members of the tribe. The sense of the collective immortality of the tribe is a result of the tribe's covenantal relationship with its natural matrix. The bones of the ancestors are planted in the Earth as the seedbed from which the next generation of the tribe arises'. This is true of other parts of the world also, as Bruce Chatwin has shown for the aboriginal 'Songlines' of Australia. Now I'm not saying that this is the same as the Songlines, but you could consider Dinnsheanchas an Irish equivalent of the likes.

Another fact about the Dinnsheanchas that particularly fascinates me is that though some of the information is indeed historical; everyone knows where Benburb is, we know the exact spot of the Battle of the Boyne, nevertheless the vast array of the Dinnsheanchas stories are not historical at all, but mythological, or paranormal, telling in one way or another about an encounter between this world and what we call in Irish in a very matter-of-fact way, 'an saol eile' The Otherworld. Now as soon as you translate this into English a certain difficulty arises, because the English language itself, in its own post-Enlightenment way, has a built-in prejudice against this concept, and so it is very quickly reduced to 'fairies-at-the-bottom-of-the-garden' and 'where did you meet your last leprauchaun?' In Irish we are talking about the 'Sí', who are a different category altogether, at the same time more common or gardenplace, and simultaneously more serious a category of beings altogether. I often felt that if we had a database of all the Dinnsheanchas stories, a whole library of these meetings between the two worlds, that what we would have is a picture of our collective soul, writ large. Now either you believe in something beyond the ego-boundaries or you don't believe, at that point it is a question of individual choice, but if you do believe in it then the whole area of Dinnsheanchas is a marvellous picture of our repressed soul, walking around the landscape before our very eyes. Of course, an apprehension such as this is not peculiar only to Ireland. In Mac Mathuna's edition of the 'Voyage of Bran' that I was reading by chance recently I came across a fascinating footnote:

> The process of symbolic mimesis is well documented in the old Irish stories.
> In Japanese tradition ascetic priests embark on two types of voyage, voluntary and involuntary. In the former, rather than the soul of the ascetic leav-

ing the body to travel to the otherworld, rather than a shamanistic experience undergone, the other world is projected by powerful symbolism on the landscape of our own world. If the man traverses the transferred landscape in mind and body it is tantamount to his soul travelling to the Otherworld as in a vision.

The way 'depth psychologists' go on about the subconscious you'd swear they had invented it. It is a little like us Europeans going on about Columbus discovering America. I know the native populations of the New World would have a completely different viewpoint on the matter. Likewise knowledge of the subconscious is not new in Ireland, in West Kerry even 'madraí an bhaile' (the dogs of the village street) know about the 'otherworld' and have evolved a delicate barking protocol for dealing with it! The narrative tradition of Dinnsheanchas is I think, a very valid and important way of dealing with the numinous. It is a very different tradition to that of conceptual thought, but that does not mean that very important and profound concepts and ideas are not deeply imbedded in it. Rather than a manipulation of ideas in a conceptual manner, such as thesis, antithesis, synthesis, and the likes, it is a way of playing with ideas which brings into play more than just the intellect, but other areas of the human organism, such as the heart and the imagination, as well.

If, as Hilary Richardson so aptly illustrated last night, our isolation on this island helped in the preservation of certain artistic motifs of great value from, say, the La Tène culture of Central Europe, long after they had died out in Central Europe, then likewise, the fact that Irish fell out of the dominant discourse of this island just about the time that the Enlightenment was taking off, has led to the preservation in the language of philosophical concepts, and even a complete mindset, which has been lost in the more developed major languages of Europe. I give as an example a story that I came across purely by chance in the Dept of Folklore, UCD, which happens to be about my own great grandmother, Léan Ní Chearna. The story is called 'Trí anam an duine' 'The three souls of the human being' and is told by a neighbour of ours called Seán O Cíobháin:

Trí Anam an Duine

Bhíos istigh sa leabaig im' chodladh theas i mBaile Móir agus pé rud a thug Eoghainín Fenton amach chonnaic sé mise ag gabháil amach as an dtigh.

(It was inside in the bed down south in Ballymore when whatever it was took Eoghaínín Fenton out, he saw me go out of the house.)

Ghlaoigh sé ar a bhean, Léan Ní Chearna.
'Hanamaindiabhal, a Léan', ar seiseann, 'tá stróc nó rud éigin ar Seán Tuohy. Féach taobh an tí síos é. Teir amach', ar seiseann, 'agus glaoigh air'.

(He called out to his wife, Léan Ní Chearna.
'My soul from the devil, Léan', said he, 'but there must be a stroke or something on Seán Tuohy. Look at him going down the side of the house. Go out',
he said, 'and call him'.)

Ach chonnaic sé a' casadh aníos aríst mé agus ag dul isteach 'on tigh. Níor
ghlaoigh Léan in aon chor orm. Ach bhíodar á reá liom lárnamháireach agus
ní chreidfinn in aon chor Eoghainín mura mbéad Léan á reá. Dúrtsa nár fhágas an leabaig ó chuas innti go dtí gur fhágas ar maidin í ach mé im'chodladh
go sámh.

(Then he saw me turning up the way again and going into the house. Léan did
not call out to me at all. The next day they were telling me this and I wouldn't
believe Eoghainín at all if Léan hadn't been telling it too. I said that I had not
left the bed from the moment I went into it until I rose up out of it in the morning, but that I had slept soundly all night.)

'Bíonn a leithéid i gceist' arsa Léan, 'agus do chuimhníos-sa air. Dá nglaofainn
an uair sin air', arsa Léan, 'd'fhanfadh sé ann go deo. Ach táim á chlos riamh
go bhfuil an duine ina thrí chuid. Tá an t-anam anáile ann, an t-anam mothála
agus an t-anam síorraíochta. Fanfaidh an t'anam síorraíochta ionnat go dtí go
gcailltear tú'.

('Such things do happen', said Léan, 'and I thought of it. If I had called out to
him then, he'd have remained out. I have always heard tell that the human
being has three parts, the breathing soul, the feeling soul, and the immortal
soul. The immortal soul remains with you until you die'.)

N'fheadar ab é an t-anam anáile nó an t-anam mothála domhsa bhí lasmuigh
agus mé féin im' chodladh. N'fheadar é sin.

(I don't know if it was my breathing soul or my feeling soul that was outside
when I was lying fast asleep. That is something I still don't know.)

Now how could Léan Ní Chearna, my great grandmother who was
completely illiterate, knew very little English and was ignorant in the
sense that Michael Hartnett said about his own grandmother:

ignorant, in the sense
she ate monotonous food
and thought the world was flat

how could she have known about something which is straight out of the
Táin (Cú Chulainn kills his armour bearer for waking him too suddenly)
and goes back as far as the Egyptian Book of the Dead, with its 'ba' soul
and its 'ra' soul etc? The answer is to be got in what I've just said, how
Irish, because of its very isolation, has been able to preserve things which
have got lost in mainstream discourse, and as in this case, preserved only
in the Gnostic tradition. In these days where a major problem is the can-
cerous growth of an Anglo-American monoculture which reduces every-

thing to a level of the most stupendous boredom the preservation of alternative mind-sets contained in minority languages such as Irish is as important to cultural diversity as the preservation of the remaining tropical rainforests is to biological diversity. Indeed, in these times where a major change of heart, a 'metanoia', a conversion to other values seems to be every moment more on the cards, if we are to survive at all as a species on this planet, then the reality of alternative mindsets, such as exists in Irish, is a very important reminder that yes, things can be different, and therefore the preservation of each so-called minority language, with its unique and unrepeatable way of looking at the world, is not just a necessity, but a question of sheer common sense.

12. IRELAND, BRITAIN, EUROPE: BEYOND ECONOMIC AND POLITICAL UNITY

Garret FitzGerald

The issue which this Conference is asked to address is how, at a time when there is a powerful momentum towards political and economic unity, can we simultaneously accommodate the resurgent national and ethnic identities clamouring for recognition and autonomy.

The States and regions of Europe have retained a powerful sense of their individual identities – not merely in the Eastern part of our continent where old identities, some of them long submerged, are currently being vigorously, sometimes violently, reasserted, but in the West also. For while membership of the European Community may have dulled old enmities, it has yet to emerge that it has anywhere weakened the strength of national or regional identities. To the extent that these identities have been undermined in the past half-century, this has been the product of American culture and of the growing international preeminence of the English language rather than because of anything in the development of the European Community. For my own part at least, my complaint would rather be that the Community, far from having had too *much* cultural influence, has unfortunately had too *little*; it has failed to halt or even to slow the pervasive Americanisation of all our societies.

Indeed I am not sure whether, left to myself, I would pose the cultural identity issue as being one of how a united Europe can accommodate national and ethnic identities. For it seems to me that in Western Europe, at least during the last four decades, this has been achieved with remarkable success. At this point only one national identity – that of England – and, so far as I am aware, *no* regional identity, has found any real difficulty with this process. While from time to time some States may have momentary problems with some particular aspects of the process of building a European Community, in general the member States work comfortably within this new framework.

Secondly the many regional identities in the Community also seem comfortable with it; indeed some of the regions seem happier working with the Community institutions than with their own national structures.

And finally, and perhaps a little surprisingly, most, though not all, national Governments, which might have been expected to be a little suspicious and uneasy about direct links between their regions and the Community institutions, seem quite relaxed about the way these Brussels-to-region links, which in some measure bypass Government, have developed. This seems true not only of States with decentralised structures like Germany, but even of France, with its strong tradition of centralisation. So far as I am aware – although I am prepared to be corrected on this – it is mainly in these islands that serious attempts have been made by national Governments to intervene between Brussels and the regions.

The fact that by and large the triangular relationship between regions, States and European institutions has turned out to be so relatively untroubled has for me been one of the surprises of the way the Community has developed.

Equally remarkable, perhaps, has been the fact that as the countries of Eastern Europe have recovered their freedom, or in some cases acquired it for the first time in many centuries, they have turned instantly to the Community seeking early membership of it without any apparent hang-ups about 'giving up' their new-won sovereignty.

It seems to me, therefore, that the problem is not so much one of how the Community can accommodate national and ethnic identities as one of how the Community can provide not merely a framework for the economic development of our Continent, but also a cultural and moral dimension that will enlarge the horizons of the parallel national and regional cultures. How, in other words, can the Community offer us an inspiration that will in some sense morally validate the decision to merge our economies while retaining our identities? What, in the end of the day, do our countries share in common, over and above a pragmatic recognition of the economic advantage of working together rather than separately? To what concept of Europe can its peoples, each with its extraordinarily powerful sense of its own identity, rally, giving to it some of the loyalty they have hitherto reserved for their own regions and States?

This question is inherently difficult to answer because the concepts with which one has to grapple in seeking such a rationale are much less easy to pin down in words than the economic issues involved, which lend themselves to both words and figures.

In attempting to sketch out some answers to these fundamental questions, albeit in a rather roundabout way, I should like to start by asserting unambiguously that economics, and indeed politics also, are merely means by which societies seek to achieve social and cultural ends; they are not ends in themselves. And this is obviously as true at the European level as at the national or regional level.

Let me start with the last of the questions I have just posed: to what concept of Europe can its people be expected to transfer some of the sense of identity and loyalty that they have hitherto directed towards their own nation, in the form of their national States?

There are some, I think, who would go so far as to deny such a possibility, believing that no entity beyond or above the nation or State can or should command any loyalty. I would answer this objection in several ways.

First, there is nothing inherently problematic about the focussing of senses of identity or loyalty at more than one level.

Thus we all have a primary loyalty to our own families, a secondary one to the area in which we have grown up and live, as well as the third, to our nation or State. Indeed within the second level there can again be several sub-levels – to one's village or town, to one's country and to one's region.

Moreover some of these loyalties are in practice often more strongly felt by many people than their national loyalty – loyalty to the family and, in Ireland especially, sometimes also loyalty to the locality.

In this context let me recall a survey of opinion carried out some decades ago in relation to industrial location in the Irish State. Asked whether they would prefer an industry employing 100 people in their own area or one employing 200 'some distance away' (which was defined as 6 miles or more), 96% opted for the lesser number in their own area, 2% for the higher number 6 miles or more away, and 2% were 'Don't knows'! To me that demonstrated dramatically the strength of local loyalties in Ireland and the extreme difficulty our people experience in extending more than a nominal, and what one might describe as 'non-operational', loyalty to anything as remote and abstract as the Irish State.

And, I have to add, that impression of intense 'localism' has been confirmed for me during my period in politics as I have observed so many of our people more concerned and exercised about having their own constituency 'represented' in Cabinet than about whether the most effective people are appointed to that body!

Let no one try to tell me in the light of my experience that people can cope with only one level of loyalty – viz. – to their nation or State; if that were in fact the only, or even primary, loyalty of Irish people, and if our State could as a result have been governed in the interest of its people as a whole rather than in a perpetual attempt to accommodate local interests seeking priority over the interests of the whole community, it would have been far better governed than in fact it has been.

But, it may be objected, even if there are such powerful local loyalties competing with loyalty to the nation or State, this does not mean that people can give their loyalty to any *higher* political level than their State, in which sovereignty is vested.

That brings me to my second point. The thesis about the unique role of the Sovereign State as the ultimate repository of final loyalty, is an historical accident and is of comparatively recent origin. In the mediaeval period people had no difficulty with a complex system of layers of loyalty – to their local lord; to *his* superior lord; to the King; in many parts of Europe to the Emperor also; and for much of the period to the Pope, who claimed and was often accorded temporal as well as spiritual dominion over rulers, a claim accepted by King John of England, for example, who paid homage to the Pope as his temporal lord in the early 13th century.

Of course such a system led to endless conflicts of loyalty and I hasten to add that I am not recommending it – with or without the Pope! I am merely making the point that the concept of different levels of loyalty, in contrast to the later concept of absolute sovereignty at one level, is one that people can cope with – and have operated.

I believe that the concept of absolute sovereignty originated with the absolute monarchies that replaced feudalism; later as the absolute power of the monarch became mitigated by the emergence of representative institutions, sovereignty shifted to democratic institutions, which for a period claimed a similar absolutism in the form of a demand for exclusive loyalty from their citizens and the unfettered right to use war as an instrument of policy against the peoples of other States, whether democracies or otherwise.

This concept of absolute sovereignty has been moderated since the end of the last century by the evolution of international institutions like the International Court of Justice in the Hague and by Conventions such as the Geneva Convention, and then by the emergence of the League of Nations and its successor institution, the United Nations. To the UN all States on entry cede a considerable share of their sovereignty by accepting the right of the Security Council to enforce peace with the aid of military units that can be levied compulsorily from member States.

The idea of absolute sovereignty has thus long since disappeared, and in face of the threat that now exists to the global environment even further inroads on sovereignty will have to be accepted. The issue to-day is what elements of sovereignty can be most usefully exercised at the level of States, which are the building blocks of the emerging global system, and what can most usefully be exercised at another level – including, most particularly in the case of our Continent, at the European level.

It is, perhaps, relevant to add that there have recently been signs of the emergence of a global regional system, through which the UN would exercise some of its functions, including perhaps regional peacekeeping functions. The manner in which the UN, the CSCE, the EC and WEU have worked together in handling the Yugoslav crisis in recent months may prove to be a harbinger of the way UN peace-keeping and peace-making will evolve through a regional structure in the period ahead.

It is against this background of an increasingly complex world political structure that I turn now more specifically to the European Community.

This Community was founded over 40 years ago by idealists from different and, until a couple of years previously, mutually hostile States. These men's primary objective was to exorcise for ever the horror of war from a Continent where a millennial fragmentation of peoples and cultures had combined with technological advances in weaponry to create a recurring and increasingly intense nightmare of genocidal violence.

These founders of the Community had a sense of a common European heritage that made them see this cycle of war as fratricidal.

There were, of course, other ancillary motives for the move towards European unity: fear of Soviet aggression and of American economic domination. But without the catalyst of the will to abolish war in Western Europe, there would have been no Community.

That the means employed to achieve this goal were economic rather than primarily political, was largely a matter of chance. Two of the first three attempts to achieve European integration were in fact in the political sphere: the establishment of the Council of Europe in 1950 and the attempt to create a common Western European Army in 1953. The Council of Europe survived in an attenuated form, but at that early stage many of its members – including Ireland and Britain – opposed integration, preferring a weaker co-operative relationship. And the attempt to integrate European defence in 1953 collapsed.

Meanwhile six countries had gone ahead on their own along an economic path towards integration and the resultant Coal and Steel Community of 1951 proved a success. Six years later that effort to secure European unity through limited economic integration was widened into a far more ambitious effort in the form of the Rome Treaty that established the European Economic Community.

In the 35 years since this latter Treaty was signed many have come to see the Community – which, after all, was known until quite recently as the European *Economic* Community – as a purely economic enterprise, one of interest to businessmen and farmers, but of little or no cultural significance, and providing no real focus for the kind of loyalty that local regions and nation States command. This view is, however, unhistorical and dangerously under-rates the motivation and significance of the whole European process. But from a practical point of view it has another undesirable consequence: it inhibits the emergence of grass-roots support for a democratisation of the European-level decision-making process.

For we should be quite clear that in terms of democratic control over the decisions of its Executive organs the present decision-making structure of the Community compares unfavourably with the domestic structures of its member States. There are good reasons for this: the founders of the Community knew that if they endowed the embryonic Community with a fully-democratic political structure from the outset, it would be strangled at birth by a whole range of vested interests which, fearing change, would use all their influence through the democratic process to frighten their politicians into abandoning such a revolutionary concept. For, let us recall, the national lobbies of industrialists and farmers and trade unions were for the most part totally opposed to the European idea at the outset; they all wanted to hold on short-sightedly to their own protected national vested interests.

This danger was guarded against by creating an independent

Commission which alone would have the power to initiate legislation; a Council of Ministers which after a period of some years would be able to take many decisions by a weighted majority; and a Parliament that would have only a consultative role. The weighted majority for decision-making would have the effect of frustrating the vested interests which, when decisions are taken by unanimity, can usually twist some Government's arm to say 'no'. Where there is majority voting this is clearly more difficult, especially because it gives every Government an alibi for not blocking action, because each Government can say: 'I was outvoted', or even: 'I would have been outvoted'.

Such a less-than-fully-democratic system was tolerable in my view during the period of this European Revolution – for it was a revolution – but as this process approaches effective completion, as, I believe, is now the case there is a clear need to move towards a democratically-controlled decision-making structure to administer and further develop over time the new European policy put in place over the preceding half-century.

Obstacles to such a democratisation of the Community institutional structure have, however, arisen from the decision by its founders at an early stage to choose the more effective indirect economic integration route rather than a direct political route towards European Union, and also from the fact that this whole process has taken much longer than they expected. (This delay has in large measure been because of De Gaulle's veto on the use of the majority voting system, which in effect lasted for 22 years, from 1965 until the Single European Act came into effect in 1987).

During this long period there was a marked decline in public understanding of the fundamental *political* purpose of the whole exercise – the Community coming gradually to be seen as almost exclusively economic in character. Of course the public recognises and welcomes the extraordinary economic benefits that the integration of member States' economies has brought about. But in the absence of a clearly visible political component the Community that has emerged does not command the kind of loyalty that people accord only to what they recognise as being a *political* structure – whether that structure be at the level of the nation State or at a regional or local level.

This absence of a sense of political loyalty to the Community is in turn reflected in the absence of strong public concern about democratic control of its activities. There is thus a danger that what was intended to become a democratic European polity that would command the loyalty of its citizens – just as at another level the people of a region extended loyalty to a State of which their region forms part – could remain what it necessarily was during the long transition period, viz. a not particularly democratic and primarily economic institution.

This raises the question as to whether at the European level there now exists a political content sufficiently inspirational to provide a focus for the kind of loyalty and even enthusiasm that is needed to give life and purpose to a dynamic political structure?

I believe that there is such a political content, but unhappily it is not yet sufficiently present to the minds of European citizens to provide an effective focus for their loyalty. I want therefore to use this opportunity to spell out a rationale for a European loyalty in which the peoples of this Continent can readily share.

This rationale lies, I believe, in the contribution Europe has been making during the past half-century to an emerging revolution in political thought which, as it develops, has, I believe, the capacity during the next century to change for the better the nature of world society. Most people who have lived through this period are unconscious of the nature of this revolution – but then this had been true of many such intellectual revolutions.

This one has five components that I can clearly identify – each of them contributing significantly to changing the way we look at the world. And four of these components are European in their origin. Let me identify them.

First, the emergence through the Council of Europe of a concept of human rights that transcends the sovereignty of States;

Second, the emergence through the European Community of a profound rejection of war as an instrument of policy (which is *not* quite the same thing as concern for the sacredness of human life), and the closely associated appearance of a 'zone of peace' in Western Europe;

Third, the abandonment by European States of colonialism and the substitution for it, in political rhetoric at least, of a commitment that the rich should *aid* the poor rather than *exploit* them;

Fourth, the growth in recent times of ecological consciousness through the Green Movement; this has created a new moral imperative at a global level.

The fifth revolution has been the challenge posed by feminism to the patriarchal norms that have prevailed throughout much of the world – notably, perhaps, in civilisations like ours which derive from the Indo-European culture.

Each of these five revolutions involves a radical reversal of traditional thinking.

Each of these revolutions is profoundly moral in its impetus. And only what is technically known as 'second-wave feminism' is non-European, with most of its roots in another Continent, North America.

Half-a-century ago none of these revolutionary concepts was conceivable as an idea that would inform the practical policy of governments.

Thus human rights were not then an issue in international politics.

War was then a normal – if increasingly apocalyptic – instrument of governments, including in particular, Governments in Europe; for some of these indeed, despite the post World War I creation of the League of Nations, war even seemed a *preferred* instrument in cases where it could be expected to yield a more decisive outcome than diplomacy.

And although from early in this century many colonial regimes were becoming more benevolent, these regimes nevertheless remained based on a fundamental unspoken assumption that European countries had a right to rule the world and to draw, where they could, substantial material benefits from the poorer countries they ruled or dominated.

And, finally, 50 years ago the ecological and feminist issues had not even been posed.

Let me take each of these in turn.

1. Human Rights Transcending National Sovereignty

The last half-century has seen the emergence of the European Convention on Human Rights, to which many European States have subscribed and to the Commission and Court of which the citizens of these States can apply for remedial action when their own courts have failed to protect their rights. In a much wider area than the more geographically circumscribed European Community these institutions transcend the sovereign power of governments. And, in part at least because of the lead given by Europe in this matter, e.g. through the introduction of a human rights clause into the Lome Agreement between half the developing world and the European Community, the UN is now starting to contemplate a re-consideration of its hitherto sacrosanct principle of refraining from intervention in the internal affairs of member States even when they commit gross breaches of human rights.

2. The European Zone of Peace

War as an instrument of policy remains such in many parts of the world and not least, as we have recently seen daily on our television screens, in a corner of Europe, the Balkans, that has yet to recover from the consequences of the later mediaeval Turkish conquest. But who now believes that States in *Western* Europe will ever again seek to settle disputes amongst each other by violence? And has not this beneficent virus shown signs of infecting much of north-eastern Europe at least; Hungary, Czechoslovakia and Poland, for example?

Moreover this rejection of war as an instrument of policy in Western Europe has, I believe, begun to spread from the realm of intra-European disputes to that of disputes external to Western Europe. For we cannot ignore the incomprehension, even incredulity, that British *enthusiasm* for the Falklands War – as distinct from the actual decision to resist aggression there by force – aroused in much of Continental Europe. Nor should we ignore the patent reluctance of European countries other than Britain and France to involve themselves more than marginally in the recent Gulf War – an attitude that evoked dismissive and contemptuous reactions from some *macho* British and American circles. Here we can see clear signs that in much of Continental Western Europe there is today less and less stomach for armed conflict, even when it can reasonably be presented as being in the cause of resisting external aggression – although this revulsion against war has yet to translate into an abandonment of the manufacture and sale of armaments.

This development, which I believe to be one of the greatest revolutions in world history, is a distinctively European phenomenon – deriving directly from the horrifying experience of the two European Wars in the first half of this century. For those wars will, I believe, be seen by later generations as the catalyst of a late 20th century Western European rejection of war as an instrument of policy.

The coincidence of this development with the abandonment by European governments of capital punishment – even in defiance of majority opinion in some countries – reinforces my belief that in recent decades we have witnessed in Europe, largely without realising it, the beginning of one of the most fundamental revolutions in human history, involving a rejection of State violence. And I believe that this revolution will ultimately (although perhaps not for a century or more), become a world-wide phenomenon.

3. Aid Replacing Colonial Exploitation

My third revolution is the replacement effectively within two generations, of colonial exploitation as a prevailing orthodoxy by acceptance of the *principle* of transfers from wealthier countries to poorer ones. I am not pretending that such aid is in any way adequate or even that much of it is well-directed. And I am not challenging the fact that in the case of many developing countries flows of aid are still more than offset by capital *out*flows to industrialised countries. I recognise also that much that is described as 'aid' still consists of armaments. Moreover much official government aid is 'tied' in a self-interested way – i.e. may be used only to purchase goods or services from the donor country.

I know all these arguments well. What I am interested in, however, is the revolution that has taken place in public *attitudes* to the relationship between rich and poor countries, and the pressures and constraints that this revolution has started to impose on government policies.

This shift, not merely in the emphasis but also in the *direction* of policy, has been primarily a European phenomenon. America's aid programme is extremely limited as a share of that country's GNP and is overwhelmingly strategic in motivation, most of it consisting of credits for the purchase of US armaments. The shift in public attitudes involved in the US case has thus been relatively small by comparison with the psychological revolution that has taken place in European public and political opinion in relation to this issue; there is indeed widespread opposition to development aid in the US. As for the other main industrial countries, until recently at least Japan has had a very limited aid programme, which is overwhelmingly regional in orientation, and the USSR, when it existed, was even more niggardly than the US, in the credits it extended to developing countries, and just as militarily orientated.

Today a Europe shorn of almost every colony it ever possessed is *par excellence* – together with Canada – the principal provider of non-military aid to developing countries; some countries of the Protestant north of Europe, viz. the Netherlands and the Scandinavian States, allocate 1% or more of their GNP for this purpose.

Although some European Governments still practise forms of neocolonialism, and although none, perhaps, the Irish Government included, fails to protect in some respect its own commercial interests vis-a-vis low-cost competition from developing countries, no one in Europe now *defends* the exploitation of these countries for the benefit of wealthy industrial States. And, however inadequate the aid programmes may be, opposition to them in Europe is never expressed in terms of objections to such transfers *per se*, but rather in terms of such aid being useless in certain cases, or even harmful to the inhabitants of the recipient country.

In other words, the former prevalent un-selfconscious language of colonialism has been universally replaced in Europe by the language of philanthropy – partly, one must accept, in order to hide other motivations, but at a more fundamental level reflecting, I believe, a real shift in public attitudes.

This is as great, and as sudden a reversal of attitudes as has taken place in this same Continent with respect to war.

I should, perhaps, emphasise in respect of these last two revolutions; the rejection of war and the acceptance of the principle of transfers from the strong to the weak rather than the other way around; that these two processes have certainly not been completed or fulfilled. What I am suggesting is merely that they have *begun*; that where they have taken root they are *irreversible*; and that they are benevolent *infections*, the spread of which will ultimately prove as irresistible as the most potent plague.

4. The Ecological Movement and the Environment

The fourth major initiative that has emanated primarily from Europe in recent decades is the ecological movement, concerned with the preservation of the global environment. This is an issue which carried no resonance in the Soviet Union or Eastern Europe during the Communist period when industrialisation proceeded at the cost of appalling pollution that will take many years and many hundreds of billions of pounds to eradicate. Nor has Japan been actively concerned with these issues, which pose special problems for that country because of the high concentration of population in those parts of the islands of Japan that are habitable.

And so far as the United States is concerned, while many Americans are conscious of environmental issues, there seems to be relatively little enthusiasm at Government level in the USA to face these issues. Indeed in relation to the Rio de Janeiro Environmental Conference this summer, the United States is currently under strong pressure from Europe; pressure to which, I understand, it has begun to show some signs of sensitivity in recent weeks.

The identification of the preservation of the global environment as a fundamental moral issue has, I believe, been primarily a European achievement.

5. Feminism

The fifth revolution in political thought in recent decades has been the 'second-wave' of the feminist movement, but in this instance Europe cannot reasonably claim to have been the prime mover, for much of the impetus of the process of re-evaluating the relative roles of men and women in society has come from the United States.

It seems to me significant, however, that four of what appear to be the five major and fundamental shifts in political thought in the second half of the 20th century have emanated from multi-cultural Europe, which has shown in these matters an intellectual vitality foreseen by few in the aftermath of the Second World War.

Surely if one is seeking a moral dimension to European culture, and a focus of sentiment and loyalty amongst Europe's peoples towards an evolving European polity, it is in these contributions of Europe's to an emerging global political morality, however tentative and incomplete at this stage, that they are to be found.

I believe that as the new Europe comes to be seen by its peoples more clearly for what it already is in embryonic form, viz. the seat of a potential global revolution designed to give primacy to human rights, to the abandonment of force as a means of settling disputes between States, to a global re-direction of resources in favour of poorer regions of the world, and to a movement to save the global environment – it will gradually become a political reality, engaging the sentiments and loyalties of its inhabitants.

At present these elements of a future European policy are not being presented in this way to the peoples of Europe. Instead the political elements of the new structure are being described in limited, and to many people not particularly attractive, terms – as the development of a common foreign and defence policy – without ascribing any particular content to these policies.

What is needed now is the emergence of a much wider consciousness of the moral content of the European ideal that is reflected in the four revolutions in political thought which I have identified, and of the fundamental political role of the Community that has hitherto been obscured by the over-emphasis upon the economic elements in the integration process. Upon these elements there can be built a democratic political structure at the European level to which we can give part of our loyalty without diminishing in any way our sense of national and cultural identity.

Let me conclude on a somewhat different note. Our native cultures in this island, Irish and English, together with the Latin and Greek of our classical tradition and their modern descendants, the Slavic, Germanic, Baltic, Albanian language groups of Europe, and the Iranian and Indic languages of Southern Asia, are all descended from the same 6,000 year old source vis. the language of a people who lived in South Russia 6,000 years ago and made the crucial technological breakthrough of domesticating the horse. The languages of our Continent have thus come down to us through 250 generations of nomads and settlers in various parts of our Continent – each of these generations contributing some modification to their particular share of this linguistic inheritance, while passing on in their folk-lore, right down to the present century, memories of our common past.

Thus when in Irish I count 'aon, do' I could be speaking Danish; when I say 'tri, ceathair' I could be speaking Albanian; when I say 'ocht, naoi' I could be speaking Tocharian – an extinct language of Central Asia.

It is worth recalling this essential unity of our linguistic heritage – I recognise, of course, that what unites us in Europe today is not so much vestigial common memories of a distant past nor traces of a common ancestral tongue, but rather the fact that for several millennia we have shared this Continent together in the context of a Christian tradition that even today provided European Christians and post-Christians alike with a common point of reference, and the basis of a common value system – albeit one that often finds expression in divergent moral judgments on specific issues.

Our manner of sharing European space has often been combative rather than co-operative – marked by aggression towards each other rather than affection. But as we flinch from the memory of the violence our differences have often evoked – and still evoke in our own island – we should also reflect on the richness and variety of our common culture which has found expression through so many divergent, if ultimately related, languages.

I believe that the continued intellectual and moral vitality of Europe owes much to this richness and variety of local cultures. Other monolingual cultures have their own achievements, which are not to be depreciated or diminished. Thus the United States and Australia amongst modern States, China and Japan amongst ancient ones, have made and are making immense contributions to world culture. But, without succumbing to banal Eurocentricity, it is, I think, fair to say that multi-cultural Europe still holds a lead in the world of political ideas, as I have endeavoured to demonstrate in this address. And despite its chequered and often violent history, and its relative numerical decline vis-a-vis the rest of the world in this century, Europe still has the capacity to provide a substantial part of the intellectual and moral leadership that the world needs on the eve of the twenty-first century of this era.

CONTRIBUTORS

James Mackey is Professor of Theology at the University of Edinburgh. He has written, edited and contributed to theological and philosophical publications.

Maíre Herbert lectures in Early and Medieval Irish at University College Cork. She is author of *Iona, Kells and Derry: The History and Historiography of the Monastic Familia of Columba.*

Gwenaël Le Duc is Professor of Breton at the University of Rennes.

Fiona Stafford is Lecturer in English at St Anne's College, Oxford. She is author of *The Sublime Savage, James Macpherson* and the *Poems of Ossian.*

John Barkley is former Principal of Assemblies College, Belfast.

Marilyn J. Westerkamp is Associate Professor of History at the University of California at Santa Cruz. She is author of *The Triumph of the Laity: Scots-Irish Piety and the Great Awakening.*

Stewart J. Brown is Professor of Ecclesiastical History at the University of Edinburgh. He is author of *The Life of Thomas Chalmers* and *The Scottish Presbyterian Churches and Irish Immigration 1922–1938.*

Declan Kiberd is Lecturer in English at University College Dublin, and a television presenter. He is author of *Synge and the Irish Language, Revival or Revolution?, Modern Irish Writing and the Socialist Tradition*, and the Field Day Pamphlet, *Anglo-Irish Attitudes.*

E.A. Markham is a Caribbean poet and lecturer in creative writing. His published collections include *Human Rites; Living in Disguise; Lambchops in PNG; Towards the End of a Century* and (stories) *Something Unusual.*

Christopher Whyte is Lecturer in Scottish Literature at the University of Glasgow. Among his published collections of poetry is *Uirsgeu/Myth.*

Nuala Ní Dhomhnaill is a poet. Her published collections include (in translation) *Selected Poems* 1986, (dual language) *Selected Poems/Rogha Danta* 1988, *Pharaoh's Daughter* 1990, and (in Irish) *Feis* 1991.

Garret FitzGerald is former leader of the Fine Gael party, and former Prime Minister of Ireland. His autobiography has recently been published.